The Glass Ceiling Delusion:
the _real_ reasons more women don't reach senior positions

The Glass Ceiling Delusion attacks head-on the militant feminist myth that men and women have the same interests and capabilities. Reviewing a wide range of evidence, Mike Buchanan shows that the under-representation of women in senior positions in business has nothing to do with discrimination and 'glass ceilings', and that attempts to impose quotas are therefore fundamentally flawed. A polemical book with an important message.
Peter Saunders Emeritus Professor of Sociology, Sussex University

At long last, someone has taken on the myth of discrimination against women who aspire to senior positions in business, including the boardrooms of major corporations. _The Glass Ceiling Delusion_ demythologizes each of thirty elements the author has identified of the now generally accepted claim that women are discriminated against in the world of white-collar work. Much has been accomplished recently in disclosing the half-truths about women and domestic violence, for example, but Buchanan illuminates an area that other critics of ideological feminism have not considered.

Buchanan's analysis is based partly on his experience of working as an executive for major British and American multinational corporations for over 30 years until 2010. His book should inspire research on settings of corporate power everywhere. Always witty and sometimes even biting in style, Buchanan's text is grounded in important texts in psychobiology, sociology, history and politics. It is an impassioned yet not angry argument that deserves the careful attention of policy-makers and a general readership.
Professor Miles Groth PhD Editor, _New Male Studies: An International Journal_

Equality of opportunity is a fine thing but equality of outcome is another matter entirely. There is little doubt that men and women have, on average, different talents and interests that make gender quotas in the workplace unfair and impractical.

The Glass Ceiling Delusion is a welcome, well-argued addition to the debate about whether women should be pushed up the social ladder just because they are women, and thus at a presumed disadvantage. This is rather an insult to women and Margaret Thatcher, for one, would not have agreed. Individuals should be treated as individuals, not as members of a particular race, class or gender. Whatever the historic injustices, this is the only way that social structures can evolve naturally.

Glenn Wilson Visiting Professor of Psychology, Gresham College, London

The Glass Ceiling Delusion is an important and brave book, the best book on social economics and society in general published for decades. It's irresistibly compelling, cogently argued and superbly put together. It should be in all our school and college libraries. It should be compulsory reading for social science, economics and politics students. It should be force-fed to male and female politicians. This is definitely a five-star book.

Brilliant. Brilliant. Brilliant. Brilliant. Brilliant.

Dr Vernon Coleman bestselling English author

David and Goliatha:
David Cameron – Heir to Harman?

Mike Buchanan has courageously taken on the radical feminists. For too long this group has dominated the public policy agenda. Pay equality, gender balance in the boardroom, all women shortlists have been given far too much prominence in public life. We needed the other side to be put, and in his book Mike Buchanan does just this. His description of the Prime Minister having a 'female-pattern brain' is an interesting aspect of David Cameron. Without being insulting, it explains some of the current direction of Conservative policy.

The book calls for a fight back against the radical feminists. It deserves to succeed. Women had a long hard justifiable fight to obtain the vote in our democracy (see my book *Our Fight for Democracy*), but now they have it the radical feminists want special treatment. This is not acceptable, each person's vote should have an equal value regardless of gender. Manipulating parliamentary candidate short lists to give preference to women is a distortion of democracy, and anyone who believes in democracy should oppose it.

John Strafford Chairman of the Campaign for Conservative Democracy

(Note: *David and Goliatha* is out of print, although second-hand copies are sometimes available to buy. All the content of the book – and a good deal more – is contained in *The Glass Ceiling Delusion*.)

FEMINISM

By Mike Buchanan:

For LPS publishing (Lpspublishing.co.uk)

2015 general election manifesto
Feminism: The Ugly Truth
The Glass Ceiling Delusion:
The <u>real</u> reasons more women don't reach senior positions
David and Goliatha: David Cameron – heir to Harman?
The Joy of Self-Publishing
Buchanan's Dictionary of Quotations for right-minded people
The Marriage Delusion: the fraud of the rings?
Two Men in a Car (a businessman, a chauffeur, and their holidays in France)
Guitar Gods in Beds. (Bedfordshire, a heavenly county)

For Kogan Page (Koganpage.com)

Profitable Buying Strategies: How to Cut Procurement Costs
and Buy Your Way to Higher Profits

FEMINISM
The Ugly Truth

Mike Buchanan

LPS publishing

This paperback edition was first published in 2016 by LPS publishing.

Lpspublishing.co.uk

ISBN 9780956641694

British Library cataloguing-in-publication data.
A CIP record for this book is available from the British Library.

This paperback edition is distributed internationally by Lightning Source Inc.

The sleep of reason breeds monsters.
Francisco de Goya 1746-1828 Spanish artist

CONTENTS

APPENDICES

ACKNOWLEDGEMENTS

My first acknowledgements – as distinct from thanks – must go to the militant feminists who've driven me to write three books to date about their dire influence. One of the most dismal examples is the Labour MP Harriet Harman. If men were not so deferential towards women – and successive governments were not institutionally pro-feminist – she'd have been locked up years ago for the harm she and her kind inflicted upon British society over the terms of the last three Labour administrations, 1997-2010. The Conservative / Liberal Democrat coalition currently in power continues to pursue feminist agendas with some enthusiasm.

[Update: David Cameron's Conservative party won the 2015 general election, and he promptly continued with all the feminist-friendly anti-male policy directions he had pursued whilst in coalition with the Liberal Democrats (2010-5). He won our 'Toady of the Year' awards in 2012, 2013, 2014 and 2015.[1]]

My thanks to all the writers whose books I cite in this one. Particular thanks must go to the writers of three highly insightful books which I draw upon at length in places: Esther Vilar's *The Manipulated Man* (1971), Steve Moxon's *The Woman Racket* (2008), and Swayne O'Pie's *Why Britain Hates Men: Exposing Feminism* (2011). Esther Vilar received death threats from feminists after the publication of *The Manipulated Man*, and the author of *Why Britain Hates Men* uses a pseudonym due to fears over death threats. What times we live in.

My thanks to Erin Pizzey, a fearless exposer of the manipulation carried out by feminists in relation to the

---

[1] http://tinyurl.com/davidcamerontoadyawards

women's refuge movement, for her campaigning over many years, and for penning the Foreword. She, too, received death threats from feminists, in this case protesting (ironically) at Pizzey revealing that women were as responsible for as much domestic violence as men.

My thanks to the psychology professors and writers about psychology, whose books form much of the bedrock upon which my own theses are built: Simon Baron-Cohen (*The Essential Difference*), Louann Brizendine (*The Female Brain*, *The Male Brain*), Oliver James (*Britain on the Couch*, *How Not to F*** Them Up*), Steven Pinker (*The Blank Slate*), and his sister Susan Pinker (*The Sexual Paradox*).

My thanks to Professor Keith Hawton of the Centre for Suicide Research in Oxford for his contribution to the chapter on the link between unemployment and suicide, and to Professor Stefan Priebe and Dr Alfonso Ceccherini-Nelli for their illuminating paper on the subject.

My final thanks to you, for buying this book. I hope it at least meets your expectations. I should be interested to read your opinions in relation to any of the topics covered in it, and I invite you to contact me (mike@j4mb.org.uk).

FOREWORD

This book details many radical feminist myths and barefaced lies, and explores the damage radical feminism has wrought on relationships and the family in our Western world. It often does this with some humour, but its message is very serious.

Like so many women of my age I became involved in the very early days of the newly emerging women's movement and I would have called myself an 'equity' feminist. I was interested in making sure that men and women could compete with each other on a level playing field. Radical feminists are now – as they were then – different from the majority of feminists, and they're highly unrepresentative of women in general. They hate men and they want equality of gender outcomes at any cost, regardless of what men and women choose to do in their personal and working lives.

I was rapidly disillusioned when I recognised that the women's movement was *never* meant to be a movement for most women. It was an attempt by militant women in the Marxist movement to wrest power from men and to create a movement of their own. They simply moved the political goalposts and instead of capitalism being the enemy it was now patriarchy i.e. all men. It didn't take them long to hijack the entire domestic violence debate and use the money to fill their coffers and state that 'all women are victims of male violence.'

Mike Buchanan is a very brave man. I've known other men who've tried to draw the public's attention to the damage done by the radical feminist movement. Many lost their jobs and none of them were able to find publishers for their books. Men have been thrown out of their own houses and unjustly accused of domestic violence towards their partners, and some of sexually abusing their children. The legitimate interests of men in Western society have been systematically assaulted by radical feminists, as this book explains.

Men are starting to campaign more effectively for their interests, though they still have a long way to go before they halt the tide of feminist influence, let alone start to reverse it. Feminists can expect more challenges from another quarter. With every year that passes, more women are becoming aware of the damage that men-hating and family-hating feminists have wrought (and continue to wreak) on society in general, and on women's interests in particular. An increasing number of women are summoning up the courage to openly criticise feminists. This shouldn't surprise us, given that the vast majority of women don't share the feminists' political ideology.

How much more damage will radical feminists be allowed to wreak before they're more widely recognised as the evil women they are?

Erin Pizzey
London, 23 January 2012

Whiteribbon.org

INTRODUCTION

An invasion of armies can be resisted, but not an idea whose time has come.
Victor Hugo 1802-85 French poet, novelist, and dramatist: *Histoire d'un Crime* (written 1851-2, published 1877)

Almost four years have passed since this book was first published in an ebook edition. I should like to thank David Power for funding the publication of this paperback edition, and Robert Wills[1] for executing the cover design. David asked me to retain the front cover from the ebook edition, and I was happy to do that, because feminism is demonstrably an evil and ugly ideology. A photograph of a waxwork female vampire seems to me as suitable an image now as it did in 2012.

A great deal has happened in the intervening four years, for those with an interest in the human rights of men and boys. Across the developed world – and increasingly the developing world, too – there has been a rapidly growing public recognition that the human rights of men and boys are systematically assaulted by the actions and inactions of states, usually to advantage women and girls.

Shortly before the publication of the ebook edition of this book in 2012, I launched the Anti-Feminism League.[2] Shortly after that I launched Campaign for Merit in Business (C4MB).[3] To the best of my knowledge, C4MB remains to this day the only organization in the world dedicated to challenging a government with respect to its bullying of companies into appointing more women onto their boards.

---

[1] http://robertwills.com
[2] http://fightingfeminism.wordpress.com
[3] http://c4mb.wordpress.com

Longitudinal studies show a causal link between increasing female representation on boards, and financial decline. I provide links to the evidence in the (updated) chapter, 'The feminist assault on capitalism'. In the same year I presented the evidence to House of Commons and House of Lords inquiries.

Over the course of 2012 I became ever more interested in the output of an American website, A Voice for Men (AVfM).[1] Founded in 2009 by Paul Elam, who leads the associated organization to this day, AVfM is without question the most-visited and most influential men's human rights advocacy website in the world. In December 2012 AVfM published the first of my articles for them, 'Let's get practical'.[2] The site has since published more than 60 of my articles,[3] including 'Let's get political',[4] the declaration in February 2013 that I was launching a political party, Justice for Men & Boys (and the women who love them) – J4MB.[5]

J4MB remains the only political party in the English-speaking world campaigning for the human rights of men and boys on many fronts. The party's 2015 general election manifesto explored 20 areas where those human rights are assaulted by the state's actions and inactions, usually to advantage women and girls.[6] A speedy insight into many of the 20 areas can be gained by reading a selection of pieces on the party's 'Key Posts' website page.[7] In the UK there are no areas where the human rights of women and girls (specifically) are assaulted by the state's actions and inactions.

---

[1] http://avoiceformen.com
[2] http://tinyurl.com/avfmletsgetpractical
[3] https://j4mb.wordpress.com/articles-published-by-a-voice-for-men/
[4] http://tinyurl.com/avfmletsgetpolitical
[5] http://j4mb.org.uk
[6] http://tinyurl.com/j4mb2015manifesto
[7] https://j4mb.wordpress.com/key-posts/

J4MB fielded two candidates in the 2015 general election, and plans to field 20 candidates in the 2020 general election. The party's strategy for that election is contained in an Appendix. Funding streams to pay for the candidates' £500 deposits were in place a month or two after the 2015 general election.

The J4MB website has updated lists of recommended books[1] and websites.[2] The party's YouTube channel[3] contains 100+ appearances on mainstream radio and television, along with other material likely to be of interest to people concerned about feminism and men's issues.

In 2014 AVfM hosted the first International Conference on Men's Issues, in Detroit. The event proved a resounding success, and I was honoured to be invited to give a talk.[4]

In association with AVfM we are planning to host the second International Conference on Men's Issues, in London, currently (December 2015) scheduled for dates in July, 2016.[5] The associated blog post will be updated from time to time. The speakers will include many of the most prominent men's human rights advocates in the world. At least four will be women, including Erin Pizzey (the keynote speaker).

19 November 2015 – International Men's Day – was a momentous day in the UK for people interested in the human rights of men and boys. A Conservative MP, Philip Davies, had applied to a House of Commons committee to set aside time for the first ever debate on men's issues in the House of Commons, on International Men's Day. A Labour MP, Jess Phillips, blocked the application. None of the other MPs on the

---

[1] http://tinyurl.com/j4mbrecbooks
[2] http://tinyurl.com/j4mbrecwebsites
[3] https://j4mb.wordpress.com/youtube/
[4] http://tinyurl.com/mbspeechicmi14
[5] http://tinyurl.com/j4mbicmi16

committee – all of them men – dared to challenge her.[1] She was presented with a J4MB Toxic Feminist of the Month award for her actions.[2]

Following a public outcry, a debate of four hours' duration was scheduled by the committee. It started with a 43-minute introduction from Philip Davies, in which feminists repeatedly tried to control the direction of his speech, and wasted time over irrelevant matters.[3] He pressed on with his trademark humour and robustness, and won the day. In the description panel under the video there's a link to the full debate.

The same afternoon in Parliament Square, just a few yards away from the men's issues debate in Westminster Hall, J4MB supporters joined a protest organised by Men Do Complain,[4] a group campaigning for an end to non-therapeutic male circumcision (Male Genital Mutilation, MGM).[5]

J4MB presents a range of awards to feminists and their male collaborators. They include Lying Feminist of the Month,[6] Whiny Feminist of the Month,[7] Gormless Feminist of the Month,[8] and Toxic Feminist of the Month.[9]

Toady awards are presented to men in positions of authority, who drive or support feminist agendas. David Cameron, leader of the Conservative party since 2005 and prime minister since 2010, has won the Toady of the Year award four years in succession, 2012/13/14/15.[10]

---

[1] http://tinyurl.com/j4mbphilipdaviesapplication
[2] http://tinyurl.com/jessphillipstoxicfeminist
[3] http://tinyurl.com/philipdaviesdebate
[4] http://mendocomplain.com
[5] http://tinyurl.com/j4mbimd2015protest
[6] http://tinyurl.com/j4mblyingfeminists
[7] https://j4mb.wordpress.com/whiny-feminists-of-the-month/
[8] http://tinyurl.com/j4mbgormlessfeminists
[9] https://j4mb.wordpress.com/toxic-feminists-of-the-month/
[10] http://tinyurl.com/j4mbdavidcameron

I frequently recommend to people wishing to understand the history and modern impact of feminism, the output of an important British anti-feminist blogger, Herbert Purdy.[1] He will be speaking at the 2016 conference, and it is anticipated that his book *Their Angry Creed* will be published beforehand.

I also frequently recommend the output of a second British blogger, William Collins. In my view – and that of many others – Collins has set the gold standard for articles exploring the many assaults on the human rights of men and boys.[2]

As I was nearing the end of preparing this paperback edition, Amnesty International refused to consider our party's application to book their conference facility in London, on the basis that J4MB is an anti-feminist party. Details in Appendix 9.

I end this Introduction with a request that you support the work of J4MB. The party couldn't survive without external financial support, and I invite you to become a party member.[3] You don't need not to be a UK resident to become a member, we have members (and donors) around the world. If you don't wish to become a party member, your one-off donations would be very welcome.[4]

Thank you for your support, and for caring about men and boys (and the women who love them).

Onwards and upwards.

Mike Buchanan
Bedford, Old England
1 January 2016

---

[1] http://herbertpurdy.com
[2] http://mra-uk.co.uk
[3] https://j4mb.wordpress.com/party-membership/
[4] https://j4mb.wordpress.com/donate/

INTRODUCTION
(2012 ebook edition)

The fact that an opinion has been widely held is no evidence whatever that it is not utterly absurd; indeed in view of the silliness of the majority of mankind, a widespread belief is more likely to be foolish than sensible.
Bertrand Russell 1872-1970 British philosopher, historian, logician, mathematician, free trade champion, pacifist and social critic

On the evening of 15 September 2011, two women were being interviewed by Gavin Esler on the BBC's flagship late night television news programme *Newsnight*. One was the dour feminist Labour politician Angela Eagle. She'd obviously chewed on a thick slice of lemon before the interview, to set her customary expression for the day.

The other was Charlotte Vere, a businesswoman and former prospective Parliamentary candidate for the Conservative party for Brighton Pavilion at the 2010 general election. The seat was unfortunately won by a Green MP, Caroline Lucas.

I cheered Ms Vere upon hearing her state the following in a piece recorded to camera before the interview:

> 'I think feminism is a toxic, battle-hardened and arrogant philosophy which has been manipulated by those at the extremes of politics. Feminism has had its day. We need women to stand up and shout, 'Feminism? Not in my name!' '

At last, I thought, at long last… *people are starting to get it!*

A warm welcome to *Feminism: The Ugly Truth*. I should start with a few words about terminology. In her book *Who Stole Feminism? How Women Have Betrayed Women* (1994) Christina Hoff Sommers made a useful distinction between 'equity' feminists who seek equality of opportunities, and 'gender' feminists who seek special treatment for women with a view to gaining advantage over men. She herself is in the former camp.

In a sense, aren't we *all* equity feminists now? Women have worked hard and achieved so much in the workplace and elsewhere that very few people in developed countries in the modern era wouldn't support equality of opportunity. But I don't know people (other than through email correspondence) who advocate equality of outcomes – in senior executive positions, say – *regardless of the relative numbers of men and women able and willing to undertake those positions.* Yet equality of outcomes remains a key gender feminist objective, and gender feminists are making relentless progress towards that goal.

This isn't about gender equality, it's about relentless special treatment for women. Feminists aren't troubled when women enjoy *superiority* of outcomes, as they now do in a growing number of fields. How do a small number of feminists, in a modern democracy, manage to exert so much influence over legislative and public policy agendas? This book seeks to answer that question, along with many others.

For the avoidance of doubt the focus of this book is on gender feminism, often termed militant feminism or radical feminism. From this point onwards I shall use the word 'feminism' to mean gender feminism, and the word 'feminists' to mean gender feminists. It's these feminists – who constitute a small but highly influential proportion of feminists – who are having such a dire impact in so many areas. Where I'm making a point about *equity* feminism I'll make it clear I'm doing so.

Feminism has at its core six elements: misandry (the hatred of men), baseless conspiracy theories, fantasies, lies, delusions and myths. When women adopt hatred as a core value – which is a fundamental requirement of feminism – the results can be ugly.

Feminism attracts little serious criticism in the mainstream media in the developed world, which is extraordinary given that it's systematically and progressively assaulting and undermining the nuclear family, government, public bodies, the legal system, the education system, the media, academia, capitalism, and much else. It's killing men in large numbers, through depriving them of employment. It's forcing women to eschew caring for their children at home, in favour of becoming wage slaves, to pay for strangers to bring up their children. It's a leading cause of misery and mental health problems in both men and women. It's arguably the most dangerous 'ism' in the developed world today, following the widespread defeat of fascism and communism in the 20th century.

I'll be using the term 'Leftie' as both a noun and an adjective. In the United Kingdom it denotes someone who is 'left-of-centre' politically. The equivalent term in North America and elsewhere might be 'Liberal' but in the United Kingdom that word means something more nuanced, albeit still left-of-centre on most issues. The UK, in common with many countries in Europe, has had numerous Leftie (Labour) administrations since the Second World War, but few as incompetent as the one in power over 1997-2010, led in its final three years by the ill-fated Gordon Brown, a man whose photograph I featured on the cover of *Buchanan's Dictionary of Quotations for right-minded people*. For any non-British reader wishing to gain insights into Gordon Brown I recommend Vernon Coleman's *Gordon is a Moron*. Brown was a firm supporter and personal friend of Harriet Harman, a radical feminist Labour MP.

What's new in the United Kingdom, and highly unwelcome to Righties such as myself, is that David Cameron, the leader of the traditionally right-of-centre Conservative party for which I once worked (2006-8) – and currently the leader of a coalition government with the Liberal Democrats – is a Leftie. In the United States he'd be regarded as having political persuasions well to the left of those held by most Democrats.

Perhaps Cameron's most shameful act in his first year of office, which started in May 2010, was the enactment of The Equality Bill just two months after taking office. The Bill was the brainchild of Harriet Harman, a militant feminist politician from the preceding Labour administration, and it was surely the crowning glory of a dismal career dedicated to a feminist agenda, none of which was to be found in her party's election manifestos. In 2008 she passed legislation enabling political parties to force all-women prospective parliamentary candidate ('PPC') shortlists onto their constituency parties *for the ensuing 25 years.* Cameron announced his intention to employ that legislation some six months before the 2010 general election, and I resigned my party membership as a result. I was informed by a senior official in the party that many other members had done likewise.

In *David and Goliatha: David Cameron – heir to Harman?* I argue that Cameron's support for feminist agendas stems partly from his clearly having a female-pattern brain. One of his most eminent predecessors as Conservative party leader was Margaret Thatcher. To many traditional Conservatives (including myself) she was the most impressive peacetime prime minister (of any party) in the 20th century, and possibly had a male-pattern brain. [Update: I no longer believe she had such a brain, after reading Charles Moore's biographies of her.] The chapter, 'The different natures of men and women' in this book covers the topic of gender-patterned brains. *David and Goliatha* is being withdrawn from sale, its content is contained in my later book *The Glass Ceiling Delusion.*

To people who ask why I chose the image of a female vampire for the cover of this book, I explain that the image reflects two defining characteristics of feminism: anger and ugliness. Feminists' anger is founded upon and fuelled by their misandry, and this book has a good deal to say on that topic. And to my mind any ideology based upon hatred of half the world's population is emphatically ugly.

There is of course another meaning of the word 'ugly', that relating to physical appearance. It would be dishonest to deny the evidence before us – that feminists *are* generally less attractive than normal women – and the link between female unattractiveness and feminism is covered in this book.

To the charge that my book makes feminists look ridiculous I happily plead guilty, but in my defence I point out that the group which has most successfully made feminists look ridiculous has been feminists themselves.

There are encouraging signs of growing consciousness among men – and women, for that matter – of the damage being wrought by feminists, and a backlash against the ideology is surely approaching. The question is not whether this backlash will take place, but rather what forms it will take, and when.

Until the next time.

Mike Buchanan
Bedford, Old England
1 February 2012

1 | FEMINISTS ARE LIARS

Truthfulness has never been counted among the political virtues, and lies
have always been regarded as justifiable tools in political dealings.
Hannah Arendt 1906-75 German-born American political theorist: *Lying in Politics*, 'Crises
of the Republic' (1972)

When asked for the characteristics commonly found in
feminists, people typically cite some of the following:

- men-hating
- angry
- miserable
- whiny
- childish
- humourless
- physically unattractive
- unpleasant personality
- unable or unwilling to engage in rational debate

Less commonly, people respond that feminists are liars,
whether as the originators of lies, or the perpetuators of them.

This is the only new chapter in this paperback edition. I've
added it to give the reader some sense of the astonishing scale
on which feminists lie, particularly those running or working
for feminist organizations, who profit from their lies. They lie
relentlessly, and shamelessly, because they cannot reveal
publicly what is self-evidently the case. Feminism is an ideology
that seeks ever more gender privileging, not gender equality.
And feminists' appetite for privilege is clearly insatiable.

I shall turn shortly to the Lying Feminist of the Month
awards my political party has been presenting to feminists
(many of them in the public eye) since March 2014.

Caroline Criado-Perez has won our award three times, and was recently given the Order of the British Empire (OBE). Laura Bates has won our award twice, and was given a British Empire Medal (BEM). These honours should not surprise us, because feminism is at the heart of the Establishment.

We invariably contact the award winners, and alert them to their awards. Rarely do we get acknowledgements of our communications, and we've never had any of the feminists retract their lies, let alone apologise for them.

Many of the awards have been presented to high-profile feminists. We've provided details to mainstream media outlets. Not one outlet, to date, has given any publicity to the awards.

We have a number of theories about the lack of media exposure. One is that the media give very little coverage to the activities of anti-feminists, and the lack of interest in the awards may be nothing more than a manifestation of that. Another theory is that the mainstream media are keen not to print anything which might upset advertisers, almost all of which are keen to appear uncritical of women. A third theory is that lying feminists aren't newsworthy, for the same reason that lying women in general aren't.

For an explanation of the last point, we turn to Alison Tieman, a well-known Canadian Honey Badger (female anti-feminist and/or men's human rights advocate) video maker. In one short video – Men's Rights versus Feminism explained, using magnets[1] – she explained that men are regarded as 'actors', and are duly expected (indeed, required) to demonstrate 'moral agency'. Failure to do so will be punished, usually harshly.

Conversely, women are 'acted upon', and are not expected to demonstrate much moral agency – little more than young

---

[1] http://tinyurl.com/alisontiemanmagnets

children, in truth. When they fail to manage even that (e.g. by lying to pursue their self-interest, or by committing a crime) society treats them leniently.

Very often society doesn't punish women at all. We see a reflection of this in the prison population of the United Kingdom. Only 4,000 of the 80,000 prisoners are women. As the British blogger William Collins has explained, if men were treated as leniently as women in sentencing terms, five out of six men in British prisons wouldn't be there.[1]

Women are regularly given suspended prison sentences – i.e. no punishment – for crimes such as making false rape allegations (they retain their anonymity, while their victims don't) and sexually abusing minors.

In this context, feminists lying to advance their interests, and what they perceive to be the interests of women and girls, is to be expected; and the lack of mainstream media coverage of our political party in general, and our exposure of high-profile feminists as egregious liars in particular, is also predictable.

We turn to our Lying Feminist of the Month awards. An updated list is maintained on our political party's website.[2] The award winners to date (November 2015) along with a few words explaining the nature of their lies:

Winner of three awards
Caroline Criado-Perez OBE,[3] whine merchant – the impact of increasing the proportion of women on corporate boards, domestic abuse is the largest cause of morbidity in women aged 19-44 (more than war, cancer, or motor vehicle accidents), women killed by male partners or ex-partners.

---

[1] http://mra-uk.co.uk/?p=215
[2] http://tinyurl.com/j4mblfotmawards
[3] http://carolinecriadoperez.com/

<u>Winners of two awards</u>
Laura Bates BEM, Everyday Sexism Project[1] – statistics on rape, and the women killed by partners or ex-partners.

Gloria De Piero MP, Shadow Minister for Women and Equalities – domestic violence, gender pay gap.

Sandi Toksvig,[2] lesbian 'comedienne', spokeswoman, Women's Equality Party[3] – impact of increasing the proportion of women on corporate boards, gender pay gap.

<u>Winners of one award (surname alphabetical order)</u>
Kat Banyard, professional grievance collector – sexual harassment of schoolgirls.

Samantha Beckett, Director General, Economics & Markets (Department for Business, Innovation and Skills) – impact of increasing the proportion of women on corporate boards.

Ann Francke, CEO of the Chartered Management Institute – gender pay gap.

Franki Hackett, Women's Aid spokeswoman. She won the award for making at least seven demonstrably false claims and/or misleading statements about domestic abuse during an online discussion with a men's rights advocate. We publicly challenged Polly Neate (CEO, Women's Aid) to retract the claims, and she contemptuously declined to do so.[4]

---

[1] http://everydaysexism.com
[2] Often referred to as Sandi Toxic by her critics
[3] http://www.womensequality.org.uk/
[4] http://tinyurl.com/j4mbwomensaidlfotm

Roz Hardie, CEO of OBJECT, a feminist campaigning organisation – domestic violence.

Teresa Hughes – falsely alleged that the headmaster of the primary school, where her daughter was a pupil, had sexually assaulted her daughter.

Melanie Jeffs, manager, Nottingham Women's Centre – the number of women killed by male partners and ex-partners.

Anne Longfield, Children's Commissioner for England – her organization's website continues to claim that children in the UK enjoy all the protection of the United Nations Convention on the Rights of the Child. Male minors who may be the victims of circumcision on non-therapeutic grounds don't enjoy that protection, although the procedure on such grounds is unquestionably illegal in the UK.

Emma Ritch, executive director, Engender (a Scottish radical feminist campaigning organisation, 88.6% funded by Scottish taxpayers, mostly men) – impact of increasing the proportion of women on corporate boards.

Roweena Russell, North East Feminist Gathering – the number of women killed by male partners.

Kate Smurthwaite, feminist 'comedienne' – the number of women killed by male partners and ex-partners.

Sophie Walker, leader, Women's Equality Party – claims in her party's policy launch document.

2| THE WORLD MUST
BE CHANGED, APPARENTLY

When intellectuals discover that the world does not behave according to
their theories, the conclusion they invariably draw is that the world must
be changed. It must be awfully hard to change theories.

Thomas Sowell 1930- African-American economist and social commentator: syndicated
column, 10 December 1985

The developed world is increasingly engaged in a futile attempt
to placate feminists, a small band of angry man-hating Leftie
women. The more battles they win, the more they start.
They're irrational and insatiable. They have no interest in a
dialogue with people who hold differing views. Until and unless
we stop them, they'll continue their assault on men, women,
children, the nuclear family, government, the legal system,
academia, the media, business, and much else.

We need to take the threat of feminism far more seriously
than we do, and to start fighting it. This will be a very difficult
challenge because feminists haven't acquire their power
through democratic means, nor through merit, and they exert
their power out of sight.

The first stage of the battle against feminism is to raise the
consciousness of more people about the true nature of
feminism in the modern era. Then we – the majority of men
and women, whose interests are being assaulted by feminists –
will be in a better position to demand of our political leaders
and others that they stop their spineless capitulation to these
hate-driven harridans.

This book is my personal contribution to raising people's
consciousness about the nature of feminism in the modern era.

You do what you can.

3 | ARE YOU A MISOGYNIST
IF YOU ONLY HATE FEMINISTS?

Chris Finch was in an argument once and he went, 'How can I hate
women, my Mum's one.'... Yeah? There's a lot of truth in that.
David Brent (**Ricky Gervais**) *The Office* (2001)

Any man prepared to comment objectively about women –
even about a small group of women such as feminists – is
automatically and immediately branded a sexist or a misogynist,
often both. Once denounced as a sexist or a misogynist, a man
must be reviled or avoided. So I thought I should start the
book by addressing the inevitable charges of sexism and
misogyny, knowing that feminists will take no heed of anything
I have to say on the subject. But I haven't written the book for
them; I've written it for the vast majority of people – women
included – who don't share their creed.

As people who know me are aware, I love some women, I
like others, and I dislike a small number. If my opinions about
women make me a sexist or a misogynist then most people I
know – men and women – are too.

The irony, of course, is that the charge of misogyny is most
often employed by feminists, women who are themselves guilty
of misandry: the hatred of men. I wasn't familiar with the word
before I started my research for *David and Goliatha*. Misandry is
the beating heart of feminism, as we shall see.

Are you a misogynist if you only hate feminists? Of course
not. You're normal.

4| WHAT *IS* FEMINISM
IN THE MODERN ERA?

I listen to feminists and all these radical gals – most of them are failures. They've blown it. Some of them have been married, but they married some Casper Milquetoast who asked permission to go to the bathroom. These women just need a man in the house. That's all they need. Most of the feminists need a man to tell them what time of day it is and to lead them home. And they blew it and they're mad at all men. Feminists hate men. They're sexist. They hate men – that's their problem.
Jerry Falwell 1933-2007 American Baptist cleric, televangelist and conservative commentator

Countless words have been written – the vast majority of them by women – about the meaning of the words 'feminism' and 'feminist'. I read a number of books about feminism and concluded there are as many definitions of the word as there are writers on the topic. And when words have many meanings, they arguably have *no* useful meaning. We return to a useful distinction used by Christina Hoff Sommers, the author of *Who Stole Feminism? How Women Have Betrayed Women* (1994).

Hoff Sommers is an American former professor of philosophy, and a self-identifying 'equity feminist'. Wikipedia has some interesting material on Hoff Sommers, including the following:

> 'Sommers uses the terms 'equity feminism' and 'gender feminism' to differentiate what she sees as acceptable and non-acceptable forms of feminism. She describes equity feminism as the struggle for equal legal and civil rights and many of the original goals of the early feminists, as in the first wave of the women's movement. She describes gender feminism as the action of accenting the differences of genders for the purposes of what she believes is creating privilege for women in academia, government, industry, or advancing personal agendas.'

Throughout this book (unless stated otherwise) I shall use the terms 'feminism' and 'feminist' in the same sense that Ms Sommers refers to 'gender feminism' and 'gender feminist'. After all, we're all equity feminists now, aren't we? Ever since Margaret Thatcher did such a tremendous job as prime minister of the United Kingdom over the country's golden years of 1979-90, anyway...

The great irony in the modern era is that feminism is coming under increasing criticism, not least from women themselves; yet the power this small band of determined women exerts has never been greater. We shall see that feminists prefer to wield power by operating in the shadows, not emerging into the light where their arguments would be exposed as a manifestation of extreme left-wing ideologies.

5 | MISANDRY
(THE HATRED OF MEN)

Feminism cannot exist *without* blaming and demonising men. It needs to spread misandry as a necessary device to justify its existence. Misandry is the fuel that drives the feminist ideology and agenda, and keeps its Grievance Gravy-Train Industries in business.
Swayne O'Pie *Why Britain Hates Men: Exposing Feminism* (2011)

Misandry has been well documented in the modern era, most notably in a series of books by two academics at McGill University in Canada, Paul Nathanson and Katherine K Young. The first two in the series were *Spreading Misandry* (2001) and *Legalizing Misandry* (2006). Both are well worth reading.

I covered the topic of misandry at some length in *The Glass Ceiling Delusion* and I didn't plan to return to it in this book. But just two months after that book's publication in July 2011 a book focusing on the topic of misandry, within the context of feminism, came to my attention. It was written by the British anti-feminist campaigner Swayne, O'Pie and titled *Why Britain Hates Men: Exposing Feminism.* The ebook edition, and the paperback edition outside the UK, are titled *Exposing Feminism: The Thirty Years' War Against Men.*

The remainder of this chapter is drawn from *Why Britain Hates Men* with the writer's kind permission. He shares my opinion of David Cameron, the current British prime minister, a highly unconservative leader of the Conservative Party, the senior partner in the coalition currently in power.

LAY OFF MEN,
LESSING TELLS FEMINISTS
(*The Guardian*, 14 August 2001: Fiachra Gibbons)

Doris Lessing, who became a feminist icon with the books *The Grass is Singing* and *The Golden Notebook*, said a 'lazy and insidious' culture had taken hold within feminism that revelled in flailing men. Young boys were being weighed down with guilt about the crimes of their sex, she told the Edinburgh book festival.

'I find myself increasingly shocked at the unthinking and automatic rubbishing of men which is now so part of our culture that it is hardly even noticed', the 81-year-old Zimbabwean-born writer said yesterday.

'I was in a class of nine- and ten-year-olds, girls and boys, and this young woman was telling these kids that the reason for wars was the innately violent nature of men. You could see the little girls fat with complacency and conceit, while the little boys sat there crumpled, apologising for their existence, thinking this was going to be the pattern of their lives.'

Lessing said that the teacher 'tried to catch my eye, thinking that I would approve of this rubbish'.

She added: 'This kind of thing is happening in schools all over the place and no one says a thing. It is time we began to ask who are these women who continually rubbish men. The most stupid, ill-educated and nasty woman can rubbish the nicest, kindest and most intelligent man, and no one protests. Men seem to be so cowed that they cannot fight back. And it is time they did.'

Universities have a great deal to answer for by producing ideologically-driven teachers who prejudice the minds of children against their fathers and their brothers, against the male half of the population. Totalitarian states, fascist and communist, also used the education system to create an ideologically-complicit populace, to create a compliant conventional wisdom. We don't expect it to be so used in Britain.

Misandry and Men's Lesser Worth
The stereotyping of a group as 'bad people' makes us callous to the death of its members.

IT'S SO HARD BEING A MAN
(*The Sunday Telegraph*, 7 November, 1993)

Last week the chief executive of the Samaritans drew attention to the growing number of young men committing suicide. There was little reaction...

Men are the last group that can be freely prejudicially denounced. It is perfectly acceptable to make general slurs about men that could never be made about an ethnic group, and certainly not about women.

That was written in 1993. Nothing has changed since. The male suicide rate is *still* four times greater than the female suicide rate. Do a gender switch... and imagine the media and political outcry that would ensue. Suicide is overwhelmingly a male issue; deliberately ignoring it is a misandric 'policy' (as is the neglect of other male issues).

On Monday, 22 March, 1999, the *Bath Chronicle* carried a small article (only about 8cm long by one column in width) entitled, 'Three bodies found in Bath over weekend'. During the course of one weekend three bodies – all male – had been found in different locations in Bath, all having died of ill-health and exposure.

If it were three *women's* bodies that had been found in similar circumstances, in *one* city, over *one* weekend, it would have been a national news feature, questions would be asked in the House, Feminist MPs would be masochistically delighted at finding yet another example of misogyny, a Commission would be set up. But these were only *male* corpses... so only 8cm in a local paper.

Widespread misandry dehumanises men. In numerous ways, men in modern Britain have become disposable, have become of lesser worth than women. A female columnist writes:

A HYMN TO HIM: MEN ARE SEXY, SMART AND GOOD FOR WOMEN

(*The Sunday Times*, 12 July, 2009: Minette Martin)

Are men really necessary? That was the question that raised its ugly head following reports that scientists had created human sperm from embryonic stem cells. A team from Newcastle University claims to have produced fully mature mobile sperm in the laboratory, which may soon be able to create a living child. If men are no longer needed for producing sperm, perhaps they are no longer needed at all – that was the suggestion humming in the media and the blogosphere last week, often rather nastily disguised as humour, with lists of ways in which men are worse than useless. Misandry – the hatred of men – is a powerful force.

With the feminisation of the media and of education and with decades of so-called positive discrimination favouring women, we have seen a growing female triumphalism; it has been accompanied by a growing bewilderment and displacement of men. There is an increasing sense that women can do well enough without them, and more and more women are embarking on a life to which men are only incidental.

Misandry, demonising and dehumanising men, has devalued men's worth compared to that of women's; it has made society blasé about the disposability of men. It is responsible, for example, for the shocking bias in the lack of attention to men's health in general. It is responsible for our blindness towards domestic violence against men. Britain today cares more about saving whales than about saving males, more interested in the rights of foxes than in the natural right of divorced fathers to see their children.

Almost anything can be said about men, or done to men, without the expectation of a public outcry.

The Public are Unaware of Misandry

Both men and women fail to see misandry as a problem. This is because 'sexism' has been defined exclusively in terms of misogyny. So nobody is looking for 'sexism' against men, for misandry, and people don't find what they're not looking for. Have they even heard of the word or concept? Everyone would admit to noticing examples of men 'perhaps losing out' now and again, here or there, occasionally. But because Feminism has never been exposed to public debate, to questioning and analysis, people have failed to see the pattern, they fail to see the intended political strategy... because of this heavy censorship people have been *deliberately* denied the knowledge and the political insight to see Feminism for what it has become.

After decades of society's and the state's relentless searching and probing, exploring in every nook and cranny of society, culture, education, the law, the media, employment, politics, to seek out misogyny and sexism against women, it can be very difficult for individuals steeped in this conventional wisdom, conditioned in this monopolistic, blinkered search, to see the dangers of widespread man-hating.

Here is one reason why this book needed to be written. Part Four offers the reader the knowledge and the insights to see the pro-Feminist / anti-male pattern in sexual politics, to see how modern Britain expresses institutional misandry; to expose the Feminist fraud.

In the Preface we saw how Feminist students (already well entrenched in their *own* political groups) aggressively attempted to prevent male students at the Universities of Manchester and Oxford from forming even non-political, innocuous, Men's Societies.

People have, so far, been unaware of how misandry has been employed as a major sexual political weapon in the Feminist armoury:

- in condemning and demonising men (and thereby legitimising the institutional 'punishment' of men via laws and policies, and by ignoring male-specific problems and issues)
- how it is used to ease and facilitate the implementation of the Feminist agenda

And neither are people aware of how Feminism's Quiet Revolution is being cleverly orchestrated. Or they may purposely have chosen not to be aware of these aspects of misandry. Male Feminists are particularly deserving of opprobrium for their lack of concern for men, their obsequious refusal to address misandry, and their obdurate refusal to even acknowledge its existence. Male politicians, male trade union leaders and male academics should be particularly singled out for condemnation.

CAMERON: ABSENT DADS
AS BAD AS DRINK DRIVERS
(*The Sunday Telegraph*, 19 June, 2011)

David Cameron today launches a full-scale attack on
fathers who abandon their families, calling for them to
be 'stigmatised' by society in the same way as drink-
drivers.

The Prime Minister's intervention – in an article for
The Sunday Telegraph to mark Father's Day – is one of
the most outspoken he has made in defence of
traditional family life... He says, 'It's high time
runaway dads were stigmatised, and the full force of
shame was heaped upon them. They should be looked
at like drink-drivers, people who are beyond the pale.
They need the message rammed home to them, from
every part of our culture, that what they're doing is
wrong, that leaving single mothers, who do a heroic
job against all odds, to fend for themselves simply isn't
acceptable.'

He says fathers must make the decision to support
'financially and emotionally' their children even if they
have separated from their mothers, spending time with
them at weekends, attending nativity plays and 'taking
an interest in their education'.

This is an attack on men, not just fathers. Cameron chose
Father's Day to make his words especially painful for those
divorced men who are desperate to see their children but have
been prevented from doing so, sometimes for many years, by
vindictive ex-wives.

Four out of five divorces are petitioned for by wives;[1] It is
fathers who are ditched and required to leave the family home.
How can this fact possibly be construed as 'runaway dads'? Such
dishonesty could only be alchemised in the warped perspective of
the Feminist and the Male Feminist. It isn't *fathers* who are
breaking up traditional families, but wives and mothers... but this
dare not be openly admitted in our politically correct culture. So
men are used as the scapegoats; in a misandric culture it is easier

---

[1] Social Trends 31 (2001) and Social Trends 32 (2002), Office for National
Statistics, London: The Stationery Office. Reported in Rebecca O'Neill,
'Experiments in Living: The Fatherless Family', Civitas (2002).

to demonise men than to face the wrath of Feminists by being truthful.

Or is Mr Cameron thinking of young men who irresponsibly impregnate girls and then refuse to commit? Well hang on, there are two sides to this story. Young women are *just as culpable* as young men with their sexual behaviour. For every male youth who impregnates a girl and then disappears from the scene there is an equal number (if not more) of young women who have had children *by numerous fathers* and who refuse to live with any of them because this would reduce their single-parent benefits, including jeopardising their state-provided flat or house. In addition, there is extensive and compelling evidence to show that young women actually *choose* to become single-parent mothers.[1] Senior research fellow Patricia Morgan states:

> 'Most unwed mothers conceive and deliver their babies deliberately, not accidentally.'[2]

Senior research fellow Geoff Dench:

> 'The existence of state benefits as a source of economic security seems to be encouraging young mothers not to bother with male resident partners.'[3]

And Cameron's *own* research team, a body specifically set up to investigate the breakdown of the traditional family, reached the same conclusion. Iain Duncan Smith speaks for the Social Justice policy group 'Breakdown Britain':

> 'However, over the lifetime of this working group we have been concerned by the extent to which it appears that the current benefits system incentivises lone parenthood and acts as a driver towards family breakdown.'[4]

---

[1] For example: 'Fractured Families' (2006) and 'Breakthrough Britain: Ending the Cost of Social Breakdown' (2007), The Social Policy Justice Group, chaired by Iain Duncan Smith, 'Broken Hearts: Family Decline and the Consequences for Society', Centre for Policy Studies (2002).
[2] 'Farewell the Family? Public Policy and Family Breakdown in Britain and the USA', Patricia Morgan, IEA Health and Welfare Unit (1999).
[3] *Daily Mail* 26 February 2010.
[4] 'Breakthrough Britain'.

So young men *don't* leave single mothers to fend for themselves. Today, single-parent motherhood is mostly driven by young women. It is not caused by 'runaway dads'. By disregarding all the evidence and all the research, including his own, we can see that Cameron is bloody-minded in his determination to blame men, fathers, for the supposed 'victimhood', and the huge public cost, of the single-parent mother phenomenon.

Cameron goes on to say that divorced fathers should be involved with their children and have an emotional input. He suggests 'spending time with the kids at weekends, taking them to football matches, going to the nativity play, taking an interest in their education.'

The man's an idiot. He has no idea just how difficult it is for the majority of divorced fathers to even *see* their children, let alone be permitted to participate in their emotional care (this ostracism is also experienced by many *unmarried* fathers). These loving fathers spend £1000s desperately trying to have some sort of meaningful contact – against the combined might of their vindictive ex-wife (free legal-aided to keep him away from 'her' children), the Feminist-friendly Family Courts and successive Feminist-sympathetic governments (both the latter supporting and encouraging the cruelty of the ex-wife). Cameron offers not a word of comfort, in the form of father-friendly policy, for these seriously distressed and desperate men.

Cameron's statement is virulently anti-male. It is not *accidentally* insensitive; he deliberately chose Father's Day to inflict his cruelty on already-hurting divorced fathers. So not only is his attack on men delusional; it is despicable. And it encapsulates (and proves) the thesis of this book – that modern Britain hates men; and that this systemic misandry is not only *cultural* but *institutional.* Here we see man-hating from the very top.

Why did Cameron perpetrate this deliberate hurt, this planned misandry? Two reasons. By blaming and demonising men, by further hurting and tormenting divorced fathers, he appeased and pleased the Feminists. It is dangerous for a politician today to incur the wrath of the powerful Feminist lobby, sycophancy is a much easier policy to keep these influential ideologues 'on side'. Secondly, by cuddling up to and flattering single-parent mothers he hopes to glean and secure the 'women's vote'. Cameron's motives were political, dishonest, devoid of integrity, insensitive and lacking in compassion.

Cameron did it because he could. Today anything can be said about men, or done to men, and nobody protests. Men are the whipping boys, they are an easy target. Modern Britain hates men.

6 | HOW FEMINISTS VIEW THE WORLD: WELCOME TO THE GRIM WORLD OF DUALISM

Four legs good, two legs bad.
George Orwell 1903-50 English novelist: *Animal Farm* (1945)

Feminism springs from the same intellectual tradition as Marxism, both sharing a core belief in dualism. There's an oppressing class (the bourgeoisie, in the case of Marxism, and men, in the case of feminism) which is by definition *always* in the wrong, and is to be overthrown; and there's an oppressed class (the proletariat and women respectively) which is by definition *always* in the right, and must overthrow its oppressors. Adherents are taught and encouraged to see the world through the lens of this dualism, and of course it's *possible* to make some sense of the world in this way. Carefully selected examples could be found to prop up *any* creed based on dualism.

But why, you have to ask yourself, might anyone *want* to think in this way? In the case of feminists the answer is obvious: misandry. They *hate* men. Feminists are angry so they wish to bring men down, which requires less effort than beating men on the grounds of merit. Any strategy or tactic is permissible, indeed laudable. Adverse consequences are acceptable even if it's women in general who suffer (as it often is).

I've all but given up trying to debate with feminists. They have well-prepared scripts they stick to through thick and thin, and seldom engage their brains. On occasion I've said to a feminist (or written in an email), 'You really *believe* this crap, don't you?' The line always goes down well, I find.

The sequence of events when one tries to engage with feminists is invariably the same, and differs only in how far along the road you manage to travel. The most common response is no response at all; as I was to discover, even invoking the law in the form of The Freedom of Information Act to obtain the prospectuses and reading lists of Women's Studies and Gender Studies courses generally produced no response.

The few feminists who respond to people challenging them will almost invariably be rude and condemn them as sexist, misogynistic, blah, blah, blah. They fly into rages when you calmly try to engage them in any sort of nuanced arguments. My theory is that many feminists are profoundly stupid as well as hateful, a theory which could readily be tested by arresting a number of them and forcing them – with the threat of denying them access to chocolate – to undertake IQ tests. My suspicions on the matter are only reinforced by the lengthy terms with which feminists pepper their conversations. Normal women don't employ terms such as 'epistemological advantage' or 'patriarchal hegemony', do they?

Perhaps the most curious feminists are feminist academics, which is ironic because they're so incurious. They've built their castles in the air, and are busily adding to them. Not one of the feminist academics I contacted had the *slightest* interest in engaging in an exchanges of views. They appeared to me to be propagandists of the worst sort.

Feminists often refer to the process of indoctrinating people with their creed as 'raising their consciousness'. Dualism has an immediate appeal for people seeking a simple explanation of the world's ills, at least for people unable or unwilling to accept that nuances exist and are inevitable in a complex world: broadly speaking, in the case of feminism, that explanation is,

'Women good, men bad'. This reduction to absurdity is surely an example of consciousness *lowering* rather than raising, and is an assault on naturally enquiring intellects.

7 | WHY MEN HAVE NIPPLES, AND MY SEX CHANGE STORY

How beautiful maleness is, if it finds its right expression.
DH Lawrence 1885-1930 English author, poet, playwright, essayist and literary critic

Why do men have nipples? It's an age-old question to which we now have the answer, but before I reveal it I'd like to present the result of a Google search I undertook in September 2011, using that very question. The search purportedly found 1.81 million 'hits', which is surely a testament to the dysfunctional times we live in. The first 'hit' was a page on the *Guardian* website where people post questions and others post answers. The question, 'Why do men have nipples?' was posed by one Hilda Bird of Lagos, Portugal.

The following is a selection of my favourites from among the answers posted by visitors to the *Guardian* website, and I should like to thank them warmly.

'Why do men have nipples?

To help our creator to put the breastbone right in the middle.
Louis van de Geijn, Renkum, Netherlands

Because we are built to a common pattern. But in the process, female breasts happen to be more prominent!
Jhune Catubag, Parañaque, Philippines

Men have nipples because they'd look plain wrong without them.
Morven Gailey aged 7, Stroud, England

Men's nipples are purely there to indicate temperature, and a jolly good way of chastisement, a good tweek can stop even the naughtiest behaviour.
Janine Bailey, Oxford

I was short on male platty fish so I stole one from where I work. After about a month it turned into a female. Evidently some creatures can change gender after birth. Nipples are there just in case.
Peter Johnson, Stockton, Cleveland

I'm not really sure why but I'm so glad I have mine to tweak, at work or on the bus. Sometimes on the toilet reading the paper or while watching my neighbours through their window. They bought a rowing machine.
Andrew Anderson, Pakuranga, Auckland, New Zealand

The same reason women have beards!
Graham Foskett, Treakle, Bumstead

Men have nipples because they help men find water. Walk to where they point and when they cross, you're above water! Simple. Mainly why men drink so much beer, I guess.
Aaron Goodwin, Middle of England

Because people like me need something to play with when bored...
Adam Newsham, Preston

Because nipples are a turn-on.
Malika Othman, Scunthorpe

Something else for the female to suck on. ;P
Lucy Campbell, Rugby, Warwickshire

So when there's no boobs around you can pretend your a woman and play with yourself ;D
Dean, Jack and Connor, Derby, England

So if a man decides to have a sex change it makes the surgeon's job easier?
Harry Machin, Burslem, UK

Because without them men would get jealous.
Bethanie Lucas, Manchester

So my girlfriend (with her Jedi powers) can flick them both square on and make me cry like a girl.
Louis Wood, Wellington, UK

Oh my, some people are odd...
Sara Rickard, Newry, Ireland

Vestigiality – one of the strongest evidences for the Theory of Evolution. Creationism can never explain nipples in men, wisdom teeth, vermiform appendix etc.
Steve Martin, New York USA

The male nipple is an erogenous zone; manipulation of it during sexual interaction greatly increases the pleasure. I am an older male posing naked for art classes; never mind erections... my nipples (enlarged over the years from being handled) have been found more of a sexual turn-on during these sessions.
Edo Deweert, Rimbey, Canada'

[Author's note: Edo, have you never heard of the expression 'too much information'?]

Needless to say, someone then had to spoil it all with the correct answer:

'All humans begin life in the womb as females. If no Y chromosome is present in the foetus, then the embryo will continue to develop as and be born as a female. If there is a Y chromosome present in the embryo, the male sex hormone testosterone restricts the full development of breasts to just nipples, the labia fuse to become the scrotum and clitoris develops fully to become a penis. If the Y chromosome prevails in producing a male, this is not done without a fight. Male babies are weaker as a result than female ones, accounting for the slightly higher death rate in male babies.
Terence Hollingworth, Blagnac, France '

Terence Hollingworth: a fine French name. So let me get the details of my sex change right. In the womb I started off being of the female persuasion, but having a Y chromosome meant I converted to the male persuasion. Phew. That was a close shave. I have a contrary nature – as my ex-wives might possibly confirm – and without a Y chromosome I might have been called Michaela, become a feminist, and admired Harriet Harman. It's the stuff of nightmares.

8 | ARE FEMINISTS LESS INTELLIGENT THAN NORMAL WOMEN?

I happen to feel that the degree of a person's intelligence is directly reflected by the number of conflicting attitudes she can bring to bear on the same topic.
Lisa Alther 1944- American authoress: *Kinflicks* (1975)

Ms Alther makes a very good point, and by her criterion feminists – who studiously avoid challenges to their faith positions – are unintelligent. We've already seen the appeal of dualism to people seeking a simple explanation for the ills of a complex world.

From my communications with feminists I've concluded that they're markedly less intelligent than normal women. Not one of them was willing to engage in a serious exchange of views, and almost all of them rapidly brought out what they evidently considered a winning argument – to call anyone challenging them, including myself, a sexist or a misogynist.

Maybe there's a sampling issue. Maybe only the less intelligent ones are willing to communicate with me. Maybe the more intelligent ones avoid me. Maybe they look like supermodels, and play beach volleyball in their spare time. It's possible.

There's an obvious and simple way to discover whether or not feminists are indeed less intelligent than normal women, which is to have prominent feminists take IQ tests. Then we'll be able to compare their IQs with the IQs of normal women. I plan to write to the feminist politicians Harriet Harman, Yvette Cooper, and Angela Eagle, and ask if they'll take IQ tests to provide the necessary data. I'll offer to pay for the tests, so I'm not anticipating any objections.

9 | WHY ARE FAT WOMEN FAT?

It's a mystery,
Oh, it's a mystery.
Toyah Willcox 1958- English actress and singer: 'It's a Mystery' (song, 1981)

As an overweight man, I have accepted for many years the relationship between my 200-pound weight and my fondness for good food, beer and wine. Other fat men of my acquaintance were equally accepting of the relationship. Last year at the age of 52, on my doctor's advice, I embarked on a programme to lose weight and reduce my blood pressure. I cut down my calorie intake and undertook more exercise: two games of pool a week, nothing too onerous. Over six months I lost over 50 pounds. My blood pressure fell to target levels.

Women's weight problems appear to be different to men's weight problems. I never cease to be amazed at how many fat women believe there isn't a direct relationship between the calories they consume, and their weight. A fat woman recently declared to me, 'I only have to look at a chip to put on weight!' The next day I saw her in a local carvery, where customers can eat as much as they like. With a plate heaving with high-calorie food items she should have changed her plea to, 'I only have to eat ten roast potatoes to put on weight!' Half an hour later I was at the bar when she ordered a drink: Diet Coke.

With impeccable man logic I've sometimes pointed out to overweight ladies that every atom in their bodies was either present when they were born, or had since been ingested. With peccable lady logic they always beg to differ, but to date none has yet come up with a working hypothesis on womanly weight gain. Some years ago a woman told me, 'I'm overweight because of my hormones.' Quick as a flash I replied, 'Oh yes, the hormones that make you eat family-size pies!' I woke up in hospital two days later.

So it falls to me to introduce a theory which I confidently expect to land me the Nobel Prize in Physiology or Medicine. A simple observation was the key to solving the riddle of why fat women are fat. Fat women often have fat children, and their fatness generally stays with them into adult life. Their fat sons obviously eat and drink too much, but what of fat daughters? Might there be a genetic component to their weight problems?

I haven't ironed out all the details of my theory yet, but let's accept, for the sake of argument, that some women *are* genetically predisposed to putting on weight, regardless of what they eat and drink. The most obvious scientific explanation for this phenomenon is that the women are photosynthesising. The tissues under their skins contain carotenes.

Carotenes (a family of chemicals in plants which account, among much else, for the colour of carrots) contribute to photosynthesis by transmitting the light energy they absorb to chlorophyll, enabling plants to gain mass by converting carbon dioxide from the atmosphere into organic compounds, especially sugars.

Evidence to support my theory includes the fact that many fat women – in England at least – are orange.

In September 2011 a feminist emailed me about the cover of *The Glass Ceiling Delusion*, complaining that it played to the stereotype of feminists being unattractive.

In an effort to 'disprove' the stereotype she then bizarrely emailed me a photograph of herself, but being conscious that in the photograph she was very overweight, she informed me of a book which 'proved' that for many women obesity was the result of neither excess calorie intake nor inadequate exercise. We then had the following email exchange:

'Self: Every atom which is present in obese people, as in non-obese people, was either present at birth or was ingested later.

Feminist: You're wrong. You need to read the three books by this author which TOTALLY discredit the calories in/out model of weight gain.

Self: I lost over 50 pounds over six months simply by reducing my calorie intake and taking a little exercise.

Feminist: As a man you don't have the hormonal problems women have with respect to weight control.

Self: It can have nothing to do with hormones, unless they induce you to eat and drink too much, or exercise too little. The claim of there being no link between calories in/out and weight control is an absurd denial of two fundamental laws of nature, the Laws of Conservation of Energy and Mass.

Feminist: You're a f***ing endocrinologist and a physicist now, are you? Typical arrogant man! You misogynistic pig!!!

Self: Thank you. I've much enjoyed our chat, but I must dash.'

In early October 2011 I had an exchange of emails with an authoress who wanted some advice on publishing her forthcoming book on dieting. She'd lost 145 pounds in weight 'and I've kept it off for a year so far'. She wrote:

'I'm quite excited about my book <title redacted> and can see lots of spinoffs with this – maybe change my focus onto health as losing the weight has certainly changed my life. I used to say I was happy fat – I lied! It's fantastic to be able to wear normal size clothes and to have so much energy, and apparently men like my new bottom! There's something on Facebook with a picture of a chubby woman who says she is so large because of all the wisdom that can't fit in her head!!!'

10 | ARE FEMINISTS LESS ATTRACTIVE THAN NORMAL WOMEN?

Feminism is just a way for ugly women to get into the mainstream of America.
Rush Limbaugh 1951- American radio host and conservative political commentator

Many years ago, as a young man, I went to a nightclub late one evening, and made an observation which mystified me at the time, but which suddenly made sense when I came to write this chapter. There were perhaps 20 to 30 young women in the club, many of them inebriated in the British manner, which tends to shock those of the American persuasion. The behaviour of the young ladies ranged from attention-seeking on the dance floor to being slumped moodily in the darker corners of the room.

If I'd lined up the ladies in a line reflecting their apparent levels of confidence – an action to which they might have objected, to be fair – the line would have accurately displayed a spectrum of attractiveness, ranging from the least attractive woman in the room to the most attractive. There was clearly some sort of hierarchy based on attractiveness, in a way that was far less true of the young *men* in the room. Why might this be? We'll return to the question shortly.

Are feminists less attractive than normal women? In general, yes. Oh, come on. A number of feminists contacted me after the publication of *The Glass Ceiling Delusion* to complain that the woman on the cover pandered to the stereotype of feminists being unattractive.

Ironically, they themselves were reinforcing the stereotype. It hadn't occurred to me that anyone might think the woman was a feminist. The image had simply been one of more than 7,000 photographs on an internet photograph library[1] which appeared after I'd employed the keywords 'angry woman'. From memory it was the only photograph which showed an angry woman looking upwards into the viewer's eyes, thereby intimating that she was looking *through* the glass ceiling at the viewer, by implication a senior executive. The responses I received from a number of the feminists to this explanation might best be described as unladylike.

The fact that *some* feminists are physically attractive doesn't alter the fact that most aren't. There often seems to be a link between the degree of a feminist's unattractiveness and her commitment to feminist ideology. The late Andrea Dworkin comes inevitably to mind. Until and unless we accept the link between unattractiveness and feminism we can't begin to understand one of the prime reasons feminists are so angry, unless there's some truth in an alternative explanation I outline in the next chapter, that feminists might suffer from PPS (Permanent Premenstrual Syndrome).

British author Steve Moxon in his book *The Woman Racket* (2008) describes the male dominance hierarchy ('DH'). In the pre-industrial world a man's position in the DH was largely dictated by physical prowess or access to men and arms, while in the modern developed world it's largely dictated by actual or potential financial resources. Women seek partners as high up the hierarchy as possible and have their own dominance hierarchy, as Moxon explains:

> 'So how does a female DH form if it does not involve physical contest? Mostly it's simply by inheritance – including in primates and human societies. The physical attributes of

---

[1] http://bigstockphoto.com

females that are attractive to males in signalling fertility of youth and beauty are predominantly genetically based, so are well conserved from one generation to the next. Attractive women will tend to have attractive daughters. The key attribute of youth is an even more pronounced 'given', in that older age cohorts are simply not 'in the game'.

In traditional societies a woman's position in the DH is largely a product of nature, as youth and beauty are the main factors. However the existence in modern societies of multi-billion dollar cosmetics, fashion and plastic surgery industries shows that beauty can be enhanced and the ravages of age can at least be postponed. The rocketing sales of celebrity and beauty magazines show that women are indeed keen to rank themselves according to a uniquely female DH; but the great difficulty involved in attempting to overcome the limitations of nature has manifested itself in the form of modern female epidemics such as anorexia nervosa and bulimia, slimming disorders being rare in males.

Perhaps the sheer difficulty of the task of climbing the female DH (males simply have to work harder or take extra risks) explains the fascination of Victoria Beckham to a female audience – her strange elfish features and cyborg-style cartoon body are more frequently found on the front covers of women's magazines than anyone else. If such an odd-looking creature is attractive to an über-alpha male like her husband David, then women are understandably eager to re-assess their *own* DH ranking in the light of this.

Females also tend to compete by doing down other females in terms of sexual propriety – hence the common playground 'ho' and 'slag' derogations. This alerts men to a woman's propensity to indulge in extra-pair sex, and consequently might well put them off considering her as a long-term partner.'

While women bemoan societal pressures to be attractive and slim, for example by exposure to advertisements for cosmetics and skincare products, you have to ask why they respond to those pressures so much more readily than men would. The use of such products as 'manscara' and skin products for men appear limited to fashionable 'metrosexuals'. The answer is clear. Women receive special treatment in proportion to their degree of attractiveness – mainly, but not solely, special treatment from men. There's a high financial and emotional return on attractiveness for women, a great deal higher than the returns enjoyed by attractive men.

The higher up the female dominance hierarchy a woman can manage to climb, the better her chances of attaining and retaining a high status male. The 'attaining' element typically results in marriage, and given the crippling financial implications of divorce to men, women have little incentive to remain slim and attractive after they marry; which perhaps goes some way to explaining the near-universal phenomenon of women putting on weight in the months and years after they marry. While their husbands remain in fine physical condition throughout their lives, obviously…

But what of the women towards the bottom of the female dominance hierarchy, the *least* attractive women? For many of them, even a superhuman effort won't move them far up the hierarchy, so they inevitably feel a resentment towards not only the men who pay them less attention than they pay more attractive women, but also towards the women able to exploit their attractiveness. It shouldn't come as a surprise that such women will tend to have a bitter outlook on the world, and seminars on 'Celebrating and Experiencing Fatness' (which we'll be coming to later in this book) make sense in this light.

There's an intriguing irony here. The women who come the closest to attaining equality with men are the *least* attractive women, because they share men's challenge to improve their lives through the medium of work rather than relying on their attractiveness to exploit the earning power of a partner. It's little wonder unattractive women are unhappy so much of the time, or that they make up such a large proportion of the feminist sisterhood.

A final thought. I've long been puzzled at the lack of serious criticism of feminists from the vast majority of women who are not themselves feminists, and whose interests are harmed by them. What might account for this? On the one hand, there's a strong class identity among women, who typically derive much of their self-esteem simply from being women. Men, conversely, typically acquire self-esteem from what they achieve in life, often through work.

But I suspect also that attractive women are conscious that unattractive women aren't enjoying the special treatment that they themselves enjoy, and feel some guilt about that reality. Also, I suspect, many women simply find some feminists *terrifying*.

11 | DO FEMINISTS SUFFER FROM PPS (PERMANENT PREMENSTRUAL SYNDROME)?

Women complain about premenstrual syndrome, but I think of it as the only time of the month that I can be myself.
Roseanne Barr 1952- American actress, comedienne, writer, television producer, director

As a business executive, I started managing staff in the early 1980s. I well remember one female member of staff, Mary, who had time off every month so she might better cope with 'women's problems'. Ironically Mary *was* quite contrary, in accordance with the English nursery rhyme. How her garden grew, I have no idea. I digress.

Mary was a Leftie; you'd probably have predicted that. Her absences from work would last two or three consecutive days, the days generally adjoining a weekend or a bank holiday.

She wasn't one of life's sunniest characters. During the days leading up to her monthly mini-holidays she was even more difficult than usual, and the other members of staff would whisper to each other when Mary's 'time' came around again.

An acquaintance who knows a number of feminists tells me that in his experience feminists have their 'time' 365 days a year, and 366 days in a leap year. So is feminism simply a result of hormonal imbalances? We need some research on this. In a later chapter we shall consider a book by a psychologist of the female persuasion, Professor Louann Brizendine's *The Female Brain* (2006). A short extract is appropriate here:

'One day it struck me that male versus female depression rates didn't start to diverge until females turned 12 or 13 – the age girls began menstruating. It appeared that the chemical changes at puberty did something in the brain to trigger more depression in women...

When I started taking a woman's hormonal state into account as I evaluated her psychiatrically, I discovered the massive neurological affects her hormones have during different stages in life in shaping her desires, her values, *and the very way she perceives reality.* [Author's italics]

Of the fluctuations that begin as early as three months old and last until after menopause, a woman's neurological reality is not as constant as a man's. His is like a mountain that is worn away imperceptibly over the millennia by glaciers, weather, and the deep tectonic movements of the earth. Hers is more like the weather itself – constantly changing and hard to predict.'

Here's an idea. Maybe we could rid the world of feminism by regularly measuring feminists' hormone levels, then adjusting the levels until they started to think and act like normal women. Think how much happier they'd be and, by extension, how much happier the other 95% of the population would be. I'm sure feminists would look favourably on the idea if I and other right-minded men just explained it to them slowly...

12| FEMINISM: THE TRIUMPH OF EMOTION OVER REASON?

All that is necessary for the triumph of evil women is that good women do nothing.

on Harriet Harman, a British feminist politician, and her like
Mike Buchanan 1957- British writer: *The Glass Ceiling Delusion* (2011)

Are women in general more emotional and less rational than men? Of course they are. Anyone who denies the assertion is out of touch with the reality we can see all around us, all the time. Wilfully out of touch, probably.

Are feminists more emotional and less rational than normal women? Of course they are. We see that with their inability and/or unwillingness to engage with the rational arguments that demonstrably prove every element of 'feminist theory' to be one or more of the following – a conspiracy theory, fantasy, lie, delusion or myth. There is as much evidence to support 'fairies at the bottom of the garden theory' as there is to support 'feminist theory' i.e. none.

There, that's a potentially thorny issue dealt with by the razor-sharp sword of man logic. Let's move on to the different natures of men and women.

13 | THE DIFFERENT NATURES OF MEN AND WOMEN

'Mrs Merton' to Debbie McGee: 'But what first, Debbie, attracted you to millionaire Paul Daniels?'
Caroline Aherne 1963- English comedienne, writer and actress: *The Mrs Merton Show* (1994-8)

An early part of this chapter is drawn from *The Glass Ceiling Delusion* (2011) and it mainly covers the issues of why men and women tend to have different natures, and how those differences manifest themselves in relation to the world of work. In my critique of marriage in the developed world in the modern era *The Marriage Delusion: the fraud of the rings?* (2008) – later published as a paperback with the title *The Fraud of the Rings* – I covered the question of the different natures of men and women in the context of marriage, and why they are so often a problem in the modern era.

There are men among us with faces which (let's be kind) only a mother could love. Some of these men happen to be rich, famous, or powerful: 'alpha males'. They commonly share an attribute, having (or having once had) remarkably beautiful partners. One thinks of the musical theatre composer Andrew Lloyd-Webber (Sarah Brightman), the magician Paul Daniels (Debbie McGee), the entrepreneur Bernie Ecclestone (Slavica Radić, a former fashion model 11.5 inches taller and 28 years younger than lucky Bernie), the tennis player Andy Murray (Kim Sears) and the French president Nicolas Sarkozy (Carla Bruni).

Notably beautiful women do not, it would appear, fall in love with *poor* unattractive men. Perhaps they're not as beautiful as we think. *I* would look pretty stood next to some of these men.

We shall return to the important phenomenon of female attractiveness later in the chapter.

Why should we have an interest in gender-typical traits? Why can we not treat everyone as individuals, thereby avoiding the cardinal sin of stereotyping? The reason is that women campaign collectively – and effectively – for women's interests at the expense of men's interests, while men rarely campaign for men's interests, effectively or otherwise. The 'shortage' of female engineers is seen to be a problem requiring to be addressed, while the 'shortage' of male psychologists isn't. The inevitable result? A considerable amount of taxpayers' money continues to be spent 'encouraging' – in plain English, bribing – young women into engineering, and other 'male typical' fields, but with minimal impact. Even today, well over 90% of engineering graduates are men.

For the avoidance of doubt, when I refer to men and women from this point onwards I shall mean gender-typical men and women – by definition, the majority – unless I make it clear I mean otherwise. I don't consider either gender innately superior to the other, but I think it's clear that the genders are in general *different* in their habits of thinking and acting. I'm now 54, and the different natures of men and women have been clear to me from an early age. 'Nature' being a word whose meaning may be ambiguous, let me state clearly what I mean by it in the context of this book. In general, I believe, men and women differ with respect to:

- their level of interest in interpersonal relationships with family members, friends, and work colleagues
- their relative interests in work, politics and business
- their attitudes towards risk

- their attitudes towards 'work/life balance': the types of work they seek, the hours they devote to work, and their ambition to be promoted
- their styles of operating in the world of work: men being more naturally competitive, women being more naturally co-operative

If these differences are real, it follows that they will impact on men's and women's life choices and therefore their average incomes. The most commonly cited measure of the 'gender pay gap' relates to the incomes of male and female full-time workers *regardless of the equivalence of their lines of work*. The gap, while it exists, is not the result of discrimination against women. It's attributable to the choices men and women freely make in their personal and working lives, including the greater readiness of women to take career breaks to look after babies, young children and ageing relatives. If and when women in significant numbers make different choices, the pay gap will disappear.

[Update: In 2015, there was virtually no pay gap for people below the age of 40. William Collins published an important article on the matter.[1]]

If we accept for the moment that, in general, men's and women's natures are different, what might be the source of those difference? Could it be something as obvious as men's and women's brains being different? For answers to this question we turn first to a book written by an American professor, Louann Brizendine, on the time-honoured 'ladies first' principle. From Wikipedia:

---

[1] http://mra-uk.co.uk/?p=150

'Louann Brizendine is a neuropsychiatrist and the author of *The Female Brain*, published in 2006. Her research concerns women's moods and hormones. She graduated in neurobiology from UC Berkeley, attended Yale School of Medicine and completed a residency in psychiatry at Harvard Medical School. She is board-certified in psychiatry and neurology and is an endowed clinical professor. She joined the faculty of UCSF Medical Center at the Langley Porter Psychiatric Institute in 1988 and now holds the Lynne and Marc Benioff-endowed chair of psychiatry. At UCSF, Brizendine pursues active clinical, teaching, writing and research activities.

In 1994 she founded the UCSF Women's Mood and Hormone Clinic, and continues to serve as its director. The Women's Mood and Hormone Clinic is a psychiatric clinic designed to assess and treat women of all ages experiencing disruption of mood, energy, anxiety, sexual function and well-being due to hormonal influences on the brain. Brizendine also treats couples in the clinic.

Additionally, Brizendine teaches courses to medical students, residents and other physicians throughout the country, addressing the neurobiology of hormones, mood disorders, anxiety problems, and sexual interest changes due to hormones.'

Professor Brizendine is clearly far more qualified than I to make statements about the female brain and to compare it with the male brain. What startled me when I read *The Female Brain* was the sheer extent of the differences between the two brains: men and women truly do inhabit different mental worlds. Brizendine outlines how a range of hormones affect women's brains as they progress through life stages: foetal, girlhood, puberty, sexual maturity/single woman, pregnancy, breast feeding, childrearing, perimenopause, menopause, and postmenopause. She reveals in the book that during her medical education at Berkeley, Yale and Harvard, she 'learned little or nothing about female biological or neurological difference outside of pregnancy', and continues:

'The little research that was available, however, suggested that the brain differences, though subtle, were profound. As a resident in psychiatry, I became fascinated by the fact that there was a two-to-one ratio of depression in women compared with men. No one was offering any clear reasons for this discrepancy. Because I had gone to college at the peak of the feminist movement, my personal explanations ran toward the political and the psychological. I took the typical 1970s stance that the patriarchy of Western culture must have been the culprit. It must have kept women down and made them less functional than men. But that explanation alone didn't seem to fit: new studies were uncovering the same depression ratio worldwide. I started to think that something bigger, more basic and biological, was going on.

One day it struck me that male versus female depression rates didn't start to diverge until females turned 12 or 13 – the age girls began menstruating. It appeared that the chemical changes at puberty did something in the brain to trigger more depression in women...

When I started taking a woman's hormonal state into account as I evaluated her psychiatrically, I discovered the massive neurological affects her hormones have during different stages in life in shaping her desires, her values, *and the very way she perceives reality.* [Author's italics]

Of the fluctuations that begin as early as three months old and last until after menopause, a woman's neurological reality is not as constant as a man's. His is like a mountain that is worn away imperceptibly over the millennia by glaciers, weather, and the deep tectonic movements of the earth. Hers is more like the weather itself – constantly changing and hard to predict.'

From the chapter, 'The Birth of the Female Brain':

'Common sense tells us that boys and girls behave differently. We see it every day at home, on the playground, and in classrooms. But what the culture hasn't told us is that the brain dictates these divergent behaviors. The impulses of children are so innate that they kick in even if we adults try to nudge them in another direction. One of my patients gave her three-and-a-half-year-old daughter many unisex toys including a bright red fire truck instead of a doll. She walked into her daughter's room one afternoon to find her cuddling the truck in a baby blanket, rocking it back and forth, saying, 'Don't worry, little truckie, everything will be all right.'

This isn't socialization. The little girl didn't cuddle her 'truckie' because her environment molded her unisex brain. There is no unisex brain. She was born with a female brain, which came complete with its own impulses. Girls arrive already wired as girls, and boys arrive already wired as boys. Their brains are different by the time they're born, and their brains are what drive their impulses, values, and their very reality.'

From a later chapter, 'The Future of the Female Brain':

'Almost every woman I have seen in my office, when asked what would be her top three wishes if her fairy godmother could wave her magic wand and grant them, says, 'Joy in my life, a fulfilling relationship, and less stress with more personal time.'

Our modern life – the double shift of career and primary responsibility for the household and family – has made these goals particularly difficult to achieve. We are stressed out by this arrangement, and our leading cause of anxiety and depression is stress. One of the great mysteries of our lives is why we as women are so devoted to this current social contract *which often operates against the natural wiring of our female brains and biological reality.* [Author's italics]

During the 1990s and the early part of this millennium, a new set of scientific facts and ideas about the female brain has been unfolding. These biological truths have become a powerful stimulus for the reconsideration of a woman's social contract. In writing this book I have struggled with two voices in my head – one is the scientific truth, the other is political correctness. I have chosen to emphasize scientific truth over political correctness even though scientific truths may not always be as welcome.'

How, you might well ask, can 'almost every woman' seeking 'less stress with more personal time' be reconciled with women's alleged quests for senior positions in the workplace in general, and for executive directorships of major companies in particular? It can't. Professor Brizendine followed *The Female Brain* with *The Male Brain* (2010). It's larger, but less interesting. The book, that is.

Onto an important book written by Simon Baron-Cohen, an eminent British psychologist. His biography on Wikipedia:

> 'Simon Baron-Cohen FBA is a Professor of Developmental Psychopathology in the Departments of Psychiatry and Experimental Psychology at the University of Cambridge in the United Kingdom. He is the Director of the University's Autism Research Centre, and a Fellow of Trinity College. He is best known for his work on autism, including his early theory that autism involves degrees of 'mindblindness' (or delays in the development of theory of mind); and his later theory that autism is an extreme form of the 'male brain', which involved a reconceptualisation of typical psychological sex differences in terms of empathizing – systemizing theory.'

The professor's book *The Essential Difference* was first published in 2003. [Update: the latest edition was published in 2012.] He starts by summarising the theory outlined in the book:

> 'The female brain is predominantly hard-wired for empathy.
>
> The male brain is predominantly hard-wired for understanding and building systems.'

He describes empathising in the following terms:

> 'Empathising is the drive to identify another person's emotions and thoughts, and to respond to them with an appropriate emotion. Empathising does not entail just the cold calculation of what someone else thinks and feels (or what is sometimes called mind reading). Psychopaths can do that much. Empathising occurs when we feel an appropriate emotional reaction, an emotion *triggered* by the other person's emotion, and it is done in order to understand another

person, to predict their behaviour, and to connect or resonate with them emotionally.'

Systemising is described as follows:

'Systemising is the drive to analyse, explore, and construct a system. The systemiser intuitively figures out how things work, or extracts the underlying rules that govern the behaviour of a system. This is done in order to understand and predict the system, or to invent a new one...

Just as empathising is powerful enough to cope with the hundreds of emotions that exist, so systemising is a process that can cope with an enormous number of systems. I will argue that, on average, males spontaneously systemise to a greater extent than do females.'

The good professor points out here – as indeed he does throughout the book – that he does not mean 'all males' or 'all females': he is talking about *statistical averages*. I contend that success in senior positions in major organisations requires strong systemising skills, not strong empathising skills: so without positive discrimination for women we shall *never* have gender balance in the boardroom.

Gender balance in the boardroom is not of the slightest interest to the vast majority of women; it is of interest only to feminists, an assortment of people – almost all women – driven by left-wing ideology. David Cameron, the current British prime minister, is a feminist despite being the leader of the Conservative party. What times we live in.

Baron-Cohen writes about the advantages of systemising brains to human males early in the species' evolution, which fell under the categories of using and making tools, hunting and tracking, trading, attaining and exercising power, developing expertise, tolerating solitude, being aggressive, and being leaders. The advantages of empathising brains to early females are explored under the categories of making friends, mothering, gossiping, being socially mobile, and reading partners' intentions. Systemising brains are increasingly advantageous to individuals as they climb the hierarchy of major organisations, and this on its own would largely account for the enduring preponderance of men in senior positions.

Questionnaires for self-assessment of empathising and systemising natures are provided in *The Essential Difference.*

There's a large and growing body of evidence supporting Baron-Cohen's theory that people exhibiting the condition of autism – a spectrum of disorders which includes Asperger Syndrome – have 'extreme male brains'. On average, compared to both men and women on average, they are markedly less empathising, and markedly more systemising. Baron-Cohen points out that these people can lead productive lives if their work plays to their strengths rather than their weaknesses. Some autistic men are found in the top levels of IT companies, for example. Studies of identical and non-identical twins strongly suggest that autism is heritable. In people diagnosed with high-functioning autism or Asperger Syndrome, the sex ratio is at least *ten males to every female.*

Baron-Cohen puts a figure of 2.5 per cent on the proportion of the population born with an extreme male brain, but what about the extreme *female* brain, which theory predicts should be as common? He continues:

> 'All scientists know about the extreme female brain is that it is expected to arise… Scientists have never got up close to these individuals. It is a bit like positing the existence of a new animal on theoretical grounds, and then setting out to discover if it is really found in nature…
>
> People with the extreme female brain would have average or significantly better empathising ability than that of other people in the general population, but their systemising would

be impaired. So these would be people who have difficulty understanding maths or physics or machines or chemistry, *as systems*. But they could be extremely accurate at tuning in to others' feelings and thoughts.

Would such a profile carry any necessary disability? Hyper-empathising could be a great asset, and poor systemising may not be too crippling. It is possible that the extreme female brain is not seen in clinics because it is not maladaptive...

A contender for who might have the extreme female brain would be a wonderfully caring person who can rapidly make you feel fully understood. For example, an endlessly patient psychotherapist who is excellent at rapidly tuning in to your feelings and your situation, who not only says he or she feels a great sadness at your sadness or great pleasure at your pleasure but also actually experiences those emotions as vividly as if your feelings were theirs.

However, the contender for the extreme female brain would also need to be someone who was virtually technically disabled. Someone for whom maths, computers, or political schisms, or DIY, held no interest. Indeed, someone who found activities requiring systemising hard to follow. We may all know people like this, but it is likely that they do not find their way into clinics, except perhaps as staff in the caring professions.'

I have a strong suspicion that many feminists (particularly lesbian feminists) have male brains, which might help explain why so many are masculine, assertive, and work-centred.

Feminists are among those unfortunate souls genetically predisposed to hold Left-wing views, which isn't a great starting point in the lottery of life, is it? An article in *The Daily Telegraph* of 29 October 2010, 'Feeling liberal? It's in your genes':

'Holding liberal views could be in the blood, scientists said after identifying a gene that makes someone more open-minded. The 'liberal gene' opens up a person to new ideas and alternative ways of living and could influence their belief in Left-wing politics, according to the research. It may mean that liberals are born, not made, although the effect is exacerbated if an individual has many friends during their formative years.

The 'liberal gene' is a transmitter in the brain called DRD4 which is connected to dopamine, known as the reward currency. Dopamine affects the way the brain experiences emotions, pleasures and pain and can therefore influence personality traits.

When adolescents with the gene are also socially outgoing with many friends, they seek and receive other people's points of view, which triggers a pleasurable 'reward' of dopamine. This suggests that, as adults, they will be more open-minded and tend to form less conventional political viewpoints, the study said.

Published in the *Journal of Politics*, the research by scientists from the University of California and Harvard studied 2,000 Americans. It found those with a strain of the DRD4 gene seek out 'novelty', such as people and ways of living different from the ones they are used to. This leads them to have more politically liberal opinions, it found. The person's age, ethnicity, gender or culture appeared to make no difference – it was the genes that counted.

Prof James Fowler, who led the research, said: 'It is the critical interaction of two factors – the genetic predisposition and the environmental condition of having many friends in adolescence – that is associated with being more liberal. These findings suggest that political affiliation is not based solely on the kind of social environment people experience.' '

The paper's editorial on the same day contained a piece titled, 'Lifetime cure for Lefties':

'Scientists have given mankind many blessings, but the discovery of the gene for Left-wing behaviour must be foremost among them. For now there is a diagnosis, there can be a cure. Just think of it – a quick screening of the unborn infant, a mild course of gene therapy, and hey presto! The disease can be eradicated within a generation.

Perhaps we are getting a little ahead of ourselves. But even if science falls short of an outright cure, it should still be possible to ameliorate the symptoms. The gene does not automatically make the carrier a Lefty; rather, it triggers the adolescent brain's reward mechanism in the presence of novel experiences and viewpoints. The treatment is simple: lock teenage sufferers in a drab room, furnished with the works of Hayek and Friedman. True, their social skills will be somewhat stunted. But the benefits will last a lifetime.'

Canadian-American Steven Pinker is a Professor of Psychology at Harvard University and the author of a number of acclaimed books including *The Blank Slate: The Modern Denial of Human Nature* (2002). He starts the book with the following passage on 'The Blank Slate, the Noble Savage, and the Ghost in the Machine':

'Everyone has a theory of human nature. Everyone has to anticipate the behavior of others, and that means we all need theories about what makes people tick. A tacit theory of human nature – that behavior is caused by thoughts and feelings – is embedded in the very way we think about people. We fill out this theory by introspecting on our own minds and assuming that our fellows are like ourselves, and by watching people's behavior and filing away generalizations. We absorb still other ideas from our intellectual climate: from the expertise of authorities and the conventional wisdom of the day.

Our theory of human nature is the wellspring of much in our lives. We consult it when we want to persuade or threaten, inform or deceive. It advises us on how to nurture our marriages, bring up our children, and control our own behavior. Its assumptions about learning drive our educational policy; its assumptions about motivation drive our policies on economics, law, and crime. And because it delineates what people can achieve easily, what they can achieve only with sacrifice or pain, and what they cannot achieve at all, it affects our values: what we believe we can reasonably strive for as individuals and as a society. Rival theories of human nature are entwined in different ways of life and different political systems, and have been a source of much conflict over the course of history.'

From a later section of the chapter:

'Every society must operate with a theory of human nature, and *our intellectual mainstream is committed to one* [Author's italics]. The theory is seldom articulated or overtly embraced, but it lies at the heart of a vast number of beliefs and policies. Bertrand Russell wrote, 'Every man, wherever he goes, is encompassed by a cloud of comforting convictions, which move with him like flies on a summer day.'

For intellectuals today, many of those convictions are about psychology and social relations. I will refer to those convictions as the Blank Slate: the idea that the human mind has no inherent structure and can be inscribed at will by society or ourselves.

That theory of human nature – namely, that it barely exists – is the topic of this book.'

Pinker later goes on to state that, 'The Blank Slate has become the secular religion of modern intellectual life'. The Blank Slate theory of human nature is espoused by feminists, explicitly or implicitly. Pinker convincingly demonstrates that the theory is deeply flawed. From the same book:

'Contrary to popular belief, parents in contemporary America do not treat their sons and daughters very differently. A recent assessment of 172 studies involving 28,000 children found that boys and girls are given similar amounts of encouragement, warmth, nurturance, restrictiveness, discipline, and clarity of communication. The only substantial difference was that about two-thirds of the boys were discouraged from playing with dolls, especially by their fathers, out of a fear that they would become gay. (Boys who prefer girls' toys often do turn out gay, but forbidding them the toys does not change the outcome.)

Nor do differences between boys and girls depend on their observing masculine behavior in their fathers and feminine behavior in their mothers. When Hunter has two mommies, he acts just as much like a boy as if he had a mommy and a daddy.

Things are not looking good for the theory that boys and girls are born identical except for their genitalia, with all other differences coming from the way society treats them. If that were true, it would be an amazing coincidence that in every society the coin flip that assigns each sex to one set of roles would land the same way (or that one fateful flip at the dawn of the species should have been maintained without interruption across all the upheavals of the past 100,000 years).

It would be just as amazing that, time and again, society's arbitrary assignments matched the predictions that a Martian biologist would make for our species based on our anatomy and the distribution of our genes. It would seem odd that the hormones that make us male and female in the first place also modulate the characteristically male and female mental traits, both decisively in early brain development and in smaller degrees throughout our lives.

It would be all the more odd that a second genetic mechanism differentiating the sexes (genomic imprinting) also installs characteristic male and female talents. Finally, two key predictions of the social construction theory – that boys treated as girls will grow up with girls' minds, and that differences between boys and girls can be traced to differences in how their parents treat them – have gone down in flames.

Of course, just because many sex differences are rooted in biology does not mean that one sex is superior, that the differences will emerge for all people in all circumstances, that discrimination against a person based on sex is justified, or that people should be coerced into doing things typical of their sex. But neither are the differences without consequences.

By now many people are happy to say what was unsayable in polite company a few years ago: that males and females do not have interchangeable minds... But among many professional women the existence of sex differences is still a source of discomfort. As one colleague said to me, 'Look, I know that males and females are not identical. I see it in my kids, I see it in myself, I know about the research. I can't explain it, but when I read claims about sex differences, *steam comes out of my ears*.' '

The phenomenon of women becoming angry and irrational whenever their viewpoints are challenged is one that men learn to live with, often by feigning to agree with women. This leads to infantilised women, and long-suffering men.

The reader interested in the biological basis of gender differences, and how they manifest themselves in the real world, will find much of interest in *Why Men Don't Iron: The Real Science of Gender Studies* (1998) by Dr Anne Moir and her husband Bill. Truly a book well ahead of its time. Anne began her career as an academic scientist, winning a Doctorate from Oxford University for her genetic research. She's now a respected and widely published authority on the rapidly developing science of neuropsychology, and the author of three international bestsellers. Her website is well worth visiting.[1]

For an illustration of how men's and women's natures differ, we need look no further than the Women's Institutes. The combined membership of Women's Institutes in the United Kingdom is around 205,000. They 'play a unique role in providing women with educational opportunities and the chance to build new skills, to take part in a wide variety of activities and to campaign on issues that matter to them and their communities'. Membership is, not unnaturally, restricted to women.

If men had an equivalent body to the Women's Institute – the Men's Institute, say – and excluded women from its membership, doubtless the body would face demands from women to admit them, and change its name to the People's Institute.

Men happily recognise that while men and women enjoy the company of the opposite sex, at times they welcome just the company of their own sex, which is why men have no problem with bodies such as the Women's Institute, or with The Orange

---

[1] http://brainsexmatters.com

Prize for Fiction (a book competition open only to authoresses), or women-only competitions in sports, even when men don't enjoy an advantage on physical strength grounds (snooker, darts etc.). But do women accord men the same courtesy? Of course not. The media these days rarely report stories of women's hostility towards men excluding women from their activities – presumably readers are heartily fed up with the subject, and examples of men excluding women from *anything* are now rare – so we go back some years for a couple of articles on the matter, to look at feminists' thinking on the matter. The first is titled, 'Men-only clubs will not be outlawed' from the 7 December 1999 edition of *The Independent*:

'The Government last night denied reports that it has secret plans to ban men-only members clubs following admissions from ministers that clubs that barred women from membership were 'anachronisms'.

The moves were said to be being discussed by at least four ministers, including the Cabinet Office Minister, Mo Mowlam. They would lead to the end of membership restrictions from every body ranging from the 17th century St James's Club in London to golf clubs and the traditional Labour bastion, the working men's club.

It was claimed that private clubs, exempted by the Sex Discrimination Act, would be modernised under an amendment to the Equal Opportunities Bill in the next session of parliament. Senior Labour figures are said to be heartened by recent about-turns by men-only stalwarts such as the MCC which last year voted to admit women after 211 years.

A Government spokesman rejected reports of new laws in the pipeline. Many topics were covered in ministerial discussions on equality but Government plans for anti-discrimination legislation did not extend beyond public bodies.

Last night Nicholas Soames MP, the former Tory defence minister, who is a member of White's, Pratt's and the Turf, said: 'This is another sign that living under New Labour is like living in Soviet Russia. What sensible woman wants to be a member of a men's club?' '

A good point, Mr Soames, and well made. Now there's a man you can imagine tucking enthusiastically into rhubarb crumble and custard at his club. The following article was printed in the paper the next day, titled 'The Irritations of Modern Life: Men-only Clubs':

'I have often wondered what men do in all-male clubs. Million-pound deals? Homosexual rituals? Men, especially if they belong to the Garrick Club, are reticent, giving the impression that it involves little more than long lunches, at which they get slightly squiffy and eat nursery food. Yet, as soon as someone proposes changing the law to force such clubs to admit women, it is as if the very foundations of civilisation had begun to shudder.

'A grotesque curtailment of freedom of association – an almost totalitarian assertion that the state should be able to decide with whom you can spend your own free time on property private to you...' is how *The Daily Telegraph* greeted the news that the Government is thinking of banning men-only establishments. Yikes! Next thing you know, Tony Blair will be personally knocking on *Telegraph* readers' doors, pushing a female across the threshold and instructing them to talk to her.

Of course, there are few subjects so likely to fire up a right-wing leader-writer. The age-old right of the British upper classes to exclude outsiders is slowly being whittled away. The Reform Club has admitted women for years; even Lord's is not the bastion it was. What's left for the man who sometimes feels the need to be with people who, not to put too fine a point on it, aren't going to go all funny and exhibit symptoms of pre-menstrual tension?

Men's clubs are an anachronism. Their very existence institutionalises discrimination, draping it with a veil of respectability. When I witnessed the reaction to this mild move towards equality, I felt as if I'd been transported back to a time when misogyny was so firmly taken for granted that most people didn't even have a name for it. Now we do, and it's not acceptable. The bad news for club bores, tucking into bread-and-butter pudding in Covent Garden – or, indeed, a working men's club in Halifax – is that the time has come to grow up.'

Ah yes. 'An anachronism.' 'The time has come to grow up.' I don't suppose the journalist – a woman, it need hardly be said – is quite so agitated by the Women's Institute, even many years later. And with such arguments, women seek to hide the real reasons they want to stop men associating freely with one another, whatever they are. Maybe they've learned of our plan to withdraw voting rights from them. Damn. We've managed to keep that under wraps for *years*.

On to *Woman's Hour*, a staple of BBC Radio 4. From their website:

> 'October 7 1946 was the start of something big – it was the first broadcast of a programme designed to celebrate, entertain and inform women.'

I've never heard a man suggest there should be a programme for men, *Men's Hour* possibly, 'a programme designed to celebrate, entertain and inform men'. [Update: The BBC subsequently launched *Men's Hour* on a less popular channel than Radio 4, Radio 5 Live. It is unremittingly feminist-friendly in its output, and to the best of my knowledge has never acknowledged the existence of my political party, Justice for Men & Boys, which was launched in February 2012, the same month the ebook edition of this book was published.]

I often heard *Woman's Hour* when driving around the country on business, and did so on 27 April 2009. It's often an interesting programme but some topics come up with mind-numbing regularity. One is the so-called 'gender pay gap', annoyingly – to some people, at least – still a reality 40 years after the 1970 Equal Pay Act. The report concerned Harriet Harman who was putting forward the Equality Bill, which included provisions to require organisations to publish individuals' salaries. The inference, as always, was that women are discriminated against by men.

But the gender pay gap *isn't* attributable to discrimination against women once a number of factors are taken into account, such as choice of profession, career breaks for having children, many women preferring part-time work, and women taking earlier retirement than men. Not that you'll ever hear this mentioned on *Woman's Hour.* Or at least *I* haven't heard it in the past 30 years of listening occasionally to the programme.

A later discussion in the same episode concerned women giving up highly paid stressful jobs to enable them to work for themselves, often on low incomes, or to do jobs they found more fulfilling. One of the women had been a 'high-flying lawyer'. The general tone of the discussion was a celebration of women who decided to forsake lucrative but demanding jobs in favour of more job satisfaction. One woman made the following observation:

> 'So many women I know are crying themselves to sleep on a Sunday night, because they really can't bear the thought of going to work the next day.'

No connection was made by the good ladies on the programme between the gender pay gap and women voluntarily opting out of highly paid, stressful, unfulfilling jobs. Nor was it considered worth raising that even if a gender pay gap did still exist, it might be attributable to men being more willing than women to continue with such jobs. And so the myths of discrimination against women and the 'glass ceiling' roll on year after year.

The enthusiasm with which politicians – both female and male – keep perpetuating the myth of the gender pay gap is surely a testimony to its enduring vote-delivering powers among female voters. In October 2010 Prime Minister David Cameron, during a major interview on BBC television, made the ridiculous assertion that the difference between men's pay and women's pay was 'scandalous'.

Many women work to achieve financial security, but this is generally not their *preferred* option. Women's search for financial security has traditionally focused on securing a higher status partner, and this has remained unchanged into the modern era. In his 1998 book *The Secrets of Love and Lust*, Simon Andreae had some interesting things to say about women's search for 'Mr Right':

> 'Handsome men will pass their physical advantages down to the children of whoever they mate with, giving those children a head-start in the race for reproductive success. The indices of conventional male good looks – a rugged jaw, broad shoulders, a full head of hair and a healthy physique – are also indications of genetic health and strength. Yet looks in the opposite sex seem to be less important to women than they are to men, and less important than other factors.
>
> In Douglas Kenrick's study of the percentages required of potential partners before women would consent to dating, having sex, steady dating or marrying them, 'good looks' was the only criterion where women, across the board, were ready to accept a lower percentage value than men. They were even prepared to consider men of below-average physical attractiveness... as long as they had other things to offer...
>
> In Glenn Wilson's study of British sexual fantasies, men were found to fantasise more frequently about group sex than any of the other scenarios he presented to them. But women had a very different fantasy life. For them, by far the most characteristic fantasy was straight, monogamous sex with a famous personality. The argument runs that famous men today, like village headmen in the past, and successful hunters during the early period in which we evolved, would have

acquired the status and resources to furnish a woman and her children with more food and protection than the next man.

Over the incremental advances of time, evolution would therefore have favoured women who developed mental programmes which allowed them to judge the signs of status within their particular environment and culture, and calibrate their desire accordingly.

Fame is not the only indicator of a man who is high in status and rich in resources. In 1986 the American psychologist Elizabeth Hill published the results of an experiment in which she asked her students to describe what sort of clothes they considered high-status men to wear, and what sort of clothes they considered low-status men to wear. Among the former were smart suits, polo shirts, designer jeans and expensive watches; among the latter were nondescript jeans, tank tops and T-shirts.

She then photographed a number of different men in variations of both styles of dress and showed the photographs to a different group of female students, asking them to rate each one for attractiveness. Overall, the same models were found more attractive when wearing the high-status costumes than when wearing the low-status ones.

It's important to note, though, that it's not just status symbols, and resources they indicate, that women find attractive. It's also those personality characteristics which indicate the capacity to acquire such symbols in the future. In most cultures, women rarely have the luxury of being able to wait for a man to achieve all that he sets out to do before pairing up with him; as a result they have to calibrate his desirability partly on unrealised potential.

To find out what these characteristics of future success might be, and to see how they correlated with female desire, psychologist Michael Wiederman examined more than a thousand personal ads placed in various American periodicals between January and June 1992. He speculated that, in an arena where men and women were paying to attract potential mates, they would be more than usually forthright in specifying the attributes they sought, and more than usually direct in how they expressed their priorities.

Taking the various descriptions of what people wanted, and arranging them into categories, Wiederman noticed that terms denoting high status and plentiful resources (terms such as 'business owner', 'enjoys the finer things', 'successful', 'wealthy', 'well-to-do', and 'financially affluent') cropped up ten times as often in the women's wish lists as in the men's.

But there was also a considerable female preference for terms like 'ambitious', 'industrious', 'career-oriented', and 'college-educated'; in other words, for terms which clearly indicated the potential to acquire status and amass resources in the future...

Douglas Kenrick, in his study of how intelligent, attractive and so on men and women had to be before they were considered sexually attractive by the opposite sex, found that earning capacity was much more important to women than to men; and David Buss, in a massive study of mating habits which covered 10,000 people in 37 cultures around the world, found that women rated financial resources on average at least twice as highly as men did.

Some researchers argue that an evolutionary explanation is not justified here. Women only desire wealthy men, they say, because most cultures don't allow women to make much money for themselves. But the female preference for wealth seems to exist regardless of the financial status of the women in question.

There is an unprecedented number of independent, self-supporting women with resources of their own in the world today, yet their mate preferences still seem to be following the age-old, evolved pattern of looking for men who can offer more.

One study of American newly-wed couples in 1993 found that financially successful brides placed an even greater importance on their husbands' earning capacities than those who were less well-off. And another, conducted among female college students, reported that those who were likely to earn more in respected professions placed greater importance on the financial prospects of their potential husbands than those who were likely to earn less. Buss's fellow psychologist Bruce Ellis summed up the prospect for future mate choice by saying, 'Women's sexual tastes become more, rather than less, discriminatory as their wealth, power, and social status increase.' '

So there you have it. Even in an era of equal opportunities in the world of work women remain keen that in their relationships with men resources flow in one direction only: *to* them, *from* men. Where's the fairness or equality in that? Women seek fairness and equality only when they believe they'll be advantaged by it, *never* when they'll be disadvantaged by it. Which begs the obvious question: why aren't men revolting? The surprisingly simple answer to that question is to be found in a later chapter of this book, titled, 'Why aren't men revolting?'

Why are some women bothered by whether or not gender balance exists in the boardroom? In my view it's the same childish impulse to grasp what men have, which lies behind women's claims to half their ex-partners' wealth after a marriage fails: regardless of the woman's contribution to the couple's wealth, the duration of the marriage, or the reason for the marriage failure. And if that's equality, I'm a *crème brûlée*.

Let's consider the issue of female attractiveness in the workplace. While women commonly decry societal pressures to be attractive – although many are evidently immune to the pressures – attractive women themselves don't hesitate to exploit their attractiveness for all it's worth, in both their working and personal lives. You have to assume they've figured out that's a great deal easier than working hard to get ahead in the world.

In a business career of over 30 years' duration I was fortunate to know a number of women who, when younger, progressed further and faster with the help of their looks. Good looks were an advantage for them on at least two grounds. *All else being equal* senior executives would sooner promote an attractive woman than an unattractive one – just as they might reasonably promote a cheerful colleague rather than a moody one – and clients preferred to deal with attractive women, obviously. Over time these women's attractiveness faded so I was to encounter the irony of hearing them later in their careers bemoaning the promotions of younger, more attractive women than themselves.

We end the chapter with an activity which interests few men, but which has been described as most women's favourite pastime: shopping. Women's fondness for shopping is an indicator of at least two ways in which their natures differ from men's. On the one hand it indicates women's preference for spending money over working for it in the first place, which is also evident in their propensity to eschew paid employment or to work only part-time. On the other hand it reveals women's herd instinct, which is nowhere as clearly displayed as in their pursuit of branded clothing, shoes, handbags etc.

In July 2011 Prince William and his fetching bride (formerly Kate Middleton) undertook a Royal tour of Canada. The tabloid press routinely named the retail outlets from which her clothes were bought, and a television 'fashion commentator' – could there *be* a more vacuous job? – informed us breathlessly that retailers sold out of stock of the items in question within hours of their provenance being revealed. The retailers favoured by Prince William were never mentioned, and with good reason; who on earth would have been interested?

14 | THE DENIAL OF THE DIFFERENT NATURES OF MEN AND WOMEN

Life has no other discipline to impose, if we would but realize it, than to accept life unquestioningly. Everything we shut our eyes to, everything we run away from, everything we deny, denigrate, or despise, serves to defeat us in the end. What seems nasty, painful, evil, can become a source of beauty, joy, and strength, if faced with an open mind. Every moment is a golden one for him who has the vision to recognize it as such.
Henry Miller 1891-1980 American novelist and painter: *Sexus (The Rosy Crucifixion)* (1949)

Feminists contend that erroneous beliefs about the different natures of men and women partly account for the 'oppression' of women over the course of history, and continue to be used in the modern era to justify 'discrimination' against women. They invariably attribute observed differences between boys and girls, as well as men and women, to 'social conditioning', although this leads them to some farcical positions.

An example may illustrate the point. While feminists flatly deny there are differences between the brains of men and women – despite clear evidence to the contrary, including physiological evidence – they credit women with superiority in some areas of cognition, as exemplified by the bizarre 'women's ways of knowing' theory we'll be exploring later. How can the two positions be equated? They can't, unless feminists believe 'women's ways of knowing' arise from an organ other than the brain. Maybe they'll let us know some day which organ is involved.

[Update: The eminent Dutch neuroscientist Dick Swaab reported in *We Are Our Brains: From the Womb to Alzheimer's* (2015) that there now known to be 'many hundreds' of differences between gender-typical male brains and gender-typical female brains. Feminists find themselves in the company of Creationists in their denial of overwhelming scientific evidence.]

The overwhelming consensus among psychologists in the modern era is that there *are* fundamental differences in the natures of gender-typical men and women. It's important to stress the term 'gender-typical' because feminists with mind-numbing frequency point to men and women who act in non-gender-typical ways (women becoming engineers, men becoming nurses...) and would have us believe that in time as many women as men will become engineers, and as many men as women will become nurses. There's no evidence of such a trend. Women's progress has largely been in fields to which they are naturally inclined anyway (e.g. medicine), and all too often (as with medicine) the progress can in large measure be attributed to gender equality programmes.

Why do men still swallow the myth that women are an oppressed gender? For a possible answer to this we turn to a remarkable book first published over 40 years ago, Esther Vilar's *The Manipulated Man* (1971). In her new introduction to the second edition of the book, published in 2008, Vilar made the point that in the original edition of the book she underestimated men's fear of re-evaluating their own position:

'The more sovereignty they [men] are losing in their professional lives – the more automatic their work, the more controlled by computers they become, the more that increasing unemployment forces them to adopt obsequious behavior towards customers and superiors – then the more they have to be afraid of a recognition of their predicament. And the more essential it becomes to maintain their illusion that it is not they who are the slaves, but those on whose behalf they subject themselves to such an existence.

As absurd as it may sound: today's men need feminists more than their wives do. Feminists are the last ones who still describe men the way they like to see themselves: as egocentric, power-obsessed, ruthless, and without inhibitions when it comes to satisfying their animalistic instincts. Therefore the most aggressive Women's Libbers find themselves in the strange predicament of doing more to maintain the status quo than anyone else. Without their arrogant accusations the macho man would no longer exist, except perhaps in the movies. If the press didn't stylize men as rapacious wolves, the actual sacrificial lambs of this 'men's society', men themselves, would no longer flock to the factories so obediently.'

15 | FEMININITY

God gave women intuition and femininity. Used properly, the combination easily jumbles the brain of any man I've ever met.
Farrah Fawcett 1947-2009 American actress and artist

Feminists hate the very notion of femininity. They consider women taking advantage of their femininity as expressing weakness; one of many dismal conclusions arising logically and inevitably from dualism. But femininity is arguably more an expression of strength rather than of weakness. Feminine women can reliably expect appreciation and support from men.

What would feminists recommend instead? That women compete 24/7/365 with men in the home, the workplace, in politics, and elsewhere? That's already added much to the sum of human happiness, isn't it?

If men enjoyed the returns from masculinity which women routinely enjoy from femininity, they'd have no reservation in exploiting it. However the option *isn't* open to them, so they might reasonably be expected to complain about women exploiting their femininity. But *do* they complain? No, of course not. They're men.

16 | FEMINIST THEORY: BUILDING CASTLES IN THE AIR

I, on the other hand, have a degree from the University of Life, a diploma from the School of Hard Knocks, and three gold stars from the Kindergarten of Getting the Shit Kicked Out of Me.
Captain Edmund Blackadder (**Rowan Atkinson**): *Blackadder Goes Forth* (1989)

Feminist academics have been busy building castles in the air, and they have little option but to work hard to stop us noticing how ludicrous those constructions are, mainly by inventing mind-numbingly long treatises which no normal person with a life would be prepared to read. You and I, dear reader, along with the other long-suffering taxpayers in the developed world, are financing those constructions. Most of the building work is undertaken by the feminists – generally but not invariably women – who design and teach Women's Studies and Gender Studies courses, about which I shall have more to say. Let me just say at this point something which may not surprise you. Feminist 'academics' have minimal intellectual curiosity; they focus on developing and disseminating propaganda for the feminist movement.

In 1979 I was awarded a Bachelor's degree in Chemistry by one of the three most prestigious universities in the United Kingdom: Oxford, Cambridge or Reading. Exactly which one, need not detain us. I vividly recall the first lecture on the first day of the course, given by one of the four departmental professors. In those balmy far-off days (summers *were* warmer) professors were usually of advanced years, unlike the twenty-something female professors of the modern era. The professor started his talk with something along the following lines:

'Because you will be studying chemistry, a physical science, one that has a long and noble history, you probably believe that all you will learn over the next three years will be held to be equally valid in 30, 40, even 50 years' time. This is a delusion commonly held by science undergraduates. Many of the theories I myself learned as an undergraduate have been discarded or refined, and this is how science progresses. I've been responsible myself for some of that discarding and refinement, I'm not too modest to say.

Political theory, however, does *not* progress in this way. This may explain why a depressingly high percentage of you are Lefties. With luck, most of you will in the fullness of time grow out of that dismal philosophy. My sole purpose in telling you this is to recommend that you be wary of believing theories asserted as facts by academics, including scientists, and to assume that anything uttered by a political theorist is the product of a deeply disturbed mind.

What's the difference between an academic and a village idiot? The academic will calculate the speed at which an elephant needs to flap its ears in order to fly like a bird, and he will – as surely as night follows day – find support for his theory from some of his colleagues. The village idiot, meanwhile, knows elephants have never flown, they don't now, and he will hazard a wild guess that they never will.'

Feminist theories will reflect the realities of the world we live in, and the realities of human nature, the day we have flocks of elephants soaring high above us. That's just a personal opinion, however, so on your behalf I thought I'd research what's currently taught on Women's Studies and Gender Studies courses at universities in the United Kingdom.

I emailed five (female) leaders of Women's Studies and Gender Studies departments in the UK, asking for details of course prospectuses and associated reading lists. I mentioned that my book *The Glass Ceiling Delusion* had recently been published, so I wasn't trying to hide the perspective I have on feminist matters. Only one academic responded, and that was to refuse to supply the materials, 'in the light of the probably anti-feminist nature of your next book.'

I then wrote letters to the five women, and still had no response. I emailed them again, invoking the Freedom of Information Act, requiring the materials to be supplied within 28 days. I had two responses. The first was polite, from a lady writing on behalf of Professor Stevi Jackson of York University, who we shall come to shortly.

The second was from Professor Marysia Zalewski, Director of the Centre for Gender Studies in the School of Social Science, University of Aberdeen. We had the following email exchange. Ms Zalewski isn't one to exchange pleasantries with people like me, clearly. No 'Best wishes', no 'Mr Buchanan', nothing like that. The following email exchange is shown in chronological order:

From:	mikebuchanan@hotmail.co.uk
Sent:	Thursday, July 28, 2011, 11:40 AM
To:	m.zalewski@abdn.ac.uk
Subject:	Women's Studies / Gender Studies

Ms Zalewski, I hope this finds you well. Following the publication of my latest book *The Glass Ceiling Delusion*, which focused on men and women in the world of work, I am embarking on a wider critique of feminist thinking and campaigning in the modern era. I wish to give the book's readers a real sense of what is currently taught in Women's Studies / Gender Studies courses. Would it be possible to mail or email me (before the end of September, i.e. nine weeks off) details of your courses in these areas, and associated reading lists for people undertaking them? Also, could you please inform me of the gender balance among the people undertaking the courses in the last academic year? Thank you.

Best wishes,
Mike Buchanan

[Author's note: in the absence of a response a month later – to be fair, Ms Zalewski might just have been on holiday over the period – I tried again.]

From: mikebuchanan@hotmail.co.uk
Sent: Saturday, August 27, 2011, 4:27 PM
To: m.zalewski@abdn.ac.uk
Subject: FW: Women's Studies / Gender Studies

Dr Zalewski, good afternoon. I emailed you on 28 July (see above) and wrote to you on 11 August (see attached). Having not even received acknowledgement of these items, I am forced to conclude that you are simply unwilling to provide the information requested. I've taken legal advice on this matter and am therefore requesting this information through invoking the Freedom of Information Act 2000. I understand that this leaves you a maximum of 28 days so I look forward to the information by Friday 23 September latest. Thank you.

Best wishes,

Mike Buchanan

From: mikebuchanan@hotmail.co.uk
Sent: Saturday, August 27, 2011, 6:36 PM
To: m.zalewski@abdn.ac.uk
Subject: FW: Women's Studies / Gender Studies

Dr Zalewski, would you please be so good as to acknowledge receipt of the email I sent earlier today (above)? Thanks.

Best wishes,

Mike Buchanan

From: m.zalewski@abdn.ac.uk
Sent: Tuesday, August 30, 2011 5:29 PM
To: mikebuchanan@hotmail.co.uk
Subject: FW: Women's Studies / Gender Studies

No information is available as these courses are currently unavailable.

[Author's note: I then returned to the University website and spotted a course which, it seemed to me, was very much of the type I was enquiring into. So I emailed again.]

From: mikebuchanan@hotmail.co.uk
Sent: 30 August 2011 17:37
To: Zalewski, Marysia
Subject: Re: Women's Studies / Gender Studies

Thank you. Is the following course being run over 2011/2?

Abdn.ac.uk/prospectus/pgrad/study/taught.php?code=sex_gender
_violence

Best wishes,

Mike Buchanan

From: m.zalewski@abdn.ac.uk
Sent: Tuesday, August 30, 2011 5:38 PM
To: mikebuchanan@hotmail.co.uk
Subject: RE: Women's Studies / Gender Studies

This is not a gender studies course.

From: mikebuchanan@hotmail.co.uk
Sent:
To: m.zalewski@abdn.ac.uk
Fw: Women's Studies / Gender Studies

Thank you, but that wasn't what I asked. I asked if the course was being run.

Best wishes,

Mike Buchanan

Writing these words in late January 2012, four months after the nine week deadline I originally offered, I have yet to receive a response to that last email, and I have no idea if the requested materials will ever be forthcoming, despite my having invoked the Freedom of Information Act. In case the reason for the non-supply of information was my failure to satisfy some obscure protocol that a citizen would struggle to discover, I think it not unreasonable that Professor Zalewski might have informed me of the fact.

The leader of another Gender Studies course passed my request on to the office responsible for handling such matters. The lady in charge of that office supplied the requested materials but said they were subject to copyright restrictions and I would have to apply for permission to use them, as the academics running the Gender Studies course were concerned I might use them in a 'misleading' manner. I would have to present them with the material I sought to duplicate, as well as any commentary concerning it. I wasn't even permitted to divulge the book titles on the recommended reading lists without prior written permission: copyright was claimed on these lists. But I could, she added generously, state the *number* of books on those lists. You couldn't make it up.

Onto the Centre for Women's Studies at the University of York. On 14 September 2011 I received a letter from Professor Stevi Jackson which started by apologising for the lateness of the response, and continued in a polite and informative manner. I rapidly concluded she'd attended a superior charm school to the one attended by Professor Zalewski.

The letter included the following table showing the headcount for all full and part-time students on Women's Studies courses over the academic years 2005/6 to 2010/11:

Academic year	Female	Male
2005/6	35	0
2006/7	30	0
2007/8	30	0
2008/9	30	0
2009/10	40	0
2010/11	40	0

Assuming the courses were completed within single academic years, that works out at 205 females: 0 males. A strong contender to win a coveted Harriet Harman Award for Gender Balance in Higher Education.

What of the course prospectuses, which were mostly for MA courses? Taking a random sampling approach, I opened the 'Handbook for MA Women's Studies and MA Women's Studies (Humanities) 2010 – 2011' at page 22, which is the first page concerning an optional module, 'Gender and Diasporic Identities (5080006)'. The course description:

'The module centres on the ways in which diasporic identities in their intersection with gender are constructed in contemporary cultural production, in particular in film, performance, and fiction. It explores the impact of (dis)locations on perceptions of self and other in the context of diaspora as a continual negotiation between past and present, movement and stability, visibility and invisibility, tradition and transformation. It asks about the changing and diverse experiences of diaspora across generations, how diasporic experience shape gendered identities at local levels and in global contexts, and what socio-cultural issues emerge from the cultural construction of diaspora.

Following on from a session on conceptualising diaspora where we shall compare the personal experience of gendered diasporic identities and their theorisations, we shall analyse the ways in which contemporary cultural production engages with the diverse manifestations of diasporic identity to explore issues such as micro-migration, dreams and realities of 'motherlands', 'first-generation' migrants, 'lost generations', reverse migrations, nomadic identities in the global world, fragmenting and integrating identities, women's roles in global diasporic economies.'

Little to argue with there, I think you'll agree.

On the positive side I noticed on one of the course reading lists some papers produced by Dr Catherine Hakim, a sociologist formerly working at the London School of Economics (now with the think-tank The Centre for Policy Studies) whose work is mentioned favourably in *The Glass Ceiling Delusion*. There's also a session on women who commit violence so maybe – just maybe – such courses (or at least those at the University of York) aren't quite as woefully imbalanced as I'd anticipated. I should really investigate the matter further but I find that if I spend more than a brief period reading feminist literature I lose the will to live. The absence of male students on the courses suggests I'm not alone.

What is the reality of Women's Studies and Gender Studies courses beyond what we might deduce from materials such as prospectuses and recommended reading lists? I'm not aware of any books which provide an 'insider's guide' to such courses in the United Kingdom, but there's a remarkable book which lifts the lid on courses in the United States: Daphne Patai's and Noretta Koertge's *Professing Feminism: Education and Indoctrination in Women's Studies* (second edition, 2003). It's an excellent but also disturbing read, partly because it depicts a world of men-hating women determined to denigrate men at every opportunity and to isolate women from men as far as possible.

The world these women dream of creating would be a depressing one for the vast majority of men and women. I came to the regrettable conclusion that I couldn't do justice to the book without using a substantial number of very lengthy extracts, so I leave you with the suggestion that you read it for yourself. Americans might be well advised to have a stiff drink to hand, to help calm their nerves when they realise the true nature of the programmes their taxes have been funding for many years.

17 | FEMINIST ACADEMICS
AND MANGINAS

The academic community has in it the biggest concentration of alarmists, cranks, and extremists this side of the giggle house.
William F Buckley Jr 1925-2008 American conservative author and commentator: 'On The Right' 17 January 1967

Militant feminists of the American persuasion take some beating. To illustrate the point let's consider a book written by four of them: three are (or at least were at the time of their book's publication) academics, indeed professors. The book is *Women's Ways of Knowing*, first published in 1986, and is said by some feminists to be central to many feminist theories of the modern era. After reading comments on the book by the psychologist Steven Pinker I was intrigued to buy a copy, and duly bought the tenth anniversary edition. To give you a flavour of the book's content I selected a page at random. From page 54, in a section titled, 'The Emergence of Subjective Knowing':

> 'The kind of change that Inez experienced is the center of our discussion in this chapter: from passivity to action, from self as static to self as becoming, from silence to a protesting inner voice and infallible gut.
>
> For many of the women, the move away from silence and an externally oriented perspective on knowledge and truth eventuates in a new conception of truth as personal, private, and subjectively known or intuited; thus, we are calling this next position *subjectivism* or *subjective knowing*. Although this new view of knowledge is a revolutionary step there are remnants of dichotomous and absolutist thinking in the subjectivist's assumptions about truth. [Author's note: are you losing the will to live yet?] In fact, subjectivism is dualistic in the sense that there is still the conviction that there are right answers; the fountain of truth simply has shifted locale. Truth

now resides within the person and can negate answers that the outside world supplies.'

I'd like to invite you to join the four authoresses of *Women's Ways of Knowing* and myself on a journey. We're strapped into our seats in a plane just before a flight from London to New York. A young actress – playing the role of a pilot – emerges from the cockpit and announces breezily to the passengers:

> 'Ladies and gentlemen, good morning! My name's Candy. [Author's note: she seems to be of the American persuasion.] I shall be your captain on today's flight, and I'll be responsible for taking off and landing the plane. I've had no flying training but I've read *lots* of books about flying planes, and with my woman's ways of knowing, I'm sure we'll all be just fine. Now, let's get this baby into the air! Stewardess, why are the four ladies over there screaming hysterically?'

For a more sophisticated critique of 'women's ways of knowing' than I can muster, we turn to Christina Hoff Sommers, an American former professor of philosophy, and a self-described 'equity feminist'. You may recall that in her book *Who Stole Feminism?* (1994) she distinguished between equity feminists and gender feminists, the latter being feminists who believe in creating privileges for women. We turn to the start of a chapter titled 'New Epistemologies' in Hoff Sommers's book:

> 'Some gender feminists claim that because women have been oppressed they are better 'knowers'. Feeling more deeply, they see more clearly and understand reality better. They have an 'epistemic' advantage over men. Does being oppressed really make one more knowledgeable or perceptive? The idea that adversity confers special insight is familiar enough. Literary critics often ascribe creativity to suffering, including suffering racial discrimination or homophobia. But feminist philosophers have carried this idea much further. They claim that oppressed groups enjoy privileged 'epistemologies' or

'different ways of knowing' that better enable them to understand the world, not only socially but scientifically.

According to 'standpoint theory', as the theory of epistemic advantage is called, the oppressed may make better biologists, physicists, and philosophers than their oppressors. Thus we find the feminist theorist Hilary Rose saying that male scientists have been handicapped by being men. A better science would be based on women's domestic experience and practice. Professor Virginia Held offers hope that 'a feminist standpoint would give us a quite different understanding of even physical reality.' Conversely, those who are most socially favored, the proverbial white, middle class males, are in the worst epistemic position.

What do mainstream philosophers make of the idea of 'standpoint theories'? Professor Susan Haack of the University of Miami is one of the most respected epistemologists in the country. She is also an equity feminist. In December 1992 she participated in a symposium on feminist philosophy at a meeting of the American Philosophical Association. It was a unique event. For once, someone outside the insular little world of gender feminism was asked to comment on gender feminist theories of knowledge. Watching Professor Haack critique the 'standpoint theorists' was a little like watching a chess grandmaster defeat all opponents in a simultaneous exhibition, blindfolded.

Haack told the audience that she finds the idea of 'female ways of knowing' as puzzling as the idea of a Republican epistemology or a senior citizens' epistemology. Some of her arguments are too technical to review here. I cite only a few of her criticisms:

> I am not convinced that there *are* any distinctively female 'ways of knowing'. All *any* human being has to go on, in figuring how things are, is his or her sensory experience, and the explanatory theorizing he or she devises to accommodate it; differences in cognitive style, like differences in handwriting, seem more individual then gender-determined.

She pointed out that theories based on the idea that oppression or deprivation results in a privileged standpoint are especially implausible: if they were right, the most disadvantaged groups would produce the best scientists. In fact, the oppressed and socially marginalized often have little access to the information and education needed to excel in science, which on the whole puts them at a serious 'epistemic *dis*advantage'. Professor Haack also observed that the female theorists who argue that oppression confers an advantage are not themselves oppressed. She asks: if oppression and poverty are indeed so advantageous, why do so many highly advantaged, middle-class women consider themselves so well situated 'epistemically'?

Ms Haack identifies herself as an 'Old Feminist' who opposes the attempt of 'the New Feminists to colonize philosophy'. Her reasons for rejecting feminist epistemologies were cogent and, to most of the professional audience, clearly convincing. Unfortunately, her cool, sensible admonitions are not likely to slow down the campaign to promote 'women's ways of knowing'.

The gender feminists' conviction, more ideological than scientific, that they belong to a radically insightful vanguard that compares favourably with the Copernicuses and Darwins of the past animates their revisionist theories of intellectual and artistic excellence and inspires their program to transform the knowledge base. Their exultation contrasts with the deep reluctance of most other academics to challenge the basic assumptions underlying feminist theories of knowledge and education. The confidence of the one and the trepidation of the other combine to make transformationism a powerfully effective movement that has so far proceeded unchecked in the academy.'

In an effort to learn more about militant feminism in the United Kingdom I googled the keyword 'feminism'. It resulted in 'about 114,000' website hits. I gained the firm impression after just a few website visits that militant feminism is well and truly the product of, and sustained by, academics; and therefore financed by long-suffering British taxpayers. Almost all these academics are women, it need hardly be said. From the website of the Feminist and Women's Studies Association:[1]

---

[1] http://fwsa.wordpress.com

'The FWSA is a UK-based network promoting feminist research and teaching, and women's studies nationally and internationally. Through its elected executive committee, the FWSA is involved in developing policy on issues of central importance to feminist scholars in further and higher education, supporting postgraduate events and enabling feminist research. Committed to raising awareness of women's studies, feminist research and women-related issues in secondary and tertiary education, the FWSA liaises regularly with other gender-related research and community networks as well as with policy groups.'

In a later chapter we shall read of a curious seminar advertised on the FWSA website, 'Experiencing and Celebrating Fatness'. For the purpose of this chapter let's consider another:

'Celebrating the feminist within
22nd September 2010 – University of East Anglia

July 30, 2010

Feminist academics in leadership positions report difficulty pursuing feminist ideals [Author's note: at last, some positive news...], often preferring to leave their 'radical' feminist identities at home with some professing desires to unite their dual identities of scholar and activist. Black feminists are particularly marginalised within academia, although the increased diversity of the student population in the UK brings hope for a new generation of black feminists entering the academy. To counter the apparent attitudes in academia that are suspicious of feminists and feminism, the Centre for Diversity and Equality in Careers and Employment Research (Norwich Business School, University of East Anglia) is holding a one day free networking event for up to 40 female and male feminist academics, research staff and PhD students on the 22nd September, 2010. The day will:

- promote wider debate of what feminism can mean in academia and research;

- provide a platform for feminist academics from a range of backgrounds (age, class, gender, ethnicity, discipline) to share their experiences;
- bring discussions about feminism in universities into the open;
- provide networking opportunities to help reduce feelings of isolation and possibly lead to future collaborative projects, particularly for early career researchers, and;
- act as a pilot event for similar events in other regions in the UK.'

We couldn't ask for clearer evidence that the militant feminist world is a closed one. The term 'male feminist' is enough to make any man shudder, but the FWSA had posted a message from one such person on its website, so presumably believed it had some merit:

'I wonder if your research and curiosity ever brings you to look at our understanding of nuclear power and the Atomic World. Our knowledge of this subject derives entirely from a masculine way of looking and thinking about the already invisible world of the atomic particles. Our knowledge is consequently overlain with patrician and misogynist perceptions. No wonder it creates such messy issues.

I've gone some way towards developing a more balanced account. There's some surprising things to see. Nuclear fission is essentially a story of passion and romance, and finally despair. Impossible for our physicists to understand. Oh! [Author's note: a nice dramatic touch, that 'Oh!'. Nurse, fetch the fainting couch, and the smelling salts...] This whole subject dearly needs feminine insight and values, to make it whole. Please don't pass it by.

Thanks and good wishes,
\<name supplied\>'

This perspective was so reminiscent of those found in *Women's Ways of Knowing* that I felt compelled to post the following reply:

'I was interested to read your post about the Atomic World. I have a number of questions:

- in what sense is our knowledge of atomic particles 'overlain with patrician and misogynistic perceptions'?
- when I graduated with a science degree over 30 years ago, nuclear fission was already very well understood. Sorry to learn that is it now 'impossible' for physicists to understand. Do you happen to know how this unfortunate turn of events has come to pass?
- in what sense does the subject dearly need feminine insight and values to make it whole?'

A year after posting my questions I was still awaiting a reply. But maybe, just maybe, the man was smarter than we might otherwise have given him credit for. For an interesting perspective on male feminists we turn to an extract from a book published in 2008, *Men are Better than Women*, penned by the American author Dick Masterson. Let's leave the last words in this chapter to the estimable Dick:

Manginas are my heroes

Male feminists, or 'manginas' as they prefer to be called, are so misogynistic they make Andrew Dice Clay [Author's note: a notably politically-incorrect, i.e. funny, American comedian] look like The Little Mermaid. The Little Mermaid is the seashell-on-the-boobs cartoon character from Disney.

Not all men have money, good looks, talent, wit, charm, charisma, interesting stories, cultural insights, skills, athletic abilities, political acumen, macho attitudes, an ability to eat an inhuman amount of food or other non-toxic products, a sense of style, an easygoing demeanour, video games, a sweet car, a spa, or an in-depth knowledge of everything. All men, however, are still men. That means they need to get laid and will always find a way. How do these men attract women, then? I'll tell you how – by taking charge where women have failed for the last thirty years: by being feminists.

Manginas are my heroes. They fight the fight that women declared for absolutely no reason and then completely failed at. Who else but a man could convince a woman that being a male feminist is not only possible, but also not the most chauvinistic thing anyone has ever done in the history of the world?

I'll tell you who, fucking no one! But men have done that shit. Men are like hypnosis masters when it comes to telling women what they want and what they should think about everything. Manginas are the biggest and most ingenious misogynists. It's perfectly natural and perfectly manly for a man to stoop so low as to cheapen his entire gender just to get laid. Men don't need a collective pat on the ass for everything we do in life. We're born with dicks and dignity, and neither can be taken away. We don't need a sash that counts up all our achievements and chafes our necks. That's for Girl Scouts, and the only thing I want to know about Girl Scouts is when they sell their cookies.

On a personal note, I have nothing against misogynism, or whatever it's called. I wouldn't call myself a misogynist, but that's a little like not calling a square a rectangle. Manginas are some of the manliest men on earth, because they know deep down within their stomachs that women can't stand up for themselves without a firm hand firmly supporting them by the ass. It's a throwback to chivalry that says, 'Sweetheart, if you want anyone to take your rights seriously, shut up and let a man do the talking'.

18| BIG FAT FEMINIST MYTHS AND LIES: FEMALE SOLIDARITY AND FEMINIST REPRESENTATIONS OF WOMEN

The great enemy of the truth is very often not the lie – deliberate, contrived, and dishonest – but the myth, persistent, persuasive, and unrealistic. Belief in myths allows the comfort of opinion without the discomfort of thought.
John F Kennedy 1917–1963 President of the United States (1961-3)

In this chapter, by the term 'big fat feminist myths and lies', I mean, of course, bit fat myths and lies asserted by feminists. I cover myths and lies asserted by big fat feminists in other chapters. I hope this avoids any possible confusion.

One of the most malicious of the feminists' myths is that given a choice in the matter, mothers would prefer to engage in paid employment rather than bringing up their children full-time. Of course governments, forever eager to maximise their tax revenues, are happy to conspire with feminists in driving women out of the home and into paid employment. For an insight into this issue we turn to an article penned by Jill Kirby and published on Conservativehome.com on 20 September 2011. It had the snappy title, 'The media won't tell you, but what British parents really want is more time to spend with their children':

'A report has been commissioned by Tessa Jowell [Author's note: a Leftie politician, but don't worry, I won't be making a habit of quoting Leftie politicians] in preparation for Labour's forthcoming party conference. Carried out by a Labour-friendly polling organisation called 'Britain Thinks', this report questioned 2,000 adults in a representative sample and came up with some very emphatic conclusions. Yet the report, entitled 'The Modern British Family', received almost no press or media coverage, the only exception being a short item by the *Daily Mail's* assiduous Becky Barrow. Nothing on the *Today* programme, no comment in the *Guardian*. The *Times* and *Telegraph*... didn't touch 'The Modern British Family'.

Why? Perhaps because it shows that British families don't share the priorities ascribed to them by most of the modern media and almost all of today's politicians. For example, a remarkable 81% of the adults questioned said that ideally one parent should stay at home to look after children. This figure was consistent across all the adults taking part, both parents and childless, with the percentage supporting the ideal of stay-at-home parenting rising as high as 84% among 25-34 year olds. And in a rejection of touchy-feely guilt-ridden parenting notions, 92% felt that being a good parent is 'mostly about setting boundaries and good discipline'. Again, there was consistent support for this proposition amongst parents and the childless.

Where the views of families and the child-free diverged was in their feelings about their financial situation: 73% of parents said it's a struggle to make their incomes last through to the end of the month, a concern felt by only 46% of the childless. Clearly families are being squeezed most by rising living costs and are looking to government to ease the pressure.

When Tessa Jowell presents the report's conclusions to her party conference next week she will no doubt press home this last message and will seek to portray Ed Miliband as the party leader most able to respond to the 'squeezed middle' – those families who are neither rich nor benefit-dependent, but who are trying to make ends meet on average incomes. Despite ignoring these families whilst in government, favouring huge increases in welfare handouts instead, Labour is now doing its best to look family-friendly. Certainly it is the Labour-leaning think-tanks who now lead on the subject, most conspicuously the Resolution Foundation. Nevertheless, they will all be struggling to reconcile the Britain Thinks report with their favourite nostrums. Instead of demanding more childcare subsidy, it seems parents actually want to look after children themselves. And instead of calling for children's rights, an end to smacking, or lamenting the consumer society, they think good discipline is crucial.

To complete their report, Britain Thinks tested its polling data on two focus groups of parents and found robust backing for the survey's conclusions, as well as some very emphatic support for 'traditional' family life. Mothers not only wanted more time at home with children, those who had been at work also seemed to regret the time lost: 'You'll never get those years back' was one poignant comment. Fathers rejected the idea of lone-parent families as an alternative family model, believing instead that society needs to value the role of fathers much more.

And the report's overall headline conclusion? That the government should support the traditional family by providing tax breaks for parents who stay together.

Given the current cross-party silence on the subject of such tax breaks, let alone any help for stay-at-home parents, it's not surprising that the focus groups also concluded that 'No politicians or political parties are seen to represent or understand the problems and priorities of the Modern British Family.' As Labour and Conservatives prepare for their party conferences, will either be able to change that perception? 'Modern British Families' may not (yet) have grabbed headlines, but it certainly deserves to be on David Cameron's Manchester reading list.'

The British bestselling writer Oliver James is a clinical psychologist and his book on child rearing, *How Not to F*** Them Up*, was published in 2010. The excerpt that follows is drawn from the first chapter and illustrates the point that women don't represent a homogeneous group collectively requiring representation by *anyone* even in the context of the same challenges; in this case, rearing babies and children under three years of age:

'Solid scientific research, mostly based on the theories and studies of a British psychoanalyst and psychologist called Joan Raphael-Leff, reveals that mothers of small children tend to fall into three groups, in terms of their approach to mothering and the basic feeling they have about under-threes. The book is divided into three Parts, each dealing with one of them.

1. The Organiser

She tends to see it as necessary for the baby to adapt to her and the needs of the family. She loves her baby as much as any other kind of mother but her attitude is that mother knows best. To her, the baby is a creature without a proper understanding of the human world, a bundle of hungry needs that require regulation to make them predictable. Insufficiently controlled, the baby can quickly become indulged, selfish and naughty. The Organiser sees it as her job to help the baby take control of its unruly passions and bodily processes. That is an important part of how she shows maternal love. Hence, she tends to see it as vital for the baby to acquire a feeding and sleeping routine, soonest. She is happy for others to care for the baby and regards a routine as very helpful for this. As quickly as she can after the birth, she wants to get back her 'normal', pre-pregnant life.

About a quarter of British mums have this approach. They are the ones who are most likely to have a full-time paid job.

2. The Hugger

The opposite of the Organiser, she places the needs of the baby ahead of everything. She is the sort of mum who may have the baby sleeping with her in the bed at night, who tends to feed on demand (when the baby indicates it is hungry rather than imposing a routine) and who regards herself as uniquely able to meet the baby's needs. She luxuriates in motherhood, happy to put her life on hold for at least three years per child. She adores being with her under-threes.

She is least likely of the three kinds to have a paid job, although some do work, even full-time. About one quarter of British mothers are Huggers.

3. The Fleximum

She combines both Hugging and Organising, cutting and pasting the pattern of care according to what the practical situation requires. She is aware of the needs of the baby and is led by them but, unlike the Hugger, she does not lose sight of her own needs. She may have the baby in the bed if it is ill, yet also seek to establish a sleep routine. She may try imposing a feeding regime, only to drop it if it is not working. Above all, she is concerned to create a 'win-win' situation, where both her own and her baby's needs are met.

About half of mothers are like this. Many have a part-time job, though some are at home or at work full-time.

You probably recognise yourself in one of these portraits [Author's note: not really, Oliver, to be honest…] but it is vital you read all three parts of the book, in the order in which they unfold, rather than just jumping to the one which you think applies to you. About half of you will be Fleximums and since they are mostly a mixture of the other two kinds, you need to understand them. If you are an Organiser or Hugger, you can learn a lot about your approach by understanding the others.

As you will see, there are potential problems for mothers whatever their approach. Huggers can sometimes find it difficult to allow the child to become independent. Organisers may find the early months particularly trying. Fleximums can trick themselves into believing they have created win-win arrangements (in which both their needs and the baby's are being met) where in reality, one or other is losing out.

My main objective is to help you define which approach suits you best and then how to make the most of it, minimising problems. Much depends on what kind of person you are and what your circumstances require, at a particular moment in time. While arranging things so that you are reasonably happy does not guarantee you will meet your child's needs, it certainly increases the likelihood thereof. Whatever your approach, there tends to be a constant trade-off between your need to stay buoyant and your baby's needs.

Mothers vary in how precisely they adopt an approach. Those who fit one of the three groups in most respects I describe as 'classic' or 'essential'. They would conform to many of the characteristics in the descriptions provided above.

A minority I characterise as 'extreme', meaning that they take the approach very seriously and push it to the limit. An extreme Hugger, for example, might breastfeed the child until it is three and still have it sleeping in the parental bed at that age. An extreme Organiser might use day care from when the baby is three months old and strictly adhere to 'controlled crying' (leaving the baby to soothe itself) from soon after birth. An extreme Fleximum might switch patterns several times, with several children.

A proportion of mothers change their overall approach. They may start out with one approach for a year, only to move to another when it does not seem to be working with that particular child. Or they may use one approach with their first child and adopt a different one with another.

So even if you think of yourself as a confirmed Hugger or Organiser today, you may find yourself changing tack at some point in the future.

One of the hottest issues that both affects and reflects a mother's approach is her attitude to doing paid work during the early years. A conflict has broken out, dubbed the Mommy Wars by Americans. At its simplest, the warring parties divide into those doing paid work and those who stay at home. But a more nuanced division is between those who feel the care should be led by the child's needs, versus those who feel the child must adapt to the parent.

The evidence shows that, in general, all mothers are liable to feel that the wider society disapproves of their approach. Organisers who use routines are all too aware that lots of other mothers accuse them of being neglectful and cold-hearted. Huggers may feel socially deviant and accused of being over-indulgent, creating bad habits. A mother of either kind can feel torn between the verdict of her social world and what she believes is best.

My ambition is to declare a truce. With any luck, by the end of this book you will feel this is a bogus conflict which need not sap your limited supplies of emotional energy.

It is perfectly clear that mothers who stay at home when they long for the stimulation of work are at greater risk of depression. Likewise, a proportion of mothers find babies and toddlers, quite frankly, boring company, and can feel isolated and frustrated if they stay at home full-time. Many such mothers are Organisers and some are Fleximums. Since depression in mothers greatly reduces the chances of the needs of under-threes being met, it is imperative that such mothers do not feel trapped at home.

On the other hand, in general, it is a fact that offspring of working mothers do not do as well academically as those of non-working ones, and are more at risk of emotional problems. A big part of the reason for this may be the inadequacy of the substitute care. Where the substitute is adequate, there is no reason why a working mother should increase problems for the child.

So from a scientific point of view, looked at in terms of the best interests of the under-three, there is no basis for saying it is better or worse for them to have a working mother. It all depends on what kind of woman she is and if she does work, what sort of substitute arrangements are made.'

The idea that the three types of mother form a homogeneous group requiring a common form of representation is plainly ridiculous. Oliver James's ambition might be to declare a truce in the 'Mommy Wars' but you may be sure that radical feminists won't accept one. They reserve a special loathing for 'stay-at-home Moms', a group of women who understandably feel aggrieved at the feminists' relentless attacks on them.

A researcher of particular interest to anyone interested in the genders and the world of work is the sociologist Dr Catherine Hakim, currently a Senior Research Fellow with the London-based think tank The Centre for Policy Studies. She formerly worked at the London School of Economics. Dr Hakim has earned a strong reputation for her honest and non-ideological research on gender in the workplace. Three of her papers and reports are cited in the section 'References and Further Reading' in this book, and are referenced by Swayne O'Pie in *Why Britain Hates Men: Exposing Feminism* (2011) in a chapter titled, 'Women's Work Ethic and Choice of Options'. Much of it concerns Hakim's 'Preference theory', published in 2000, which uses three related work-life models to express women's preferences and choices. While these models refers to women as a whole, there are clear parallels with Oliver James's later (2010) models for mothers of under-threes. Hakim's three models are:

'Family centred: 17 per cent of women. Family life and children are the main priorities throughout these women's lives.

Adaptive: 69 per cent. This group is the most diverse and includes women who want to combine work and family. They want to work but are not committed to a working career. This is a large majority, with direct consequences for the 'pay gap' and the 'glass ceiling'.

Work-centred: 14 per cent. Their main priority in life is their career. Childless women are concentrated in this category. O'Pie comments, 'This very small percentage has huge implications for the Feminist issues of the pay gap and the glass ceiling... The 14 per cent of work-centred women are likely to be Feminists. So when Feminists demand positive discrimination and quotas to increase the number of women in top jobs they are, in fact, demanding that *they themselves* should fill these designated senior status, high salaried jobs'.'

The lack of common experience and attitudes among women is evident in many aspects of women's lives. So how can there be any 'solidarity' among women in any meaningful sense, such that they require representation as a gender? There can't. But this doesn't stop the feminists from perpetuating the myth of female solidarity.

Feminists represent only 14 per cent of women, the work-centred ones. Quite apart from their attitudes towards paid employment, very few women share the extreme left-wing views of feminists. I've spoken to dozens of women about the issue I believe most clearly divides equity feminists and gender feminists: positive discrimination to 'improve' the proportion of women in senior roles in business and elsewhere. I've yet to find a woman (or a man, for that matter) who believes positive discrimination should be used in this way.

How, then, in a supposedly modern democracy such as the United Kingdom, could such discrimination effectively be enforced by an Act of Parliament, the Equality Act 2010? As I explain in *The Glass Ceiling Delusion*, positive discrimination remains illegal in both the United Kingdom and the wider

European Union; but weasel words (such as 'positive action') are used in the legislation and (more importantly) related guidance notes which leave no doubt that positive discrimination is the order of the day. My book also explains how feminists exert their influence on the broader public policy agenda, with campaigning organisations such as the Fawcett Society participating in consultation exercises run by the ultra-Leftie Equality and Human Rights Commission; their involvement is openly acknowledged in EHRC reports. The women leading the Fawcett Society, and the chair of the EHRC himself, should be grilled by *Newsnight* presenter Jeremy Paxman until they're toast. I leave you with an article from *the Daily Telegraph* edition of 12 September 2011:

> Putting children into day care may change their brain structure and function, according to research published today. The study by Dr Aric Sigman – a British-based American psychologist, biologist and author – found that 70 to 80 per cent of children in day care centres showed increasing levels of the stress hormone cortisol throughout each day they were there.
>
> In his article 'Mother Superior? The Biological Effects of Day Care', Dr Sigman proposes that higher levels of cortisol in children could have long-term implications for their adult health. He writes that the human response to fear and uncertainty is affected by early child care experiences, and that prolonged exposure to cortisol can prove toxic to the child's nervous system.
>
> His report also says that his research shows that the amount of attention given by a child's mother in early childhood can alter the part of the brain which is involved in forming memory, and so have an impact on whether he or she suffers attachment anxiety and attachment avoidance.
>
> He concludes that the three key factors in the impact of child care on stress levels are the quality of the care, the time spent in care, and the age when the child is put into day care.

Can we *really* be surprised by Dr Sigman's findings? If we are, then we truly have become accustomed to denying human nature in general, and the nature of young children in particular.

19 | ARE FEMINISTS DELUSIONAL?
IS THE POPE A CATHOLIC?
DO BEARS CRAP IN WOODS?

If I were to suggest that between the Earth and Mars there is a china teapot revolving about the sun in an elliptical orbit, nobody would be able to disprove my assertion provided I were careful to add that the teapot is too small to be revealed even by our most powerful telescopes. But if I were to go on to say that, since my assertion cannot be disproved, it is intolerable presumption on the part of human reason to doubt it, I should rightly be thought to be talking nonsense.
Bertrand Russell 1872-1970 British philosopher, logician, mathematician, historian, free trade champion, pacifist and social critic: 'Is there a God?' (1952)

From Wikipedia:

'The Flat Earth Society (also known as the International Flat Earth Society or the International Flat Earth Research Society) is an organization that seeks to further the belief that the Earth is flat, instead of an oblate spheroid, contrary to the scientifically proven fact. The modern organization was founded by Englishman Samuel Shenton in 1956, and later led by Charles K Johnson, who based the organization in his home in Lancaster, California. The formal society was inactive after Johnson's death in 2001, but was resurrected in 2004 by its new president Daniel Shenton...

The belief that the Earth was flat was typical of ancient cosmologies until about the 4th century BC, when the Ancient Greek philosophers proposed the idea that the Earth was a sphere, or at least rounded in shape. Aristotle was one of the first thinkers to propose a spherical Earth in 330BC. By the early Middle Ages, it was widespread knowledge throughout Europe that the Earth was a sphere...

In 1956, Samuel Shenton, a signwriter by trade, created the International Flat Earth Society as a successor to the Universal Zetetic Society and ran it as 'organizing secretary' from his home in Dover, in Britain. Due to Shenton's interest in alternative science and technology, the emphasis on religious arguments was less than in the predecessor society.

This was just before the launch of the first artificial satellite and when satellite images taken from outer space showed the Earth as a sphere rather than flat, the society was undaunted; Shenton remarked: 'It's easy to see how a photograph like that could fool the untrained eye.'...

The society also took the position that the Apollo moon landings were a hoax, staged by Hollywood and based on a script by Arthur C Clarke, a position also held by others not connected to the Flat Earth Society. On hearing this, Clarke sent a facetious letter to NASA's chief administrator:

'Dear Sir, on checking my records, I see that I have never received payment for this work. Could you please look into this matter with some urgency? Otherwise you will be hearing from my solicitors, Messrs Geldsnatch, Geldsnatch and Blubberclutch...'

The most recent world model propagated by the Flat Earth Society holds that humans live on a disc, with the North Pole at its center and a 150-foot (45 m) high wall of ice at the outer edge. The resulting map resembles the symbol of the United Nations, which Johnson used as evidence for his position. In this model, the sun and moon are each a mere 32 miles (52 km) in diameter...'

It's my firm conviction that feminists are as delusional as members of the Flat Earth Society. They have a faith in a set of beliefs with an internal consistency, and that faith is best preserved by limiting contact with non-believers. I emailed a number of prominent feminists and feminist academics following the publication of *The Glass Ceiling Delusion*, offering a free copy of the book. I explained that in writing the book I'd drawn upon my experiences in leading companies over the course of 30 years. Of the few who responded most were hostile, and I didn't detect a shred of intellectual curiosity in any of them. Not one individual requested a copy of the book.

It's not so much that feminists *won't* consider the validity of arguments which fly in the face of their cherished convictions:

they *can't* do so. For an explanation of this we need to have an understanding of the phenomenon of cognitive dissonance.

Cognitive dissonance is a theory first put forward by the American social scientist Leon Festinger in 1957. In his book *Cognitive Dissonance: Fifty Years of a Classic Theory* (2007), Joel Cooper, Professor of Psychology at Princeton University, charts the progress of dissonance theory. He writes:

> Leon Festinger, whose work on social comparison theory had already made him an influential figure in social psychology, made a very basic observation about the social lives of human beings: we do not like inconsistency. It upsets us and it drives us to action to reduce our inconsistency. The greater the inconsistency we face, the more agitated we will be and the more motivated we will be to reduce it.
>
> Before formalising the definition of dissonance, let us imagine some inconsistencies that can happen in social life. Imagine that you prepared at great length for a dinner party at your home. You constructed the guest list, sent out the invitations, and prepared the menu. Nothing was too much effort for your party: you went to the store, prepared the ingredients, and cooked for hours, all in anticipation of how pleasant the conversation and the people would be. Except it wasn't. The guests arrived late, the conversations were forced, and the food was slightly overcooked by the time all of the guests arrived. The anticipation and expectation of the great time you were going to have are discordant with your observation of the evening. The pieces do not fit. You're upset, partly because the evening did not go well, but also because of the inconsistency between your expectation and your experience. You are suffering from the uncomfortable, unpleasant state of cognitive dissonance...
>
> Festinger was adamant about one point. People do not just *prefer* consistency over inconsistency... The party host does not just wish the party had gone better; he must deal with the inconsistency between the hopes, aspirations, and effort that he put in prior to the party and the observation that the party did not go well. How can that be done? Surely, if the host changes his opinion about how well the party went, then there is no longer an inconsistency. Perhaps the guests loved a

slightly blackened lamb and their quietness at the table reflected their enjoyment of the meal.

Festinger's insistence that cognitive dissonance was like a drive that needed to be reduced implied that people were going to have to find some way of resolving their inconsistencies. People do not just *prefer* eating over starving; we are *driven* to eat. Similarly, people who are in the throes of inconsistency in their social life are *driven* to resolve that inconsistency. How we go about dealing with our inconsistency can be rather ingenious. But in Festinger's view, there is little question that it *will* be done.'

An article which appeared in a Minneapolis newspaper gave Festinger and his students an ideal opportunity to study inconsistency in a real-world setting. Cooper's account of this remarkable example of cognitive dissonance is reproduced below:

'An article that appeared in a Minneapolis newspaper gave Festinger and his students an ideal opportunity to study inconsistency in a real-world setting. The article reported on a group of west coast residents who were united in a belief about a significant event: the belief that the Earth was going to be annihilated by a cataclysmic flood on December 21, 1955. All of the people would perish in the cataclysm except for those who believed in the prophecies emanating from the planet Clarion; they alone would be saved from the flood.

Festinger reasoned that if Earth survived December 21, then the people in the little group, dubbed The Seekers by Festinger, Riecken, and Schachter (1956), would face a considerable amount of inconsistency on the next morning. While the rest of the world awoke to just another day, The Seekers would face a calamitous amount of inconsistency. The world's very existence would be inconsistent with their belief that the world as we know it was to have ended on the previous evening.

The Seekers was a serious group: this was not a collection of individuals who had a mild premonition of the world's demise. Their beliefs were specific and strong. As the December day approached, Seekers members sold their possessions and quit their jobs. Some, whose spouses did not share their beliefs, divorced. The Seekers members were united in their support of their leader, Mrs Marion Keech, who believed she was the medium through whom the unearthly beings on the planet Clarion communicated their wishes. She received her messages through automatic writing – a paranormal belief that a person's hand is seized by the spirits in another world and is used to communicate messages from the Great Beyond.

Clarion was specific. The group was to gather at Mrs Keech's home on the evening of December 20. They were to await the arrival of a spaceship that would come to Earth and whisk the group away from danger.

The Seekers were not publicity hounds. They sought no attention for their beliefs or their prophecy. When the reporter whose story appeared in the Minneapolis newspaper attempted to interview them, they grudgingly gave only the briefest interview. Publicity was not their goal; protecting themselves from the cataclysmic end of the Earth was.

As a social psychologist, Festinger saw the immediate relevance to the theory he was generating. If people are driven to deal with inconsistency, how would Marion Keech and her followers react to the morning of December 21 when the sun rose, the sky brightened, and the spaceship from Clarion failed to appear? The clear and specific anticipation of the world's demise, the elaborate preparations for the group to be saved, the broken marriages and other personal sacrifices, all would stand in stark contrast to the world's having made just another turn around its axis. Festinger and his colleagues predicted that the dramatic inconsistency would create the state of cognitive dissonance and the group would be driven to find some way to reduce it. They would need to find some way of restoring consistency to their mental maps of the cosmic events.

One of the researchers, Stanley Schachter, infiltrated the group. He carefully observed the group's preparations and specifically observed the events as they unfolded just after midnight on December 20. The group gathered near midnight, waiting for the arrival of the spacecraft. Tension and excitement were high. They had followed the Clarions' instructions meticulously. Mrs Keech's grandfather clock ticked the final seconds to midnight. No spacecraft.

Someone in the group checked his watch and saw that his watch still read only 11:55. All watches were reset. At 12:05, even by the ticking of the newly set watches, there was still no spacecraft. Another member of the group suddenly realized that he had not fulfilled all of the instructions given by the Clarions. They had insisted that all metal objects be removed from the human space travellers. Thus, they came with no zippers, belt buckles, or bra straps. But now a Seeker realized that he had a metal filling in a tooth. He removed it. [Author: I imagine that at this point some of the other Seekers 'forgot' they too had metal fillings.] Still, no spacecraft.

There followed a terrible few hours following the midnight disconfirmation of the prophecy. People sobbed and wept. Had they been abandoned by the Clarions? Had they been wrong all along, just like their more cynical spouses and former friends had told them? Shortly past 4:00 am, Mrs Keech received her final message from Clarion. The message provided the answer to their questions, and also provided the opportunity to restore consistency between their doomsday beliefs and their observation that the spaceship had not come and there had been no Earth-destroying cataclysm.

The Clarions' final message was brilliant. Through Mrs Keech's trembling hand, it said:

> This little group, sitting all night long, has spread so much goodness and light that the God of the Universe spared the Earth from destruction.

So that was it. The beliefs had not been wrong after all. God had been planning to destroy the Earth. All of the preparations for the cataclysm had not been in vain. In fact, it was precisely and only because of the preparations, sacrifices, and faith of the group that the Earth still existed on the morning of December 21. The sun still shone because of them; people went to work because of them; people still had homes to return to and families to love them . . . all because of the determination of the small group of Seekers.

Before December 21, Festinger et al (1956) had made a prediction. They hypothesised that The Seekers, who shunned publicity and notoriety, would take their cause to the public following the disconfirmation. And The Seekers did that with gusto. As soon as their new belief was in place – as soon as they had generated the story that their actions had saved the world – they took their case to the public. They looked for social support for their story. They desperately wanted others to see that their actions had not been in vain, that their prophecy had not been disconfirmed, that there was no inconsistency between their belief in the cataclysm and the bright sunny day that had dawned on December 21.

The premise of dissonance theory is that people do not tolerate inconsistency very well. The Seekers had found a way, post hoc, to make their actions feel consistent to themselves and they now sought validation in having the world believe them. They printed flyers, called newspapers and magazines, offered to talk on radio programs, all in an effort to bolster their new found consistency.

There are probably many factors that influenced the group of Seekers in their actions. Who can guess what had initially influenced these individuals to believe in the prophecy and the automatic writing? Who can guess what motives each individual may have had in the wake of the disconfirmed prophecy? But one thing seems certain. Caught in a major inconsistency among their beliefs, behaviours, and observations of reality, The Seekers did just what Festinger and his colleagues predicted they would do: they were driven to find a way to restore their consistency – driven to find a new belief that would make sense of what they had done and driven to convince a sceptical world of the truth of their new position.'

The upshot of all this for the battle against feminism? It can't be won through the power of argument, and there's no point in trying to do so. If the battle is to be won it will have to be through simply *stopping* the influence of militant feminists. Imprisoning the feminist Labour politicians Harriet Harman (née Harman) and Yvette Cooper (née Cooper, but considering her husband is fellow Leftie MP Ed Balls, you must have some sympathy…) would be an encouraging start to the battle. They could share a small stinking cold cell where the only reading material would be admiring biographies of Margaret Thatcher.

20 | THE EVOLUTION OF NAGGING

Nagging is the repetition of unpalatable truths.
Edith Summerskill 1901-80 British Labour politician: speech to the Married Women's
Association, 14 July 1960

One of my more unusual habits is to speculate on the evolutionary basis of the differences between men and women. I invite you to join me in a cave in the Stone Age in the area of England which is now the county of Wiltshire, not long after the construction of the Stonehenge stone circle.

As you may be aware, archaeologists have recently proved beyond all reasonable doubt that Stonehenge was built to act as a highly visible marker to the visiting citizens of the planet Xlodić 217k where, you may recall from *The Glass Ceiling Delusion*, Elvis Presley has been performing twice nightly since his abduction on 16 August 1977. Apparently he still wears his trademark black leather jumpsuits, but these days he's usually chained to his Zimmer frame lest he stumbles during his act and displaces a hip again. I digress. Back to the cave.

Mr Ug has explained to his toothless wife all about his recent invention of the wheel. She's unimpressed, and wonders aloud what's wrong with men dragging huge stones through the mud and over hills, before ending the exchange with, 'You've always been a lazy sod. Typical man!'

Mr Ug says nothing in response, walks out of the cave in a glum mood, and kicks one of the puppies into a fast-flowing stream – which lifts his spirits a little – then goes about his day.

Now this real life story is but one example of an age-old phenomenon: women nag, and men suffer but aren't permitted to nag in turn. The tendency of women to nag, and of men to suffer as a result and to do *anything* within their power to stop their womenfolk nagging, was positively selected for over the many thousands of years of the evolution of *Homo Sapiens*.

It's a general rule in nature that species-specific phenomena have an evolutionary basis. Might there have been an evolutionary advantage for women who complained more than the average, and for men who suffered more than the average when women complained?

The most successful families would have been those where the men worked the hardest to support their wives and children. In the absence of incentives in the Stone Age – would *you* risk your life hunting a sabre-toothed tiger, if the reward for success was a couple of shiny pebbles? – women evolved to nag, and men evolved to wilt in the face of nagging.

The genes of less selfish men would be passed on more successfully than the genes of more selfish men. And what better way for nature to make men less selfish, than to have them suffer mentally at the hands of complaining women? So it is that we find men being prepared to do *anything* to stop women complaining. 'What's that, dear, you ladies want the vote? But you've never been interested in politics, nor have your sisters, your aunts, your mother... oh, all right dear, stop moaning, you can have the vote. Can I have that cup of tea now, dear? What's that, dear? I can stick my cup of tea *where?*'

The fact that women complain more than men doesn't mean they have more to complain *about*. Men in general have yet to recognize that truism.

A small number of men, myself included, are fortunate to lack whatever genetic coding is required to wilt when women nag. One of my ex-wives once nagged me non-stop for perhaps a quarter of an hour over something utterly trivial, and all I heard was, 'Blah, blah, blah...'. At the end of her speech she tapped me on the arm, frowned, and hissed, 'You haven't been listening to a word I've been saying, have you?' I replied, 'No dear, my sanity depends on not listening to you at times!' I had to iron my own shirts that week. She could be a cruel woman, when she put her mind to it.

Anyway, there you have it, the reason that feminists have been so successful. Their nagging drives men in positions of power to readily give their power away to women, rather than listen to any more nagging. Can you *imagine* a man having the mental fortitude to withstand Harriet Harman nagging for ten minutes or more? Nor me. An attractive woman, too, by feminist standards. Just don't look for too long into those violent eyes... sorry, violet eyes.

[Update: In recognition of the power that nagging confers on women in general, and feminists in particular, my organizations have been presenting 'Whiny Feminist of the Month' awards for several years.[1] Winners of the awards automatically become members of The Whine Club. Laura Bates was the inaugural member of the club. She launched and still runs the Everyday Sexism Project,[2] which we refer to as the Everyday Whining Project. She enjoys remarkable media exposure – particularly on the BBC, predictably – and she's a magnet for whiny women. We now refer to her simply as 'Special Snowflake'.

We launched the Alternative Sexism Project,[3] to show that sexism affects men and boys far more gravely than it affects women and girls.]

---

[1] https://fightingfeminism.wordpress.com/the-whine-club/
[2] http://everydaysexism.com
[3] https://thealternativesexismproject.wordpress.com/

21 | WOMEN HAVE A RIGHT TO COMPLAIN, BUT DO FEMINISTS ABUSE THE PRIVILEGE?

I personally think we developed language because of our deep need to complain.
Lily Tomlin (1939-) American actress, comedienne, writer and producer

There's an interesting difference between how we regard men who are prone to complaining, and women who are. Men who are prone to complaining are figures of fun; even if we restrict ourselves to BBC television series we have Basil Fawlty in *Fawlty Towers*, Victor Meldrew in *One Foot in the Grave*, Albert Steptoe in *Steptoe and Son*, and numerous well-known men on *Grumpy Old Men*. There have been glum female characters in television series, but few whose misery carried as much comic potential.

I've known a number of long-married couples where one of the spouses is an Olympic-standard complainer. Where that person is the husband the wife generally ignores him, perhaps nodding occasionally and muttering, 'Yes, you're right, dear', to keep the peace. But where the complainer is a woman, you'll find a haunted-looking husband. You only have to look at the husband of militant feminist Harriet Harman, fellow Labour politician Jack Dromey. Even by Leftie standards he looks glum. They married in 1982, so they've probably shared over 10,000 breakfasts by now. The man deserves a medal.

Somehow the doe-eyed Harriet makes her way into almost all my books, including *The Marriage Delusion: the fraud of the rings?* She was a senior figure in the dire Labour administrations the United Kingdom suffered over 1997-2010. The possibility of a fourth Labour general election victory in succession in 2010 was such a depressing prospect that, had it happened, I planned to emigrate to France and pay my taxes to the French government rather than the British one. I also planned to write a book on the matter, *Harriet Harman Drove Me To France.*

[Update: the Labour party lost power at the 2010 election, after which a Conservative / Liberal Democrat coalition emerged.]

22 | ARE FEMINISTS DEPRESSED, AS WELL AS DEPRESSING?

When women are depressed, they eat or go shopping. Men invade another country. It's a whole different way of thinking.
Elayne Boosler 1952- American comedienne

Lefties in general, and feminists in particular, tend to be depressing company in rough proportion to the extent of their convictions. But here's an interesting thing: they're also more likely to be *depressed* in rough proportion too, in my experience.

Perhaps we shouldn't be too surprised by these findings, given that envy lies at the heart of Lefties' and feminists' world views. The greater the envy, the greater the misery. It's obvious, when you think about it.

But I could be wrong. Please, don't write to me to protest. It's possible. It happened once before. It could be the case not that feminism makes women depressed, but that depressed women are drawn to feminism. Or maybe both are true. Maybe women are drawn to a philosophy which offers simple explanations for why the world is not as they would like it, to do with the evil nature of men, patriarchal hegemony, blah, blah, blah...

Maybe for some women it's partly to do with sex. The highly regarded English clinical psychologist and writer Oliver James has written at length in a number of bestsellers about mental health. His books are always worth reading and he often teases out some subtle nuances that other writers miss. In *Britain on the Couch* (1998) James had some interesting points to make about 'Sex and attraction as sources of gender rancour':

'Worldwide, there appear to be substantial and consistent differences between the sexes as to what attracts them, what they fantasise about sexually, and what they want in bed. Let it be said at the outset that men will probably tend to be more enthusiastic about these findings than women, that most of the research on which they are based was done by men, and that some women may even find them insulting and offensive.

Despite these disclaimers, there is not much doubt that what you are about to read is true of the average man and woman all over the world today.

COMPARED WITH WOMEN, MEN . . .
- Value physical attractiveness higher than women whether it be for marriage, a date or casual sex
- Prefer partners who are younger than them and marry younger partners
- Care less about the social status and wealth of partners if they are physically attractive or actually prefer lower status and wealth in partners
- Place a higher premium on sexual intercourse
- Are keener on the idea of casual sex, more indiscriminate when considering it, think more often about sex, are more unfaithful and have more partners in practice
- Fantasise about a greater variety of partners, masturbate more, are more explicit about sexual acts during fantasies, picturing precise features of partners' anatomies, such as genitalia, and are more likely to base their fantasies on real people and situations
- Fantasise more about 'doing things to', rather than 'having things done to'
- Are more jealous of sexual infidelity

COMPARED WITH MEN, WOMEN . . .
- Place a higher value on the wealth and status of potential mates – even if they are themselves of high status and wealth
- Prefer and marry partners who are older than them
- Are more influenced by negative information about a potential mate
- Place less emphasis on sexual intercourse as a goal, are more faithful and have fewer partners overall
- Fantasise less about sex, are less sexually explicit in the fantasies, focus more on the build-up than the climax, focus

more on the emotions and settings of the fantasies, are
more likely to ascribe the partners a profession and
personality and are more likely to base the fantasy on their
imagination than on real people or situations
- Are more jealous of emotional rather than sexual infidelity

When I began to research this chapter, I was amazed at how
abundant and robust is the evidence for these assertions, cross-
nationally and historically. Despite several decades of intense
debate and pressure for equality, apart from in a few respects,
what women and men want sexually does not appear to have
changed very much. The cliché that 'men use love to get sex
and women use sex to get love' still has more than a little truth
to it (as we shall see, it seems that you could equally substitute
'status, power and wealth' for the word 'love'). Why are men
and women still so different? Will the differences remain, say,
50 years from now? Above all, has the durability of these
differences affected gender rancour and, therefore, rates of
depression and serotonin levels since 1950?

That these differences have endured has led some
sociobiologists to go so far as to claim victory in the gender
debate: 'despite decades of feminism, genes will out'. As we
shall see, this is premature. There is still a long way to go before
we know for sure what, if any, psychological differences in this
area have been inherited. There are still good grounds for
supposing that they could be largely a matter of conditioning,
and evidence regarding the first two questions is inconclusive.
But in the meantime, I do believe that the durability of these
differences, coupled with recent social trends, is causing a good
deal of gender rancour and adding significantly to our
unhappiness.

The heart of the matter is that they cause considerable role
strain for both genders in the sexual realm. The media still
exploit these differences in films, magazines, advertisements,
popular songs and books. Put crudely, the women are portrayed
as wanting rich, powerful men, the men as wanting 'babes', and
the products sell because these narratives play to audiences' real
preferences to a surprising degree.

Yet alongside this commercial exploitation of our desires
(whether natural or nurtured), there is also another pressure
from the media which is telling us that it should not be so and
offering a new way. Men are under considerable pressure to
value women as people and as equals, and women to become

independent and thrusting. Both sexes are being pulled in two directions and this increases aggression and depression. For, if it is true that most men still basically want to have sex with young, pretty women, think about sex more, want it as often as possible and still tend to be focused on intercourse as the goal, then these desires will clash with the contrasting desires of women listed above and with the prevailing ideology that men 'should' value women as human beings.

Most men want the old traditional femininity in women and are upset by the New Woman. Some men react angrily when their predilections are criticised or rejected by women and in the media; others conceal their 'true' predilections behind a carapace of New Man attitudes and feel dissatisfied; others still feel guilty or even 'unnatural' when they find themselves fantasising about what they really want.

Meanwhile, if most women still basically want a 'good catch' – a relatively well-to-do, high-status, older man – who will make a solid breadwinner and father, and if they are less focused on sex in general and intercourse in particular, these desires will also conflict with the desires of men listed above and the prevailing ideology that the New Woman should be an independent equal with the sexual appetites of the New Woman in *Cosmopolitan* magazine articles. In some cases this leads to a self-contradictory position in which a woman may be cursing 'the lack of real men who are not just wimps' in one breath and complaining of the overbearing arrogance or intransigence of men in the next.

Some women are furious when men exhibit classically male desires; others pretend to be New Women in front of their girl friends but act Old Woman with men; and others still act New Woman all the time and guiltily nurse Old Woman fantasies. Yet again, both sexes end up losers.'

It's clear that 'both sexes end up losers' when they try to think and act in ways which don't accord with human nature. And what is feminism if not a project to deny the natures of gender-typical men and women for ideological reasons, regardless of the consequences?

Apart from problems with gender roles in their sex lives – for those who have sex lives – what else might be giving feminists the blues? Well, for those women who dream of equality in the boardroom and similar triumphs for womankind, persistence over lengthy periods must be a useful attribute – but might there be a penalty to be paid for such persistence? From *The Economist* of 27 July 2009:

'Clinical depression is a serious ailment, but almost everyone gets mildly depressed from time to time. Randolph Nesse, a psychologist and researcher in evolutionary medicine at the University of Michigan, likens the relationship between mild and clinical depression to the one between normal and chronic pain. He sees both pain and low mood as warning mechanisms and thinks that, just as understanding chronic pain means first understanding normal pain, so understanding clinical depression means understanding mild depression.

Dr Nesse's hypothesis is that, as pain stops you doing damaging physical things, so low mood stops you doing damaging mental ones – in particular, pursuing unreachable goals. Pursuing such goals is a waste of energy and resources. Therefore, he argues, there is likely to be an evolved mechanism that identifies certain goals as unattainable and inhibits their pursuit – and he believes that low mood is at least part of that mechanism.

It is a neat hypothesis, but is it true? A study published in this month's issue of the *Journal of Personality and Social Psychology* suggests it might be. Carsten Wrosch from Concordia University in Montreal and Gregory Miller of the University of British Columbia studied depression in teenage girls. They measured the 'goal adjustment capacities' of 97 girls aged 15–19 over the course of 19 months. They asked the participants questions about their ability to disengage from unattainable goals and to re-engage with new goals. They also asked about a range of symptoms associated with depression, and tracked how these changed over the course of the study.

Their conclusion was that those who experienced mild depressive symptoms could, indeed, disengage more easily from unreachable goals. That supports Dr Nesse's hypothesis. But the new study also found a remarkable corollary: those women who could disengage from the unattainable proved less likely to suffer more serious depression in the long run.

Mild depressive symptoms can therefore be seen as a natural part of dealing with failure in young adulthood. They set in when a goal is identified as unreachable and lead to a decline in motivation. In this period of low motivation, energy is saved and new goals can be found. If this mechanism does not function properly, though, severe depression can be the consequence.

The importance of giving up inappropriate goals has already been demonstrated by Dr Wrosch. Two years ago he and his colleagues published a study in which they showed that those teenagers who were better at doing so had a lower concentration of c-reactive protein, a substance made in response to inflammation and associated with an elevated risk of diabetes and cardiovascular disease. Dr Wrosch thus concludes that it is healthy to give up overly ambitious goals. Persistence, though necessary for success and considered a virtue by many, can also have a negative impact on health.

Dr Nesse believes that persistence is a reason for the exceptional level of clinical depression in America – the country that has the highest depression rate in the world. 'Persistence is part of the American way of life,' he says. 'People here are often driven to pursue overly ambitious goals, which then can lead to depression.' He admits that this is still an unproven hypothesis, but it is one worth considering. Depression may turn out to be an inevitable price of living in a dynamic society.'

The fact that so many women have embraced feminism might account in part for their higher aspirations in life, but it hasn't led to the creation of any more fulfilling and well-paid jobs to satisfy those aspirations. It follows, as night follows day, that many of these women have unrealistic expectations which – unless discarded – lead inevitably to unhappiness, and possibly clinical depression.

Through embracing feminism many women have abandoned their traditional search for happiness through attaining and retaining the love and support of a man. They've sought instead to compete with men for power; how does that contribute to their happiness?

As well as being the country with the highest rate of depression in the world (by some reports) America is by some accounts the country in which feminism is most influential.

[Update: It has become clear to me since this book was first published in 2012, that there are many countries in which feminism is more influential than in the United States, the United Kingdom being one of them.]

Might the two be connected? I haven't the slightest doubt they are, and I'm equally sure that public funds will never be made available for researchers to investigate the link.

Are there some psychological themes common to feminists which might incline them to be more depressed than most women? Feminists are notably anti-marriage and hostile to the nuclear family, and maybe this gives us a clue as to the answer.

Swayne O'Pie in *Why Britain Hates Men: Exposing Feminism* (2011) speculates on the psychology of misandric feminists and he's in a better position to do so than most, having spent time on two gender-related Masters degrees. He refers to a time in the early 1990s when he was a self-declared socialist and feminist (and had been for 'many years') and – having recently divorced and been given custody of his three children – he set up a telephone counselling service for fathers denied access to their children.

He soon recognised a pattern emerging. The men were generally 7-10 years older than their ex-wives, the ex-wives had often been an 'only child', they'd had dysfunctional relationships with their fathers, the request for a divorce came from the ex-wives, the ex-wives used denial of access to the children as a weapon against their former husbands... and more besides. O'Pie cites Nicholas Davidson's *The Failure of Feminism* (1987):

'Feminism is capable of providing an explanatory system to women who are marked by difficult relationships with their fathers. This is not the whole story of feminism, but it is an important part of it. It is my personal observation that every feminist I know has two predictable elements in her life history, the first of which is an unusually strained relationship with her father. The feminist perspective has often given these women a way out. Their personal traumas and tragedies become intelligible as part of the great tragedy which, according to the feminist perspective, men have imposed on women throughout history. Feminism has often given such 'wounded women' a way to strike back at the oppressor – superficially a less demanding route than to confront the reality of their frayed personal lives.'

23 | POLITICS AND FEMINISM: AN EXPLOSIVE MIXTURE

Politics are usually the executive expression of human immaturity.
Vera Brittain 1893-1970 English writer: *Rebel Passion* (1964)

If we accept that feminism shares many if not most of the characteristics of faiths, we should not be surprised that when mixed with politics, the result is an explosive mixture.

The removal of religion from the world of politics across much of the developed world took centuries of struggle, and cost millions of lives, and of course the struggle for that removal has yet to begin in some parts of the world. Why, then, are women permitted to introduce feminism into the political system not only without active opposition, but with the active support of politicians?

In *The Glass Ceiling Delusion* I outlined areas in which radical feminist thinking had trampled over democratic processes. One was the introduction by the feminist politician Harriet Harman in 2008 of legislation permitting political parties to use women-only prospective parliamentary candidate shortlists for the ensuing 25 years.

When David Cameron announced his intention to employ such shortlists in late 2009, in the run-up to the general election, I resigned my membership of the Conservative party in protest. I'd worked for the party as a business consultant at its London headquarters over 2006-8. I was informed that a large number of other party members had resigned their party memberships following Cameron's announcement.

We should be grateful such shortlists weren't in place when Winston Churchill was considering standing for parliament; the outcome of the Second World War might have been different if they had, and British citizens might today be speaking German as a result; and life's already difficult enough without having to speak German as well.

The second area was the introduction in the Equality Bill 2010 of the principle that public sector bodies be required to pursue equality of outcomes of gender, race etc. as opposed to equality of opportunities. The Conservative-led coalition which came to power in May 2010 enacted the legislation, and did so within two months of the general election.

Readers familiar with the commitments made in Labour party general election manifestos over the past half century will not be surprised to learn that the possible introduction of either of these measures weren't contained in the 2005 general election manifesto, unlike the following statement which *was* in it:

> 'The new European Union Constitutional Treaty is a good treaty for Britain and the new Europe. We will put it to the British people in a referendum.'

The failure of the Labour government to honour that commitment was perhaps the greatest betrayal of a general election manifesto commitment in my lifetime. Without doubt, popular anger over the issue contributed to Labour's defeat in the 2010 general election. But rivalling it as an abuse of democracy were the plans to permit political parties to employ women-only prospective Parliamentary candidate shortlists for 25 years, and to introduce the concept of equality of outcome in the 2010 Equality Bill. Both led to remarkably little comment even in right-of-centre newspapers, to their eternal shame.

24| WHY DO LEFTIES NEVER LEARN?

Your liberal is an eternal sixteen-year-old, forever rebellious, forever oblivious to the nasty realities of life, forever looking forward to some impossible revolution in human nature.
Tony Hendra 1941- English satirist and writer: *The Book of Bad Virtues* (1995)

Historians estimate that communism, the roots of which can be traced back to before Karl Marx's and Friedrich Engels's *Communist Manifesto* (1848), was responsible for the deaths of between over 90 million people in the 20th century, mostly in the former Soviet Union and China. The number dwarfs the number of deaths attributable to fascism. Yet all around us Lefties assault our ears and intelligence with their views. What might explain this incredible state of affairs? Why do Lefties never learn?

Lefties have an infinite capacity for not learning the lessons of history. All but the most stupid of them now accept that the state cannot create wealth, it can only destroy it. But if we put that to one side, Lefties in the modern era hold essentially the same beliefs that Lefties have held for over 150 years.

Whatever Marxist theorists and their like might have said or written, the appeal of Leftie philosophies and Leftie parties to the population at large has always rested fairly and squarely on individual citizens' desire to improve their standard of living at the expense of other citizens, and this is often manifested in a desire for the state to provide 'just a little bit more'.

A friend who lives in London managed somehow to attain a council flat in 1989. At the age of 60, having lived in the flat for over 20 years, he now pays neither rent nor local taxes. Bizarrely he maintains that through his taxes he effectively financed the accommodation in which he now lives. I point out to him that other citizens have paid taxes too, but there's one small difference. They had to buy their homes with the money left over *after* they'd been taxed. None of this makes the slightest impression on him. Did I mention he's a socialist? I hardly needed to, did I? He's always moaning that the state should do 'just a little bit more' for him. I challenge him to find someone willing to pay just a little bit more tax for that purpose, but he's yet to track down such a person.

As if to press home the madness of the socialist philosophy, the other day he ranted for a time about the obscenity of a world in which top earners were paying 'only' 50% income tax on the portion of their annual earnings in excess of £130,000 'while kids are starving in Africa – higher taxes on the rich would finance more foreign aid.'

A year or two ago he earned a sizable lump sum for a small amount of work, and was paid in cash for his troubles. I asked him whether he had paid tax on the sum, thereby doing his 'bit' for poor African children. 'F*** off,' he replied eloquently, 'I paid taxes for *years* when I was working!'

25 | SHOULD WE TREAT FEMINISTS AS WE TREAT OTHER DIFFICULT PEOPLE?

She's the sort of woman who lives for others – you can always tell the others by their haunted expressions.
CS Lewis 1898-1963 English scholar, writer and novelist: *The Screwtape Letters* (1942)

The first rule of dealing with difficult people – at work, in the home, and elsewhere – is not to reward them for being difficult, because you only encourage difficult behaviour. The default setting of our political classes is to cave in to feminists' demands. Feminists only have to stamp their feet, screech and say something is 'outrageous' and they get their way.

At the time of writing (September 2011) there's a campaign underway in the United Kingdom to force companies to have women constitute a minimum of 30% of board directors. You'd have to have the IQ of a dim-witted tree frog to think they'll stop at 30%. Men need to strap a pair on and say to individual feminists, 'Look, sweetheart, we're not going to have quotas. We're going to carry on appointing directors on the grounds of merit. A crazy idea, I know, but it seems to have worked well in the past. Now off you go....'. That should do the trick.

When they decide to become feminists, women dedicate their lives to the pursuit of unhappiness. That imposes no obligation on the rest of the population – normal people – to turn the world upside down in a futile attempt to make them happy.

26 | WHY IS FRANCE ALMOST A FEMINIST-FREE COUNTRY?

In Paris they simply stared when I spoke to them in French; I never did succeed in making those idiots understand their language.
Mark Twain 1835-1910 American author & humorist

Given that French citizens on the whole are more left-wing, more secular, and less socially conservative than most American citizens, you might reasonably assume that feminism is more enthusiastically espoused in France than in the United States; but you'd be wrong. The opposite has long been the case.

A useful barometer of the level of interest of a country's womenfolk in feminism is the incidence of women's studies or gender studies courses. There's only one women's studies course at a university level in France – in Paris, predictably – while in the United States a survey conducted by the National Women's Studies Association in 2007 included 576 institutions offering women's studies or gender studies at some level. 576 institutions. Do statistics get any more depressing? What might account for the relative disinterest in feminism in France?

The United Kingdom lies between France and the United States in its citizens' attitudes towards feminism, and its number of gender-related courses. For an intriguing account of the differences between the United Kingdom and France we turn to Lucy Wadham, an English writer. She left England at the age of 18 to live with a Frenchman in Paris; they later married, had a number of children, and eventually divorced. 25 years after her move to France Wadham penned *The Secret Life of France* (2009) from which the following is drawn:

'There is no 'sisterhood' in France and for many years this was something I missed profoundly. With time, however, I realised – as I did of most areas of French life – that in losing one thing I had found another. I learnt that the extraordinary female friendships I had known in Britain were part of a wider landscape, itself not so pretty – a landscape ravaged by a low-level and persistent war between the sexes. The absence of gender conflict in France has become a source of relief to me... There is no tradition of gender separation in France because men enjoy the company of women... There is no such thing here as a 'ladette' because French women are happy to be admired for their femininity...

Feminism, when it came, sat far better in our two Protestant cultures [the United Kingdom and the United States] than it ever could in France's Catholic one.

The cross-gender tension that permeates both British and American society is not easy to describe, precisely because it is everywhere. In England, at least, I can feel it at dinner parties, on the radio, on the street. An unspoken agenda seems to exist between men and women in Anglo-Saxon Protestant societies that produces a certain carefulness in men – or else an irritating defiance – and in women a kind of guardedness, brittleness, even a sanctimoniousness. I have noticed that the tension is often camouflaged by that chumminess, which is not only unsexy but also slightly disingenuous. I'm not suggesting that men and women hate each other in Britain or America any more or less than they do in France, only that there is a lack of ease in their relations that is the direct result of having tried – and to some degree succeeded – in extending the rules of our contractual, mercantile society to the sexual playing field. In our otherwise laudable quest for transparency, we have managed to sabotage one of the greatest pleasures of life: the experience of enjoying being a woman in the company of a man or a man in the company of a woman. In Britain and America this pleasure has become shot through with a whole new kind of post-feminist guilt, and no one, it seems – neither man nor woman – is entirely free of it.'

I'm informed by an Italian lady friend that feminism has made as little headway in Italy as in France, and the Italian family remains a strong institution. American and British men and women – unlike their French and Italian counterparts – have sacrificed pleasure on the altar of feminism. What have they gained by way of compensation? Nothing. Absolutely nothing.

A worrying article in the 28 September edition of *The Daily Telegraph* titled, 'Mademoiselle? Don't be so insulting, say French feminists':

> 'Coming from a Frenchman, the term 'Mademoiselle' is normally a compliment, suggesting a woman is young and attractive. Not for some feminists, however, who have decided the Gallic equivalent to 'Miss' is sexist and should be removed from French official language.
>
> Yesterday two women's groups, *Osez le Feminisme* (Dare feminism) and *Les Chiennes de Garde* (Guard Bitches) [Author's note: they sound nice...] began a campaign to have the term struck off state and company forms. They say it is condescending and bolsters latent machismo because it stems from an old word for 'virgin'.
>
> Others called the campaign a stunt, saying it would be better to concentrate on sexual harassment. Even supporters of a ban, like the author Laurence Waki, conceded it had one drawback: "We will no longer be able to single out imbeciles who try to find out whether you're free with the chat up line, 'Madame or Mademoiselle?' '

It's sad to see the generally reliable *Daily Telegraph* pandering to political correctness. Laurence Waki is an authoress, not an 'author'. It appears feminism is becoming more influential in France, a bad development for mankind. For French mankind, anyway.

27 | ARE SOME FEMINISTS (E.G. TRACEY EMIN) A PAIN IN THE ARTS?

Art is making something out of nothing and selling it.
Frank Zappa 1940-93 American composer, singer-songwriter, electric guitarist, record producer and film director

The vast majority of the most talented artists up to and in the modern era have been men, a phenomenon that has been explored by numerous writers including Steve Moxon in *The Woman Racket*. The domination by men has existed for centuries despite the uncanny ability of lady researchers on the BBC radio programme *Woman's Hour* to find 'female artists who are all mysteriously unknown now but who were at least as good as and as well-known as the top male artists were at the time no really they *were* ' for any art form, in any country, in any century.

Is the existence of women-only artistic competitions (such as the Orange Prize for Fiction) the ultimate testament to the superiority of men in the arts? No. The ultimate testament is the feminist artist Tracey Emin, a Professor of Drawing at the Royal Academy, despite her obvious inability to draw any better than the average five-year-old. She is the creator of such works as *My Bed*. From Wikipedia:

> '*My Bed* was first created in 1998 [Author's note: by this definition of 'create' I myself have created works of art every morning for over 50 years...] and was exhibited at the Tate Gallery in 1999 as one of the shortlisted works for the Turner Prize. It consisted of her bed with bedroom objects in an abject state, and gained much media attention. Although it did not win the prize, its notoriety has persisted.

The artwork generated considerable media furore, particularly over the fact that the bedsheets were stained with bodily secretions and the floor had items from the artist's room (such as condoms, a pair of knickers with menstrual period stains, other detritus, and functional, everyday objects, including a pair of slippers). The bed was presented as it had been when Emin had not got up from it for several days due to suicidal depression brought on by relationship difficulties.

Two performance artists, Yuan Chai and Jian Jun Xi, jumped on the bed with bare torsos in order to improve the work, which they thought had not gone far enough. They called their performance *Two Naked Men Jump Into Tracey's Bed*. The men also had a pillow fight on the bed for around fifteen minutes, to applause from the crowd, before being removed by security guards. The artists were detained but no further action was taken. Prior to its Tate Gallery showing, the work had appeared elsewhere, including Japan, where there were variant surroundings, including at one stage a hangman's noose hanging over the bed. This was not present when it was displayed at the Tate.

My Bed was bought by Charles Saatchi for £150,000 and displayed as part of the first exhibition when the Saatchi Gallery opened its new premises at County Hall, London (which it has now vacated). Saatchi also installed the bed in a dedicated room in his own home.

Craig Brown wrote a satirical piece about *My Bed* for *Private Eye* entitled *My Turd*. Emin's former boyfriend, former Stuckist artist Billy Childish, stated that he also had an old bed of hers in the shed which he would make available for £20,000.'

Had 'works' such as *My Bed* been produced by a male artist, we'd never have heard of him.

28 | DOES HARRIET HARMAN SUFFER FROM MAD COW DISEASE?

The problem with political jokes is they get elected.
Henry Cate VII

My mother has long been a devoted reader of the *Daily Mail*, a newspaper which is a frequent critic of the feminist politician Harriet Harman, 'Mad Hattie'. In early October 2011 I was having lunch with her (my mother, that is, not Harriet Harman) and, as is her habit, she passed me a number of articles she'd cut out of the paper. Pointing at the article at the top of the pile, she remarked, 'She's mad, you know. Quite mad.' She could only be referring to one woman, I thought, and sure enough she was. The article was titled, 'Hattie's not for turning over Mrs Thatcher':

> 'Harriet Harman, the high priestess of political correctness, is leading the drive for Labour to change its rules to ensure that a woman is either leader or deputy leader in the future, irrespective of their ability or popularity. [Author's note: it was, unfortunately, to be a 'successful' drive.] It will be the ultimate act of positive discrimination from the party that first championed all-women short lists for Labour seats.
>
> But despite her pro-women policies, Harriet still can't bring herself to say anything positive about Britain's only female Prime Minister, Margaret Thatcher (who, incidentally, became Tory leader in 1975 without any such help from the party's rule book).
>
> When I asked who her female role model in politics was, she said, 'There isn't one.' What of Margaret Thatcher? 'But she was a Tory,' said Harman, her lower lip curling in distaste. 'I am terribly tribal. Thatcher was saying: "I'm doing it despite the fact I'm a woman." She spoke to women with her shopping basket and had the advantage of being an outsider and was seen by women as an outsider.'

All you need to know about Harman's attitude to Tory women MPs emerged shortly after she entered Parliament in a by-election in 1982 at the age of 32. Hattie caused a stir by breast-feeding in the Commons, before going into the division lobby to vote while still cuddling her baby. 'Mrs Thatcher spotted me with the baby and came over. I was in great conflict.'

'I wanted her to see my baby and the Prime Minister was obviously going to admire my baby. But I was torn. I did not want the eyes of a Tory Prime Minister to fall on my baby.'

So what did she do? 'I walked away as fast as I could.' And did Thatcher see the child? 'No.'

So much for the sisterhood sticking together.'

I've long been a subscriber to the daily broadsheet newspaper *The Daily Telegraph*, the deliverer of daily doses of truth to British citizens of sensible right-of-centre opinions, mainly gentlemen. [Update: Shortly after this book was first published, the paper started becoming feminist-friendly. Their journalists, both male and female, attacked my party and myself before the 2015 general election.] Some of their finest columnists happen to be of the female persuasion, and one such is the estimable Liz Hunt. From the 5 August 2009 edition of the paper, her article about the feminist politician Harriet Harman, at her most influential at the time:

'Harriet Harman once cracked a joke. Yes, I know, it's hard to believe. Humour is not one of Miss Harman's chief attributes, nor is self-awareness – and this, remarkably, was a joke against herself. Asked, at the height of the leadership crisis last summer, about her own chances of becoming prime minister, Miss Harman said: 'It will not be possible, because there aren't enough airports in the country for all the men who would want to flee.'

One year on, she could confidently rewrite the line to include all the women who would join the stampede, too: desperate to escape a Britain shaped by her politically correct zealotry. The news that she has been slapped down by No 10 over a policy announcement is the culmination of a disastrous few days for

Labour's deputy leader, although an entertaining time for the rest of us. As an end-of-pier turn, she is starting to rival John Prescott in his gaffe-prone heyday.

Topics of national and international import – the swine flu pandemic, doctors' hours, bankers' bonuses, the war in Afghanistan, turbulence in Iran – are of no concern to the woman in charge while Gordon (Brown) chews his nails in a sodden Lake District and rues the political necessity of having to take a holiday at home. Instead, Miss Harman's fixation with 'equality' continues – although her ranting has taken on a disturbing shrillness of the 'all men are rapists' school of feminism.

She does 'not agree with all-male leaderships' because men 'cannot be left to run things on their own', she told an interviewer at the weekend. This eye-popping statement came alongside reports that, after winning the deputy leadership in 2007, she tried to change Labour's rules to ensure that a woman was always in a top job.

Undeterred by the ridicule this generated – not least from many prominent women – she turned her fire on the bankers, suggesting that if the girls, rather than a horde of testosterone-fuelled Gordon Gekkos, had been in charge, the global turndown might not have been as serious. I think she has a point about the macho culture of high finance, but she negated it almost immediately with a crass reference to 'Lehman Sisters rather than Lehman Brothers'. It prompted one minister to say that 'Harriet has literally gone bonkers'. [Author's note: it also prompted a comedian to quip that a similar point could have been made in favour of 'Gay Men Brothers'.]

Yet it is the timing of these ill-judged headlines that really shows how out of touch she is with the public mood. Under Labour, we have had more women MPs than ever before, and more women in government. Yet their success rate in high office has been abysmal, largely through their own ineptitude. The demeaning departure of Jacqui Smith (porn and sink plugs), Hazel Blears (flipping houses) and Caroline Flint ('female window dressing') is kept fresh in our minds by the vengeful recriminations that continue to surface on chat shows or in interviews. Even the old guard – Patricia Hewitt, Estelle Morris, Margaret Hodge, Clare Short – displayed a general lack of achievement that lingers in our consciousness. So what made Miss Harman think that either sex would sympathise with her renewed demand that a woman should be guaranteed one of the top jobs in the party for reasons of equality rather than ability?

In fact, it rather throws the spotlight on Harriet herself – and makes you wonder what, other than a thick skin and a bludgeoning tenacity that wears others down, she brings to the Cabinet table.

To me, she belongs to a particular breed of Labour women who claim to have the best interests of other women at heart. In reality, their concern is rooted in a blinkered ideology that panders to a particular faction of their party, and is ultimately self-serving.

There is no question that Miss Harman has her eye on a forthcoming vacancy [Author's note: the vacancy in question was the leadership of the Labour party, in the event that Labour lost the subsequent general election]. But she may come to regret her outburst this week. It has alienated a majority of women who know, instinctively or through experience, that without merit there can never be a meritocracy.'

Harriet Harman's official title for a number of years was 'The Rt Hon Harriet Harman QC MP'. The 'QC' element stood for Queen's Counsel, denoting a senior legal figure appointed within the legal profession on the grounds of merit, but in the case of Ms Harman it was purely an honorary title, resulting from one of her many appointments.

In stark contrast, Margaret Thatcher – a trained barrister – would have been entitled to use the term 'QC' after her name on professional grounds, but never did.

29 | CAUTION: WOMEN AT WORK

There is nothing wrong with discontent at having a modest place in the scheme of things. That very discontent produced the ambition that built the culture of yesterday and today. But the discontent of those times was accompanied by discipline, willingness to work hard, and ready acceptance of a competitive society.
William A Henry III 1950-1994 American cultural critic and author: *In Defence of Elitism* (1994)

In my last book *The Glass Ceiling Delusion* I argued that the glass ceiling is one of many assertions concerning men and women in the world of work which are variously conspiracy theories, fantasies, lies, delusions or myths; and that initiatives to 'improve' the proportion of women on executive boards, regardless of the number of women with the experience and expertise to make a success of those roles, could only harm the business sector and by extension wider society.

I thought it might help the reader if I were to summarise a number of the key elements of the book, not in order to promote *The Glass Ceiling Delusion* (heaven forbid) but to provide the reader with some of the bases on which the arguments in this book rest. There's some material common to both that book and this one, and I point out where this is the case on a chapter-by-chapter basis.

After the chapter summaries I explore a major 'successful' gender balance initiative – equalising the number of male and female general practitioners ('GPs') – followed by remarks made by our current Prime Minister, David Cameron, about gender balance in the boardroom. I end this chapter with some insightful responses to those remarks, from members of the Great British public.

Chapter 1 – The world of work: feminist fantasies, lies, delusions and myths

Women are highly selective about the fields in which they seek equality with men, seeking to avoid work which is unpleasant, dangerous, or requires long periods being spent away from home. (In his book *Why Britain Hates Men* Swayne O'Pie refers to such jobs as being in the 'glass cellar'). This is true for single women as well as for women with responsibilities for children.

30 assertions commonly made by women (and by feminists in particular) about the genders in the world of work are identified, and they are explored over the course of the book. These assertions aren't held to be valid by the people who appoint senior executives. Examples of the assertions include:

1. Unlike men, women are gender-blind when it comes to recruiting and promoting staff. They make selection decisions based solely on individual candidates' merit
2. Talented women with the experience, ambition and qualities required to reach senior positions and the boardroom share a common cause with less talented women, and the career prospects of the former will not be impaired if they campaign for gender balance initiatives with the latter
3. The key psychological differences between men and women result from differences in their social conditioning (nurture) rather than in their biology (nature)
4. A higher proportion of women in senior positions can be expected to enhance organisations' profitability
5. Equal numbers of men and women are able and willing to take on senior positions including board directorships
6. Men and women are equally interested in the world of work; women are no more likely than men to seek a satisfying 'work/life balance'
7. Women are likely to be more emotionally intelligent than men, and emotional intelligence helps foster a productive working environment
8. The rate of *capable* women's progression into senior positions is being enhanced by the activities of militant feminists

9. Women would be more likely to seek high office if there were more role models to inspire them (but who will be the role models' role models?)

10. Men and women are equally likely to be innovative and risk-taking, and are therefore equally likely to behave in an entrepreneurial manner

Chapter 2 – The different natures of men and women

The content of this chapter is also in this book.

Chapter 3 – Astrology, guardian angels, crystal healing, underpants and stuff

The markedly greater propensity of women than men to believe in phenomena with no basis in reality is explored. There's a double standard at play here, a sexist one which ironically plays to women's advantage: men who believe in astrology would be regarded as unintelligent and/or uneducated, while women who believe in astrology would be indulged. Why might that be?

Chapter 4 – What makes women happy?

It's argued that the prime driver of happiness / unhappiness for most women is their interpersonal relationships rather than their work, and they are accordingly less inclined than men to devote the time and effort required to reach the highest offices in business and in other fields.

Chapter 5 – What are women interested in?

Compared with men, women are more interested in their close interpersonal relationships – friends, family, colleagues – and less interested in areas such as business and politics.

This is evident not so much in what women *say* they're interested in – they're usually careful to portray a serious and professional image – but in how they spend their time and money when free to pursue a range of options. In support of this proposition the chapter offers an analysis of the content of 'women's interest' magazines. Women are far less likely than men to be readers of magazines covering current affairs in depth, such as *The Economist*, *New Statesman* or *The Spectator*, and far *more* likely than men to be readers of magazines with titles such as *Let's Knit!*, *Hair Ideas* and *Soul & Spirit (your spiritual life coach)* along with other riveting publications. Although – irony of ironies – the monthly magazine *Riveting* (which explores new developments in the art of attaching metal plates to one another) has an almost exclusively male readership. I digress.

The chapter ends with a section drawing on material in Steve Moxon's *The Woman Racket* covering the issue of male dominance hierarchies (in the modern developed world, largely based on actual or prospective financial resources) and female dominance hierarchies (since time immemorial based on attractiveness and youth).

Chapter 6 – *Women and leadership*
Few men possess the characteristics required for the highest levels of leadership, but they outnumber the women who do. Margaret Thatcher possessed them in abundance.

Chapter 7 – *Are women more emotional and more rational than men?*
Yes, of course they are. The implications in the world of work are explored. Women are more likely than men to seek to be liked rather than respected, which is a problem for gender-typical women seeking to ascend corporate ladders.

Chapter 8 – The Empress's new clothes

The societal tendencies to avoid hurting women's feelings, and to boost their self-esteem, are explored. It's asserted that the tendencies – albeit the result of women's behaviours – serve to infantilise women. The link between persisting with unrealistic goals and depression, also covered in this book, is mentioned.

Chapter 9 – Why are fat women fat?

This chapter is also included in this book.

Chapter 10 – Feminists in academia

The curiously isolated world of feminist academics is explored, a world in which wishful thinking (feminist epistemologies or gender feminist theories of knowledge, anyone?) not only survives, but thrives. Don't laugh. Your taxes have been financing this nonsense for many years. The chapter ends with two pieces of material also included in this book, one on 'manginas' (male feminists), the other on the seminar titled, 'Experiencing and Celebrating Fatness'.

Chapter 11 – Militant feminism (gender Marxism)

Feminism arises from the same intellectual roots as Marxism, and is both a very radical and (in historical terms) a relatively new ideology. The chapter includes material from a leading textbook on human evolutionary psychology to show why such an 'unnatural' philosophy can be expected to be problematical.

Feminists' use of false logic is explored, such as their habit of taking rare examples of women with certain characteristics (e.g. entrepreneurial flair) and asserting they are commonplace among women, despite all the evidence suggesting otherwise. There follows material on cognitive dissonance, replicated in this book. The chapter ends with an extract from a textbook on the subject of misandry (hatred of men).

Chapter 12 – Political correctness (cultural Marxism)

Political correctness arises from the same intellectual roots as Marxism, and is equally based on dualism. There's an oppressing class (men) and an oppressed class (women). The former class are deemed always to be in the wrong, the latter class always in the right. Political correctness, despite being ridiculed in certain quarters, has become a major mode of thinking for many people in the modern era, and is one of the key phenomena that stops feminist assertions and initiatives being challenged.

Chapter 13 – Why does Fairtrade coffee always taste like mud?

A mystery explained.

Chapter 14 – Women and politics

How the suffragettes delayed universal suffrage – material replicated in this book. Why women sought the vote despite having no interest in politics, and women's continuing disinterest in politics other than 'women's issues' (and even then, only for a few women). The dangers inherent in having so many people voting in response to emotional rather than rational arguments. The problems of being a bald political party leader. Two pages of material on the irrepressible Harriet Harman.

Chapter 15 – Politicians and the fairness question

What is fairness? Equality of opportunity, or equality of outcome? It can't be both, so why do politicians pretend it can? The material is replicated in this book.

Chapter 16 – How fair is Britain? Men and women at work and the glass ceiling myth

The manipulation of the political system by militant feminist politicians with no democratic mandate to seek equality of outcome. A detailed analysis of the 'gender pay gap' concludes that it exists but it has nothing to do with discrimination against women, and is explainable by men's and women's choices in relation to the world of work as well as other factors unrelated to discrimination against women.

The glass ceiling doesn't exist today, and probably never did.

Elvis Presely's abduction by aliens and his transportation to the planet Xlodić 217k.

A lengthy extract from Steve Moxon's *The Woman Racket* drawn from a chapter titled, 'Sex at work: why women are not in love with work, yet the pay gap is so small.'

Chapter 17 – Gender balance in the boardroom: an assault on the foundations of a free society

Women have been taking up more and more managerial jobs but remain in a significant minority in the boardroom. The reasons for this are explored, including women's reluctance to take on such roles, as reported by a female psychologist in her insightful book.

The 'Top 20' reasons why female executives are uncommon in the most senior levels of major businesses are explored, including:

1. Many women have alternative options to work for attaining a high standard of living
2. Women seek a satisfying work/life balance
3. A private sector worker is 43.3% more likely to be a man than a woman
4. Women take educational choices unlikely to lead to senior executive positions

5. Women don't like to make decisions for which they might be criticised
6. Women are more likely to have empathising natures than systemising natures
7. Women value happiness over power
8. Women don't like working for women
9. Women who require role models to inspire them are followers, not leaders
10. Women prefer to promote women rather than men so are themselves regarded with suspicion as potential directors

Chapter 18 – How have militant feminists become so influential?

Some of the material in this chapter is replicated in an earlier chapter of this book.

Chapter 19 – The Equality Act (2010): the triumph of Harriet Harman

For the first time in Britain public sector bodies are required to seek equalities of outcome (e.g. of gender) rather than equalities of opportunity, regardless of the relative numbers of (for example) men and women seeking senior positions. The Labour party's Equality Bill (2010) was enacted by a Conservative-led coalition just two months after taking office in May 2010.

Chapter 20 – David Cameron – heir to Harman?

It's argued that David Cameron, the leader of the Conservative party and head of the current Coalition government, has a female-pattern brain, so his support for militant feminist initiatives such as the Equality Act 2010 should come as no surprise. His dominant decision-making style is based on emotion rather than reason, and he is fixated with style over substance. His only job before he entered politics was in Public Relations, a female-dominated field. He is poorly qualified on the grounds of either experience or personal characteristics for the position of prime minister.

Chapter 21 – Why aren't men revolting?
Men – or at least the vast majority of them, who are of low status – are manipulated by legislation favouring women. Men are reluctant to recognise just how powerless they have become in the modern era. The chapter includes extracts from Esther Vilar's classic work *The Manipulated Man* (1971).

Chapter 22 – Are women revolting?
Women are increasingly seeking a better 'work/life balance' which for women always means less work and more life. This runs counter to the direction in which militant feminists are urging them to travel.

Chapter 23 – Conclusions
More women will progress into senior positions when they stop seeking special treatment as a group, and compete effectively as individuals. The time has come to stop supporting feminist efforts to increase diversity in the boardroom, and leave board appointments to be made solely on the grounds of merit.

Appendix 1 – Quotations
A different selection of quotations to that found in this book.

Appendix 2 – The Empathising Quotient questionnaire

Appendix 3 – The Systemising Quotient questionnaire

Appendix 4 – Harriet Harman: a biography
More information on Hattie than you probably care to know…

Appendix 5 – the first letter to The Rt Hon Harriet Harman MP
The letter seeking an audio interview on the topic of equality of opportunity versus equality of outcome in the workplace.

Appendix 6 – the second letter to The Rt Hon Harriet Harman MP
It's my habit, after buying books to use in my researches for new books, to pass them on to worthy recipients. In the course of writing *The Fraud of the Rings* I read an excellent book by the Canadian-American psychologist Susan Pinker, *The Sexual Paradox*, and duly posted it to Ms Harman. Oddly, I never received a letter of appreciation from her.

Appendix 7 – The letter to Lord Davies of Abersoch
Conservative party leader David Cameron appointed Lord Davies, a *Labour* peer, to investigate women's 'under-representation' in the boardroom. You couldn't make it up, could you? I wrote to Lord Davies seeking an audio interview (on the same topic I'd written my first letter to Harriet Harman) but never received a response.

Appendix 8 – The letter to Ceri Goddard, Chief Executive of the Fawcett Society
I wrote to Ms Goddard seeking an audio interview (on the same topic I'd written my first letter to Harriet Harman) but never received a response.

Appendix 9 – The letter to Richard Lambert, the Director-General of the Confederation of British Industries ('CBI')

I wrote asking Mr Lambert for his personal views on the gender balance in the boardroom issue, as well as the CBI's official position on the matter, and received a speedy reply.

Appendix 10 – The letter from Richard Lambert, the Director-General of the CBI

The letter from Richard Lambert, while considered, could have been written by the Fawcett Society, and in the Appendix I comment on the points he makes in his letter. The final paragraph of his letter reads, 'We at the CBI believe therefore that board gender equality, as part of a wider drive for board diversity, is key to ensuring appropriate corporate governance is exercised in the future.'

An extraordinary example of an employer's organization caving in to special interest groups with not the slightest interest in corporate performance; governance being deemed to be more important than performance, and who but Lefties have an interest in making major alterations to corporate governance? If he were alive today, Karl Marx would find little to object to in Richard Lambert's letter.

Appendix 11 – The letter to Trevor Phillips, Chair of the Equality and Human Rights Commission

I wrote to Trevor Phillips seeking an audio interview (on the same topic I'd written my first letter to Harriet Harman) but never received a response. A pattern was starting to emerge...

Appendix 12 – The letter to The Rt Hon Theresa May MP

I wrote to Theresa May, Home Secretary and Minister for Women & Equalities, expressing my concerns over the Equality Act 2010, ending my letter with the following paragraph:

'Perhaps the most invidious provision of the Act is the introduction of the concept of 'positive action', by means of which public sector organisations will meet their 'Equality Duty'. Whatever the weasel words associated with positive action might be in the Act and associated guidance, it will surely result in positive discrimination – for women in particular – and discrimination is illegal under British and EU law. Might I ask, do you personally support the concept of positive action in this context?'

In her timely response Theresa May wrote, 'My approach to these issues is set out in a speech I recently gave, available here':

equalities.gov.uk/ministers/speeches-1/equalities_strategy_speech.aspx

The link leads to the text of a speech given by Mrs May on 17 November 2010 titled, 'Political Correctness won't lead to equality'.

Given the government's determination to 'improve' gender balance in the workplace through initiatives, what does a 'successful' gender balance initiative look like? We can expect public sector initiatives to be more 'successful' than private sector initiatives because long-suffering taxpayers will always pick up the bills.

A high profile initiative has been underway for some years in the National Health Service. For some thoughts on the topic we turn to a perceptive commentator on the practice of medicine in the UK, bestselling author Dr Vernon Coleman. The following is an excerpt from *Diary of a Disgruntled Man* (2011):

'December 1 2010
15.57 p.m.
There is talk of British companies being forced to have more female directors – whether or not they can find any decent ones. This is a really bad idea. Quotas are always bad. This

sort of positive discrimination is sexist and will produce the same sort of disaster that was created when medical schools were forced to increase their intake of female students. Many of the problems with medical care today stem from this absurd piece of legislation. There were never enough good girl applicants and so medical schools started taking the dregs in order to fill their quotas.

And, today, many female doctors want to work part-time. They don't have the sense of commitment of male doctors. They expect to be home for tea at 5 p.m. and they don't want to work weekends or nights. They want long periods off to have babies. And they don't have the same sense of dedication that has always been a tradition in medicine.

Incidentally, it does strike me as rather odd that while medical schools are forced to take in more female students so that there will eventually be equal numbers of female and male doctors there is no pressure on nursing schools to take in vastly more male students. And, as an afterthought, what will be next? Quotas for the army so that we have as many female soldiers as male soldiers? Probably. And what about transsexuals and transvestites? If there are going to be quotas for women then there should also be quotas for transsexuals and transvestites. And quotas for one-legged albinos with hearing problems.'

From *The Daily Telegraph* of 27 December 2011, an article titled, 'Shortage of GPs leaves health care in crisis':

'The NHS is facing a chronic shortage of family doctors after official figures showed some GPs were responsible for 9,000 patients. More than a million people were registered with a GP who served more than 3,000 patients, almost twice the average list size of 1,600...

There are concerns that the growing number of female GPs, many of whom work part-time because of family commitments, will lead to further shortfalls. Two thirds of trainee GPs are women and research by the Royal College of Physicians has found that women GPs will outnumber their male colleagues by 2013.

Dr Sarah Wollaston, a Tory MP and former family doctor, said: 'It creates all sorts of pressures as women take time out with family commitments. There is a real risk of a shortage.'…

Dr Wollaston added that many medical students perceive hospital careers to be more glamorous. [Author's note: more glamorous – how shallow is *that*?]…

A spokesman for the Department of Health said there was 'no evidence of difficulties accessing GPs'. However, she said [Author's note: ah, not a spokesman, then, but a spokes*woman*. *Quelle surprise.*] the department planned to make training more flexible to ensure the right people became GPs. [Author's note: the 'right' people being women, presumably.]'

The Daily Telegraph is sometimes criticised for its right-of-centre leanings but it's remarkably uncritical of gender-related initiatives. In the same edition of the paper as the article mentioned above, the editorial included the following:

'Another factor is the increasing presence of women GPs. This is a welcome development in many ways [Author's note: such as…?] but surgeries are finding it hard to cope with the challenge of women doctors during maternity leave…

The new data have been published at an awkward time for the Coalition and for Andrew Lansley, the Health Secretary, whose NHS reforms are unpopular. But the truth must be faced. The familiar relationship that the British enjoyed with their GPs is beginning to die out. It can be rescued only by far-reaching and expensive measures to incentivise medical students to become full-time community doctors. Either that, or we will have to adjust to a more impersonal style of health care. As usual, there are no easy options.'

The implication is that the decline of the GP service is a price worth paying for 'improved' gender balance among GPs. Given the enormous cost of training doctors, female doctors working part-time or having lengthy maternity leave must be adding to the already heavy burden on taxpayers. I don't recall voting for that. And 'there are no easy options'? All this from a right-of-centre newspaper. Scrapping gender quotas would an easy option, and could be introduced forthwith. But that won't happen. Gender equality initiatives only increase in number and scope, regardless of the damage caused by them.

Readers not familiar with the British medical scene might reasonably think that medical students would need to be 'incentivised' to become GPs because the pay and conditions of GPs are poor. They'd be wrong. The average income for a GP in Britain today (and few are willing to work at weekends or at night) is well over £100,000 p.a. as a result of negotiations between the professional body representing the GPs and the last Labour administrations (1997-2010). The state is mugging taxpayers to make health professionals (ever more of them female) wealthy. And when did you last hear of a GP being sacked for incompetence? Only in the public sector could incompetent employees earn six-figure salaries for life.

So, who precisely are the 'winners' and the 'losers' from this particular gender equality initiative? The losers include:

- taxpayers who have to foot the bill for extra doctors to be trained to compensate for female doctors who work part-time, don't work at night or at weekends, or don't work at all (far more female doctors than male doctors withdraw from the medical profession, the same being true for *all* professions)
- patients, who suffer a poorer GP service
- men who would gain access to medical training but are denied it because of the favouring of less well-qualified women

The winners are:
- the small number of women who gain access to medical training despite being less well-qualified than eligible men

I don't know the relative proportions of people in the two groups, but there must be *thousands* of 'losers' for every 'winner'. How can such a scenario prevail in a democracy? Because the forces behind the initiatives are strong, even if ideologically driven, and they face no opposition. And if the National Health Service is an example of a successful gender equality initiative, I shudder to think what a failed initiative might look like.

Quite apart from the outcomes of gender equality initiatives, we hear little of their cost. A Civitas report in 2011, *The Rise of the Equalities Industry*, provided a rare insight into the matter. From *The Daily Telegraph* edition of 28 November 2011, an article titled, 'The £1bn cost of equality monitoring':

> 'Employers are being forced to spend up to £1billion a year complying with 'flawed and clumsy' equality laws, a report claims. A study by Civitas, the think tank, estimated that small businesses alone were losing £210million a year on unnecessary bureaucracy related to equal rights for workers.
>
> The report, written by Professor Peter Saunders, a sociologist, argues that spending on 'mindless' data gathering could be harming rather than helping efforts to increase diversity.
>
> It estimates that private sector employers are wasting up to £400million a year on monitoring exercises required to meet equalities legislation, with an even larger bill for the public sector. The report cited the example of one Government department with 2,570 employees at its main Whitehall offices that spent £231,000 a year operating a five-strong 'diversity team'.
>
> 'Originally established to underpin equality before the law, equality legislation today is perversely undermining that very principle of fair treatment,' said the report. 'This is in pursuit of a false utopia of absolute equality for all.'
>
> The report takes issue with statistics suggesting that discrimination is costing the country billions in lost productivity, arguing that differences in the make-up of the

workforce are often assumed to be the result of discrimination rather than other factors.

Professor Saunders, an emeritus professor at Sussex University, wrote: 'The only way to generate the "savings" of up to £23billion that the Government's Equalities Strategy refers to would be to force millions of women to do science rather than arts degrees, to take private sector rather than public sector jobs, to work as software engineers and architects rather than as teachers and vets, and to put their children in nurseries and crèches even if they prefer to spend time with them at home.' '

Feminists continue to assert that discrimination against women accounts for women's low representation in some areas, although they only ever highlight lines of work which are highly paid and in pleasant and safe environments, never those which are poorly paid or in unpleasant and dangerous environments.

There's a long-running feminist campaign to 'improve' the gender balance of corporate boardrooms, feminists repeatedly claiming that the historically low representation of women in boardrooms results from men's discrimination against women: the 'glass ceiling'.

I contend that the 'glass ceiling' is a baseless conspiracy theory – as are other assertions about discrimination by men against women in the workplace – but what do women *themselves* think about discrimination on the grounds of gender? To answer this question we turn to the 2009-10 Citizenship Survey report 'Race, Religion and Equalities' produced by the Department for Communities and Local Government ('DCLG'). Paragraph 5.57 of the 123 page report states:

'Males and females were equally likely to cite gender as a reason for discrimination in relation to being refused a job (in both cases 1%), while female employees were slightly more likely than male employees to cite gender as a reason for discrimination regarding promotion (2% of females compared with 1% of males).'

How can these findings be squared with feminists' claims of gender discrimination in the workplace, and the consequent need for special treatment of women, which drive government policies? They can't.

The DCLG report extract was brought to my attention in a post on 30 January 2012 on the respected 'Rights of Man' blog.[1] [Update: It's no longer being maintained.] It inspired an 'open letter' I wrote to Theresa May, Home Secretary and Minister for Women and Equality (Apx.2). I emailed copies to all 306 Conservative MPs, and posted it on one of my blogs.[2] In the event of a reply, I shall post that on the blog too.

The person behind the 'Rights of Man' blog made the following comments about the DCLG report extract:

'The key statistics from this report shows three things:

Promotion – boardroom discrimination
Firstly, the anti-male Marxists feminists who bitterly complain against discrimination against women from the gender pay gap to promotion to boards and such like are out of step with what women actually think. Only 2% of women believe they are denied a promotion (1% men) because of their gender and 1% refused a job because of their gender.

The 30% Club, Fawcett Society, Lynne Featherstone MP, and all the others are wrong when they say it is a disgrace that women are being discriminated against because women themselves do not believe so.

These people live in a fantasy world of male hatred where white fat upper middle class men are keeping the 'sisters' in the kitchen and on the shop floor. Women disagree with the 30% Club, Fawcett Society, Featherstone, and everyone else who says it is a scandal.

---

[1] http://therightsofman.typepad.co.uk.
[2] http://fightingfeminism.wordpress.com

These groups do not speak for women, they speak for female privilege for (upper) middle class women at the expense of men.

Equality Act

We know the Conservative Government had initial reservations about sections 158 and 159 of the Equality Act (2010) which allows employers to discriminate against people when it comes to training, filling jobs and promotions, however, they ended up putting it into law on 1 April 2011.

It means that while 1% of men and 2% of women claim they are being denied a promotion because of their gender, I would expect this to be reversed over the next five years and then a clear gap will emerge, perhaps 5% of men claiming they are being denied a promotion because of their gender.

This will not only affect the men themselves but also affect their wives/girlfriends, daughters, mothers etc., so this discriminations affects women as much as it does the individual men.

Sample Size

Following on from the above, the numbers of 1% and 2% are very small and could be classed as insignificant. Perhaps a lot of that is down to the fact there still remains broadly a gender split in the work roles that men and women undertake. Without wanting to be too broad brush about it, it's hard for a male car mechanic to say he is being denied a promotion because he is a man when there are so few female mechanics. Likewise, a female primary school teacher may not be able to say she has been denied a promotion when there are so few male primary school teachers. It means that while the figure on paper looks small, its significance should not be under-estimated.

In conclusion, this report undermines those anti-male Marxist feminists who with every breath they take say that women are discriminated against in the workplace, when women themselves say they are not. Secondly, the Equality Act 2010 will, I predict, see a gap created where more men than women feel discriminated in work.'

On 11 October 2011 the online edition of the *Daily Mail – Mail Online* – carried a story about female directors in the 350 most highly capitalised firms in the UK, the 'FTSE350'. It started with the following:

> 'Top companies must do more to promote women to senior positions, the Prime Minister is expected to say. David Cameron will personally write to firms warning that their lack of action will not be tolerated by the Government. He will single out the bosses of FTSE 350 companies which have so far failed to set out plans for increasing the numbers of female directors in boardrooms.
>
> In February, the Government set voluntary quotas for business leaders and called for them to more than double the number by 2015. Former trade minister Lord Davies said they must employ at least 25 per cent and gave businesses six months to outline plans to achieve this target. He is expected to this week announce that a third of FTSE 100 appointments have gone to women since the publication of his 'Women on Boards' report. But nearly half of the most successful companies still do not have a single woman on their boards...'

Visitors to the website posted over 200 comments to the story within the following 24 hours, herewith a representative sample which will take us to the end of this chapter:

> TALENT is what we need, you bumbling nincompoop, not PC quotas!
> - Bryan Wrightson, Brampton, UK

> TALENT should be the deciding criterion for ANY job – not gender, race or any other bogus 'fiddling' to appease the PC brigade. Strewth, this country has become idiotic and spineless.
> - Brian, Wellingborough, UK

> I thought he was mad now I'm convinced.
> - b street, moreton wirral, UK

> We have a CONservative nanny state coming, dave has got too much media coverage, babblings of an untrained mind.
> - MARGARET ADAMS, SIDCUP KENT, UK

Let's be professional here. IT'S THE BEST PERSON FOR THE JOB and if it is a WOMAN she should have it... However women also have to make sure that they have the same commitment as other employees. TO MAKE FIRMS employ women in top jobs is wrong... We want the top jobs because we are the right people with the right skills set and will add value to the Company... Anything less is a sell-out of our dignity.
- Diane, Peterborough, UK

It's about time there were some employers' rights. Companies are in business to make money and to do this they need to employ the best people for the job. Full stop. They should not be forced to employ a workforce with specific percentages of sex, colour, race, religion or disability. Why do these people approach this from the bottom up. I do not see any calls for 50% of supermarket checkout operators to be male. There is a good reason why most of them are female. They are quicker and relate better to the customers.
- charlie, portsmouth, uk

He's turning into Harriet Harman! Get a grip man. Perhaps you should lead by example and replace some of your ministers with women. No? I thought not.
- Still Grumpy, Derby, UK

Hello David. How are things in Noddy Land today? I do hope all those nice companies will give the ladies some lovely top jobs. But I think the men want to keep them. It's quite a problem isn't it? Never mind.
- Sue, Sheffield, UK

You know, I'm beginning to believe that Cameron is really a Labour or Lib Dem mole placed in the Tory party to subvert it.
- Dave, UK

Idiot.
- Mike, Cardiff, UK

I worry about Cameron's thought processes, I really do. He is spending all his time wildly flailing around desperately looking for bandwagons to jump on to earn a few votes here and

there instead of rolling up his sleeves and tackling the elephants in the room which have now multiplied into a vast stampeding herd. If he were to do this, then 'votes would follow, as the night the day' (to rephrase Shakespeare). But I am afraid he is serving two masters, hence his vacillation. As for the present topic, I believe that the best qualified person for the job, whether male or female, should get the job. On merit. That's what I have always believed in and that's what I have always taught my students of both sexes.
- Susan, Manchester, UK

Why doesn't Cameron involve himself in solving some of Britain's real endemic problems – the economy, immigration, welfare dependency, the booze culture etc? Is Britain in such a good state that he can concern himself with campaigning about plastic bags, gay marriage and getting more women into top jobs? The man's an idiot!
- Reubenene

More social engineering. I am obviously a woman and I believe that women should only be given the job if they are good enough. I have seen too many women being promoted beyond their capabilities. There should also be no discrimination in favour of anybody be it black, white, female, male, gay, lesbian, young or old or social background. The only criterion that should matter is ability.
- Liz M, London, UK

'But nearly half of the most successful companies still do not have a single woman on their boards'. Perhaps we should be examining this statement more. Maybe for some companies that works better. Clearly for some companies not having women has not harmed their success. The women who do better are those who think & work like men i.e. put in as many long hours as required, are hardened & don't expect special treatment. I do think though we need to be honest about some women do not always want to do the long hours needed & also want to have families and they will have needs, which is right. And you cannot give 100% to both. Something or someone else will suffer. We currently have high unemployment, it is an employers' market, why would they want to employ a woman who is juggling family commitments & requires more flexibility when they can employ someone

who is able to be more committed to work & can totally fit in with the company's requirements?
- honest girl, UK

There is no such thing as Democracy, only a choice of Dictators. Most Politicians seem this way, Power crazy from when they stamped their feet as little children. If you put a moustache on the photo of Cameron you may get a better idea of what I mean. [Author's note: I did this, and Bernard makes a good point...]
- Bernard, England, UK

Harriet Harman in drag.
- Paul, Leeds, UK

'Must do this', 'Must do that'. What a petty little tyrant Cameron is. No wonder he is well pleased with keeping us in the EU Dictatorship which is run by tyrants just like himself, albeit they are not elected. They also want to control every aspect of our lives, even to the type of light bulbs we MUST use. Cameron simply can't resist them.
- TW, London, UK

Dave listen to yourself. You pillock. The only time someone should get a promotion is if they are the best person for the job. It's not about testicles or ovaries... or keeping the numbers balanced / equal rights etc. It's about who is best suited to do the job and experience. End of.
- Wayne, facebook and elsewhere

What does Cameron know about running a successful business?
- Stratford, Hants, UK

Why does any experienced man buy into this myth that there is some club being worked in which members are anti-women? I don't believe it happens at all, it's just an excuse women have invented because males have proven more competitive, impressive candidates. If anything, women get the leg up and favouritism because they are women, but maybe their work-life balance approach hasn't convinced employers that they are a good bet for top jobs. If successful companies thrive without including women on their boards,

let them alone – they obviously made good choices for their boards. I thought this government wanted business to succeed, not be hampered by all this PC crap.
- Fox, London, UK

Women should get more top jobs? How about employing the best person for the job regardless of sex or ethnicity. The country is in enough of a mess, we don't need any more of this politically correct garbage.
- louise, UK

He is talking about women in the private sector – note PRIVATE sector. Last week, this so-called 'Conservative' said he wanted to redefine marriage to include homosexuals and now this! I thought Labour was the party of political correctness and social engineering. He doesn't have a mandate to dictate to private enterprise who it appoints and promotes to its top positions – he should butt out. If he can't, he should be booted out.
- Stu, Laholm, Sweden

For Christ's sake Dave sort out the country first… you really are a plonker.
- Toto Kubwa, Cyprus

Many woman lose out because a fast paced moving company cannot tolerate maternity leave, proposed breast feeding breaks and flexible working hours. When you are in a position such as CEO, CFO or such, a company cannot afford to wait idle. You need to be flexible, be reliable, and have no distracting influences in your life.
- Michelle, Ireland

Cameron should be promoting the idea that it is the best person for the job if we are to dig ourselves out of this economic mess we are in. Gender based recruitment is simply politically motivated and it makes Cameron look as though he is now interfering in business for his own political gain. Sure there are less women in the boardroom than men. That is because most women have better things to do like bringing up a family!
- Josephine, Lytham, Lancs, UK

There is something very odd about any man who is as pathologically obsessed with women as Cameron is.
- Bryan C, Watford, UK

Don't bother with promoting women, I have worked with them. They're OK if you want paperwork to go missing.
- Robert, Leicestershire, UK

For every 100 male junior doctors, there are 150 female. We need to cut back on female admission to medical school to rebalance this.
- Tom, Glasgow, UK

Job selection should be on merit alone. It has nothing to do with a person's sex. But don't worry, it's only Camoron flapping his lips again.
- david smith, timaru, new zealand

'But nearly half of the most successful companies still do not have a single woman on their boards.' Maybe that's why they're successful? If a woman's the best person for the job then fair enough, but women's promotion shouldn't be forced, the best candidate should get the job. Bringing political correctness into the world of business will lead to disaster.
- jon, staffs, UK

Speaking as a female, I would be thoroughly insulted if I was taken on as an employee because I was a female rather than based on merit. I agree with all the men on this page. Just stop it Cameron!! You're an idiot!!!
- Angel, Midlands, UK

30 | HOW FEMINISTS ARE KILLING
MEN AND WOMEN

I am prepared to die, but there is no cause for which I am prepared to kill.

Mahatma Gandhi 1869-1948 pre-eminent political and ideological leader of India during the Indian independence movement

With any major change in society there will inevitably be winners and losers. With the onset of feminism and the consequent move of women from the home into the world of paid employment, there have been many more losers than winners. Feminists create the conditions under which many men commit suicide, by manipulating recruitment processes to deprive them of work which they would otherwise have on the grounds of expertise and experience; and they cause the suicides of some of the women unsuited to the worlds of work and financial independence.

Is there a differential between the numbers of men and women who try – and sometimes succeed – to commit suicide? I asked this question of six acquaintances. Four said they doubted there was a significant differential, one said there was a differential but more women than men committed suicide, while one was confident that more women than men commit suicide, on the grounds that women are more likely to suffer from depression than men. So what's the reality?

It is said that across the developed world women are, on average, three times as likely as men to *attempt* suicide. There's broad agreement among mental health professionals that this reflects women's greater tendency than men to 'cry for help', often through taking drug overdoses then calling immediately for an ambulance. They *expect* to be helped, in short. When it comes to 'successful' suicide attempts, men have long outnumbered women across the developed world, generally by a ratio of between 2.5:1 and 4.5:1. In Russia the ratio is currently around 6:1.

Suicide among British women has been in decline for many years, across all age bands, while suicide among men has risen among men under 45 years of age. If the differential were in the opposite direction – women committing suicide more frequently than men – we can be sure that governments would take the matter seriously.

Another example of the phenomenon is successive governments' huge expenditure on national screening programmes for female-specific cancers – around £250 million p.a. – while there are no such programmes for male-specific cancers. In the UK, as many men die from prostate cancer, as women die from breast cancer.

In the United Kingdom the unemployment rate among men is double that among women. From the website of Mind, a mental health charity:[1]

> 'There is growing evidence that unemployment has an impact on mental health. One study has shown that approximately one in seven men who become unemployed will develop a depressive illness in the following 6 months. Another study found that unemployment may be associated with a doubling of the suicide rate. Lack of job security is also a risk factor.
>
> Unemployment and falls in socio-economic status are thought to have particularly serious effects on men. One recent study found that men who experienced downward social mobility were four times more likely to develop depression than those who had not. Among women, however, there was no marked difference in mental health between those who experienced changes in social status in either direction. As one of the researchers suggests, this reaction

---

[1] http://mind.org.uk

could be linked to the traditional expectation that the man should be the 'breadwinner' of the household, and inability to do this can lead to low self-esteem.'

From the BBC News website, an article titled, 'Suicide linked to unemployment':

'There is a strong link between unemployment and suicide, according to new research. Professor Glyn Lewis, from the University of Wales, and Dr Andy Sloggett, from the London School of Hygiene and Tropical Medicine, studied data on suicides occurring between 1983 and 1992.

They found that unemployment was associated with a doubling of the suicide rate. Lack of job security was also a risk factor. Other measures of socio-economic status, such as social class and housing tenure, were not associated with an increase in suicides. This contrasts with a strong link between depression and anxiety and low socio-economic status...

Writing in the *British Medical Journal*, the authors say, 'Employment may have a particularly important role in defining an individual's place in the community, and unemployment could lead to alienation from the rest of society. This study could not adjust for some potential confounders but provides strong support for the possibility that reduction in unemployment would also reduce rates of suicide.' '

From the World Health Organisation, suicide rates per 100,000 people in 1999 in a number of developed countries:

Country	Males	Females	Ratio males: females
United Kingdom	11.8	3.3	3.6
United States	17.6	4.1	4.3
Canada	19.5	5.1	3.8
Germany	20.2	7.3	2.8
France	26.1	9.4	2.8

In an effort to obtain information about the link between unemployment and gender-related suicides I turned to an acknowledged expert on suicide, Professor Keith Hawton, Director of the Centre for Suicide Research at the University Department of Psychiatry in Oxford. He emailed me the following:

> 'The question of differing gender impacts of unemployment suicide rates is an interesting one. In the Great Depression there was a stronger association between unemployment and suicide in men than women, but far fewer women would have been employed at that time. More recent data suggests more equal impacts on suicide in men and women. I attach a PDF of a paper which partly addresses this question. While the statistical analyses are highly complicated you will see a simple statement on page 978 in the first paragraph of the Discussion which reaches a clear conclusion on this point. Therefore, I would be cautious about necessarily assuming that unemployment has greater effects on men than women.
>
> While there may be psychological reasons why one might think that this would be so (e.g. greater effects on self-esteem etc.), with the changing pattern of employment in the two genders, mainly in women, the nature of the influence of unemployment may have changed.'

The PDF sent by Professor Hawton was of a paper published online on 22 July 2010 in the journal *Social Psychiatry and Psychiatric Epidemiology* titled, 'Economic factors and suicide rates: associations over time in four countries'. It was written by two academics based in London, Professor Stefan Priebe and Dr Alfonso Ceccherini-Nelli.

The paper reviewed evidence of associations between deaths by suicide and three economic factors: unemployment, real gross domestic product per capita (RGDP) and the consumer price index (CPI) in four countries: United Kingdom (1901-

2006), United States (1900-1997), France (1970-2004) and Italy (1970-2001).

In the following extracts from the paper I've put into italics the 'statement on page 978' referred to by Professor Hawton:

'Results
Co-integration and correlation tests showed a long-run association between economic factors and suicide rates. Increase/decrease of unemployment predicted an increase/decrease of suicide rates over long historical periods and in different nations. RGDP and the CPI were also linked with suicide rates, but this was not consistently so and the direction of the association varied.

Introduction
Although suicide can be the epilogue of many psychiatric disorders, the majority of people who kill themselves are not patients of psychiatric services (approximately 75% in England and Wales). Suicide rates significantly change over time and differ across countries and there is little evidence that these variations are predominantly caused by changes of either the sensitivity of recording suicide verdicts or psychiatric causes, i.e. morbidity and service provision. Already a long time ago, considerations had suggested the need to investigate other factors explaining these variations.

Among other factors, economic ones have repeatedly been suggested as influential... Numerous studies have analysed associations between economic factors and suicide rates. The existing evidence points towards an association of unemployment and suicide rates... The findings for other economic factors are less consistent...

Discussion
The study used time series analysis to explore the impact of economic factors on suicide rates over long periods of time and using a consistent methodology to analyse data sets from different countries. The study shows a significant association between economic factors and suicide rates almost equally in males and females. Unemployment has the largest impact on suicide rates. In all four countries and over long periods of time increases of unemployment are linked with higher suicide rates, and decreases of unemployment with lower suicide rates. RGDP and CPI were also

associated with suicide rates, but this association was less consistent and applied mainly to France and Italy...

The relationship between unemployment and suicide is probably complex and mediated by several factors. Some studies suggest that people's alcohol consumption increases during unemployment... heavy alcohol consumption is a well-known risk factor for suicide...The relative interplay of these factors have been studied by Norström: a good third of the male suicides in Sweden were attributable to the alcohol factor and the impact of unemployment was also found to be fairly strong. For the author the indirect effects of unemployment were at least as important as the direct ones.

In conclusion, our findings suggest that the heterogeneity of methods may explain much of the inconsistencies of findings on economic factors and suicide in the literature. Although we used data sets from four countries with different traditions and partly different economic cycles, we identified a similar impact of unemployment on suicide rates. Unemployment is linked to suicide rates in males and females even at times when females were less likely to seek and expect unemployment. This indicates that the impact of unemployment may go beyond those directly affected by redundancies. One may speculate that unemployment can create an overall societal atmosphere that leads to higher suicide rates in various parts of the population and through different mechanisms...'

In couples where both male and female partners are engaged in paid employment, it's possible that either the man or the woman might lose their job. The frequent responses of such couples to loss of employment of one partner is testament to the basic natures of the genders. For a married couple where the husband becomes unemployed for an extended period, and his partner continues to work, there's an unusually high likelihood of the marriage ending in divorce, with the wife filing for divorce. The likelihood of divorce is markedly lower if it's the wife who loses the job.

The obvious conclusion is that women's supposed desire for equality doesn't extend to a willingness to support a non-working partner. It follows that among couples – all else being equal – when a person is deprived of employment for an extended period, the impact on a person's life is more likely to be negative if it's a man who loses his job than if it's a woman who loses hers. Women can more reliably expect to be supported by a partner. Given all this, it would be perverse if women schemed to deprive men of employment. But that is *precisely* what is happening.

From *The Woman Racket*, a section titled, 'Women's preference for their own sex: serious sex discrimination against men':

> 'The fourfold female preference for their own sex, and the 'in-group' / 'out-group' differences between men and women means that employers entrusting recruitment to women are likely to get not the best man for the job but more likely a mediocre woman. It also means potential problems of female performance in the job, irrespective of ability. The upshot for men is serious sex discrimination against them.
>
> In recruitment, whereas women candidates will tend on average not to suffer discrimination – even if the interview panel is all-male – men candidates will probably suffer worst outcomes the greater is the proportion of female interviewers. If the panel is all-women, then not only is this effect at its maximum, but there is no male perspective to counteract it. Women interviewers will prefer women (even aside from any feminist political attitudes, or any acceptance of notions of supposed oppression of women, or pressure through equal-opportunities policies).
>
> There would seem to be two complementary reasons for this. First, the interviewer tends to feel a potential personal connection with any and every female applicant, even though she may be a complete stranger – there need be no shared 'in-group' for this to occur, as would be the case for men. Second, prejudicial preference will go relatively unchecked (compared to how men would feel) given that women have a very different sense of 'in-group', and so will be less concerned about the impact of making a decision that may not be in the best interests of the work group...

Performance in the job by female workers will tend to be problematic because of the relative failure to identify with the 'in-group' of fellow workers, and to focus instead on personal connectedness rather than the task at hand. This will reduce efficiency in the workplace directly, but there is also a further impact in that those members of the work group that the top clique of female workers do not feel personally related to, will feel rejected.

As a result, they will either become de-motivated, or work more for themselves and competitively against the group. This is the opposite of how male workers would tend to behave. Men experience a mutually reinforcing sense of belonging to a group, and competitiveness on behalf of the group (as well as individual effort within it to try to rise to the top).

The current notion, though, is that women make better employees than men. Men are thought to be 'bolshy' and women compliant. Yet the more rule-based existence of men – apparent right from the days of school playground team sports – makes them likely to be more predictable and reasonable than women. Countless television advertisements (exemplified by the excruciating BT 'work smarter' series, but long ubiquitous), proclaim a contest of male 'dimwits' versus female 'smarties'...

Some think that men are too status-orientated, without seeing that there is a problem with women employees being too person-centred. Both male and female sex-typical behaviours could be regarded either as distractions from or contributions to the work culture, but employers certainly do prefer women (as a 1996 Rowntree report showed).

Yet it is men who have the additional clear attributes of being both task-centred and of forming teams within the workplace, rather than personal networks that may well be more connected with life outside – though sometimes female work teams are as effective as male ones...

Conclusive evidence of widescale discrimination against men at the job application stage was uncovered in 2006 by Peter Riach and Judith Rich, 'An Experimental Investigation of Sexual Discrimination in Hiring in the English Labour Market'. They had sent pairs of resumés to employers: one from a mythical applicant called 'Phillip' and another from a no less fictitious 'Emma', differing from each other only in the most minor details, but sufficient to ensure they would not be detected as being identical. The experience, qualifications, age, marital status, socio-economic background – every relevant detail – were as near to identical as could make no difference. They awaited the offer of an interview (or a request for a telephone discussion) or a rejection note (or silence).

Nobody was prepared for the result. Not even the direction of it, let alone the size. It was not women but men who got the fewer offers, and by not a small margin but by a massive factor of *four*. Uncannily, this is precisely the same factor by which women prefer other women to men, as discovered in research into the female social psychology of 'in-group'. Have workplaces completely capitulated to basing their hiring entirely on female prejudice? (HR is a predominantly female profession.)'

When men are deprived of employment they lose more of their 'identity' than do working women. They're more likely to sink into a depressive state and 'self-medicate' against depression with drugs or alcohol, and are ultimately at a higher risk of committing suicide than women in the same position. I'm only too familiar with the potential impact of loss of employment because I encountered it myself, albeit when I was (as I remain) a single man.

In the autumn of 2009, at the age of 51, and two years after my second divorce, I was seeking a new assignment in my customary line of work as a procurement consultant. Almost all my assignments in the preceding decade had been in the private sector. In one assignment I was the Head of Procurement for the Conservative party (2006-8) at their headquarters near the Houses of Parliament in London. As a 'Mike' I felt somewhat out of place in a sea of people with names such as Giles and Petronella, but everyone was nice and friendly. Well, almost everyone, but let's move on.

Many of the ladies spoke like Joanna Lumley. Now I've always had a soft spot for posh women – if they're also tall, slim, and have a lisp, like the TV chef Thomasina Miers, all the better – so it was an unusually pleasant assignment.

The year before I started working for the Conservatives they'd lost the 2005 general election and had a leadership contest, in the final round of which were two contenders: the media-savvy David Cameron, whose only job before entering politics had been in public relations, a poor background for the potential leader of a major political party; and David Davis, a far more substantial figure with a successful career in business behind him – a rare thing in a politician in the modern era. In the final postal ballot, 68% of Conservative Members of Parliament voted for Cameron, 32% for Davis. Many of the former group must later have regretted their choice, one imagines. But whoever they'd voted for, the Conservative party would have ended up with a 'Dave' for a leader. What dysfunctional times we live in.

Back to 2009. The market for expertise such as mine was weak at the time, as generally happened during recessions, and I hadn't worked for a number of months. The only buoyant sector was the public sector where there were plenty of opportunities for people with my type of expertise. But public sector procurement staff have created a 'closed shop' for procurement professionals, for their own benefit, at the taxpayers' expense.

I once had an assignment in the public sector, in 1999. The procurement function of a major government department had maybe 50 to 60 employees. Looking back on the assignment, the only happy memory I have is of working with the head of department, an unusually tall, slim, attractive lady, with a pronounced lisp. After a few weeks there I concluded that only a small minority of the employees (including the head of department) would have survived in equivalent roles in the private sector.

The assignment was unusual in that it didn't involve any negotiation of contracts with suppliers, so it didn't require any familiarity with 'OJEU'. OJEU is the Official Journal of the European Union and it's the document which outlines the regulations for tendering contracts. Its purpose is to ensure a 'level playing field' for suppliers across the European Union, to prevent government departments favouring suppliers in their native countries.

OJEU was a gift for manipulative government employees working in procurement. It enabled procurement departments to insist in job advertisements that applicants had prior working experience of OJEU regulations, thereby preventing private sector procurement executives from working in the public sector. As well as harming the work prospects of people like myself, this ruse is – more importantly – against the public interest for two reasons. It prevents private sector procurement experience and expertise from being introduced into the public sector and, because of the laws of supply and demand, it inflates the remuneration packages of public sector procurement staff. It's been estimated that those packages are currently two to three times larger than they would otherwise be.

I recently asked an old friend, a procurement consultant with long experience of the private sector but who's worked for a few years in a major government department, about OJEU experience. This is what he had to say:

'I could teach you all you'd ever need to know about OJEU in less than an hour. Occasionally there arises a matter which isn't straightforward, but even then you'd find the answers in the published guidance, or you could ask one of the countless employees who are very familiar with the regulations. The same employees who can hardly believe they've managed to pull this trick – of keeping out private sector people – for so long without it becoming public knowledge. In terms of cost to the taxpayer, not only through inflated salaries but far more importantly through incompetent management of procurement processes and consequent waste of tax revenues, it's a scandal on a par with anything the government does.'

In 2009 I wrote to the heads of the procurement functions of the ten largest government departments complaining about this matter, asking what I had to do to become eligible for public sector work given that it was *impossible* for people such as myself to claim prior OJEU experience. Nine of the ten were men, the only woman being the one who ran the procurement function of the Cabinet Office, then headed by Harriet Harman. *Quelle surprise.* I had only one reply, from one of the men, but it didn't address the issues I'd raised, and provided the department's recruitment website address.

I had for many years been a member of the Chartered Institute of Purchasing and Supply and wrote to the incoming President (a woman) about this matter, but never had a response. I terminated my membership as a protest.

The magazine for British procurement professionals, *Supply Management*, refused to carry my letter on the subject, presumably because a sizeable proportion of its readers work in the public sector and therefore have a vested interest in the matter being kept quiet.

I raised the matter with a major recruitment agency. My contact told me the closed shop suited the agencies well as it inflated remuneration packages and in consequence their commissions. The only losers were people like myself, and long-suffering taxpayers.

In late 2009 I was surprised to be called by a recruitment agency about an opportunity in a government department. In common with my earlier public sector assignment, this one didn't involve negotiations with suppliers. Not having worked for some months in the difficult prevailing economic climate, I was keen to land the job.

My meeting with the (female) Head of Procurement was to be held in the head office of her department in Victoria, London, an area full of government offices. The meeting was at 9:00am so I had the unpleasant experience of travelling on the London Underground at rush hour, with travellers pressed together like sardines in a tin. Most of the bodies I was pressed against were owned by plump scowling women dressed in black, many of them carrying *The Guardian*. I understand it's the newspaper of choice for overweight Leftie women who suck on a slice of lemon first thing every morning, to fix their expressions for the day.

The woman who was to interview me hadn't shown up by the time of the interview – maybe she'd run out of lemons and had gone to buy some – so I was interviewed instead by a nervous thin woman who explained she'd only started in her job the previous week, but she knew about the role in question. I took her through my working experience and after about half an hour she said, 'Mike, you could clearly do this job standing on your head. I'm sure it will be a formality.'

A huge woman dressed in black then burst into the room. Her expression suggested she'd tracked down the lemons. The nervous woman gulped, looked terrified, and started to stammer something. Goliatha glared at her then waved her hand imperiously to indicate she wasn't to utter another word. She then scowled at me, and asked a question on some trivial matter. I replied with what I considered an uncontroversial reply. She frowned deeply and told me I was wrong, without explaining why. The same thing happened with two further questions, and before I knew it, I was out of the building wondering what had gone wrong. I was in a daze and walking towards the Underground station a few minutes later, when my mobile phone rang. It was my contact at the interim agency, calling to let me know I hadn't landed the assignment. I asked for some information on the decision and the man said he'd call me back ten minutes later. He did so, and this is roughly what he had to say:

> 'Mike, I'm using my mobile phone and calling you from my car. Sorry I couldn't talk more in the office but most of my colleagues are women, and they'd go *apeshit* if they overheard me telling you what I'm about to. I only learnt just before your interview that the woman you met today has rarely recruited any men. She's well-known for being a militant feminist, and she's a big fan of Harriet Harman. She's careful to interview as many men as women so her records look OK, but the men stand very little chance of landing a job. She'd sooner take on an inexperienced and incompetent woman than an experienced and competent man.
>
> Because it's the public sector we're talking about, she's at liberty to do that, of course, and who's going to notice a bit more inexperience and incompetence in the public sector? Lots of women in senior positions in the public sector are like her. Sorry about that. Good luck finding another assignment, but don't be too hopeful of landing one in the public sector.'

I was so furious over the sheer injustice of this matter that over the ensuing days and weeks my spirits slowly sank. For the first and possibly only time in my life I became deeply depressed. I refused to recognise at the time that I was depressed, despite having seen a good deal of depression in others over the years. My work had been a bigger part of my identity than I'd ever realised, and without work I felt a terrible hollowness.

In the absence of work I filled my days over this period writing books, and I now see that being fully occupied mentally in this way during those dark days probably saved my life. But the evenings and nights were difficult to get through. In the early hours of one morning, I resolved to commit suicide by jumping off the roof of a local car park one lunchtime.

I've just recalled that I'd planned to have a T-shirt printed on the front and back with a message, the idea being that my death might *possibly* serve some purpose. I couldn't recall what the message was, so I've just looked it up on my computer. The document was filed under 'Suicide' (how organised is *that?*) and reveals the T-shirt was to be printed with the following:

JUST ANOTHER UNEMPLOYED MAN KILLED BY BLOODY FEMINISTS

I considered making a formal complaint to the head of the government department in question, but eventually I forced myself to consider my options, and recognised I was fortunate in being able to take early retirement at 53 years of age. I'd become increasingly exhausted by a line of work which entailed a great deal of pressure, long hours, and lengthy commutes. I decided to cash in my pensions and continue pursuing full-time what had by that time become a passion, writing books.

My business book *Profitable Buying Strategies* had been published internationally by Kogan Page in 2008 and sold moderately well, and I'd much enjoyed subsequently writing and self-publishing *Guitar Gods in Beds. (Bedfordshire: a heavenly county)* and the travelogue *Two Men in a Car (a businessman, a chauffeur, and their holidays in France)*.

I've never regretted the decision to 'downsize'. I was fortunate in being able to survive financially on my company pensions and earnings from book sales. In the absence of this income I should have faced financial ruin, and the chances would then have been high that in the grip of a severe depression, I'd have worn that T-shirt and jumped. I was lucky – nothing more – to not have been another suicide victim.

In the United Kingdom today, suicide is the leading cause of death of men under 50. Men are almost four times more likely than women to commit suicide, and the unemployment rate among men is higher than among women. Worklessness among men is a prime driver of suicide. The manipulation of recruitment processes by feminists is clearly leading to a considerable number of men sinking into depression and ultimately committing suicide. The cruel irony is that many of these men leave behind dependent wives and children, while the jobs that are rightfully theirs (on the grounds of merit) are often taken by women with no family responsibilities.

The increase in the suicide rate of men caused by the manipulation of recruitment processes by feminists is a readily understood phenomenon, but what of the positive correlations between the suicide rate of *women* and the worklessness of both men and women? The correlation of female suicide with men's worklessness has been attributed in part to economic deprivation, particularly in eras when women were wholly financially dependent upon men. The correlation with women's worklessness may partly be due to the potentially catastrophic financial impact of worklessness on women with no partner to rely on financially, a problem possibly fuelled by alcohol; in the United Kingdom, alcohol consumption by women has increased markedly over recent decades, and we have seen that heavy alcohol consumption is a risk factor for suicide.

I suspect there's another factor at play when it comes to female suicide. While some women may have been helped psychologically by the move from the home to paid employment, it would be surprising indeed if there were not a cohort of women – possibly a large cohort – for whom the move was a problematical one. I've known quite a number of women who suffered very badly from stress in the work environment, to the point they suffered depressive illnesses.

Some sought relief with anti-depressants, which women tell me doctors in the modern era effectively prescribe upon request. For other women, their depressive symptoms were relieved by leaving the world of work. My suspicion is that many women in former times were helped psychologically through being spared employment-related stresses, and having lives almost wholly focused on family and friends.

This isn't a plea for women to leave the world of work and return to household duties; merely an assertion that the move from the home to paid employment wasn't a positive move – psychologically speaking – for all women. So the feminist campaign to drive women into paid employment must logically be a contributor to female suicide; how significant a contributor, I have no idea. It's difficult to imagine public funds being used to support the research necessary to investigate the phenomenon.

The idea that for some women the world of work is an inherently stressful one is possibly supported by the higher frequency of anxiety disorders among women than among men. We might reasonably expect this phenomenon to manifest itself most clearly in anxiety induced by the world outside the home. From Wikipedia's entry on agoraphobia:

'Agoraphobia is an anxiety disorder defined as a morbid fear of having a panic attack or panic-like symptoms in a situation that is perceived to be difficult (or embarrassing) from which to escape. These situations can include, but are not limited to, wide-open spaces, crowds, or uncontrolled social conditions. Alternatively, social anxiety problems may also be an underlying cause. As a result, sufferers of agoraphobia avoid public and/or unfamiliar places, especially large, open spaces such as shopping malls or airports from which they cannot easily escape if they have a panic attack. In severe cases, the sufferer may become confined to his or her home, unable to leave their safe haven.

Although mostly thought to be a fear of public places, it is now believed that agoraphobia develops as a complication of panic attacks. However, there is evidence that the implied one-way causal relationship between spontaneous panic attacks and agoraphobia in DSM-IV may be incorrect. [Author's note: DSM-IV is the fourth edition of the *Diagnostic and Statistical Manual of Mental Disorders* published by the American Psychiatric Association in 1994.] Onset is usually between ages 20 and 40 years and more common in women. Approximately 3.2 million adults in the US between the ages of 18 and 54, or about 2.2%, suffer from agoraphobia. Agoraphobia can account for approximately 60% of phobias. Agoraphobia, as studies have shown, has two age groups at which the first onset generally occurs – early to mid-twenties and in the early thirties – thus helping to distinguish between simple phobias in child and adolescent years…

Agoraphobia occurs about twice as commonly among women as it does in men. The gender difference may be attributable to several factors: social-cultural traditions that encourage, or permit, the greater expression of avoidant coping strategies by women (including dependent and helpless behaviors); women perhaps being more likely to seek help and therefore be diagnosed; men being more likely to abuse alcohol in reaction to anxiety and be diagnosed as an alcoholic. Research has not yet produced a single clear explanation for the gender difference in agoraphobia.'

Feminists assault women through persuading them to take on work which is beyond their capabilities, or which exhausts their natural levels of resilience. In an earlier chapter we looked at the link between persisting with unrealistic goals and depression. What is the feminist project if not an exercise in driving women in general to persist with unrealistic goals?

In *The Glass Ceiling Delusion* I related the tale of a female colleague who was regularly overcome with stress. What I didn't relate – because it wasn't relevant to that book – was that the lady in question had on an earlier occasion tearfully revealed to me that she had an overbearing and bitter feminist mother who drove her daughter to achieve the things in life which she herself hadn't. This is the story, told from my perspective:

'A few years ago I carried out a consulting assignment in the London headquarters of a major service company. The deputy Finance Director was a single woman in her mid-thirties with no children, well versed in all the accounting skills required for her job. Both she and I reported to the Finance Director, an overbearing man disliked both inside and outside his department and (being short in stature) nicknamed 'Napoleon'.

To say that working for Napoleon was stressful would be an understatement; his penchant for demanding endless revised versions of complex spreadsheets, so as to improve their accuracy by a fraction of a percentage point, would have made even a nun kick a sickly puppy into a fast-flowing river. But the pay was good, and I tried to take the stress in my stride. I found that a large measure of Talisker or Lagavulin Scotch Whisky in the evenings soon put Napoleon out of my mind. Alcohol has long been the self-medication of choice for men seeking to cope with stress, and it's increasingly the self-medication of choice for women coping with stress too.

Working in the corner of an open plan office, with her staff in close proximity, my female colleague was frequently and visibly highly stressed, often to the point of being tearful; and occasionally she *did* burst into tears. On one of these occasions I took her for a coffee and asked her why she put herself through the stress rather than confronting her boss or resigning. She replied along the following lines:

> 'I recently bought a flat and a new car, the costs of which require me to earn a good income, and that only comes with jobs like this, which are highly stressful. But I really hate this job. I'd give it up tomorrow to be a mother and housewife, if the option presented itself. Although my Mum says she'd *kill* me if I did that. I *think* she's joking.'

To militant feminists, this woman – by virtue of holding down a well-paid, pressurised job – would be viewed as a success. But the woman knew otherwise, every working day of the week. A man who was so visibly stressed during his working day would be relieved of his duties, but some misplaced sense persuades us to allow women to carry on, if they're prepared to. It's no wonder that so many female executives are absent from work on stress- or depression-related grounds.

Apart from the impact on the individual, what's the impact on the firm of allowing a person insufficiently robust for their work to continue working? Colleagues will not want to add to their stress and will shy away from dealing with them in a businesslike manner, which can only damage the efficiency and effectiveness of the firm.'

Three of the nine books I've written to date, including this one, have been inspired by the dire influence of feminists in the modern world. Ironically, I've only had the free time to write these books because of Goliatha's manipulation of a recruitment process in the autumn of 2009. Maybe I should write to her to thank her, and send a gift. Lifetime membership of Weight Watchers, perhaps?

A further reward from taking early retirement and taking up writing full-time is that I'll no longer be paying tens of thousands of pounds in income tax every year to help pay for Goliatha's salary and gold-plated pension contributions, nor to help finance the social engineering programmes in this country. If a young woman in my adopted home town of Bedford decides she's going to have a virgin birth (no father being named on the baby's child certificate) the benefits that support her won't be coming from *my* pockets. In common with other towns in the United Kingdom, Bedford has long had more virgin births than Bethlehem.

The next time a woman complains to you that she's exhausted and stressed out by her work in the senior reaches of an organisation, do what I do. Laugh. Tell her that women made the choice to enter the world of work. Tell her to become a housewife if she can't cut it in the workplace. Tell her to stop bleating. Tell her to make you a cup of tea before she does her ironing. Tell her you understand women find ironing calms them down. Tell her you've heard that women have evolved to be good at ironing. But before you say these things call for an ambulance, because you're going to need one *really* soon.

[Update: The *International Business Times* published my article on male suicide in March 2015.[1]]

---

[1] http://tinyurl.com/j4mbibt

31 | THE FEMINISATION OF
THE UNITED KINGDOM

One almost begins to feel that the reason some women worked feverishly to get into men's clubs was to have a respite from the womanised world feminists have created.
Carol Iannone American conservative writer and literary critic: *Good Order* (1994) ed. Brad Miner 'The Feminist Perversion'

I'm 54, and over the course of my life the United Kingdom has become an ever more feminised country. It's got so bad that the current leader of the Conservative party, David Cameron, is actively pursuing the feminist agendas of the previous Labour administration – with little comment in the media – as I pointed out at length in *David and Goliatha* and *The Glass Ceiling Delusion*. I concluded that one contributory factor is David Cameron having a female-pattern brain.

The influence of men-hating women in general, and of feminists in particular, has stripped the country of the colour that once helped made it such a great country. Many British people who can afford to emigrate when they retire do so – usually to France, Spain, Portugal or Italy – and I can't say I blame them. It's not just for the weather. I've often been tempted to emigrate to France myself.

I routinely open doors for women in shops and other places, but I'm increasingly disinclined to do so. Twice this year I've been snarled at by women after I opened doors for them. The first, a young woman, hissed, 'Chauvinist!', the second, a middle-aged woman, hissed 'Sexist bastard!' The attractiveness of both women would have been enhanced by burkas, hijabs and niqabs, you won't be surprised to learn. Maybe I'll only open doors for attractive women in future.

The feminisation of the country can be seen wherever we look. We're suffocated and damaged economically by a Health and Safety culture which reflects women's risk-averse natures. Taxation levels are outrageously high partly to finance the lifestyles of voluntarily single mothers, a matter I cover in another chapter. Most of the benefits that go to these women are paid for by the taxes of men who the women would never consider as partners. The state is mugging these men – mostly poorly paid low status men – on these women's behalf.

Mothers send their children to nurseries and primary schools where there are, in the modern era, few if any male teachers. A year or two ago I met a former primary school teacher at a state school, a man who'd quit the profession he loved after a number of mothers (he described them, unprompted, as 'a bunch of fat ugly feminists') had collectively met with the Headmistress and insisted that he never be allowed in a room alone with their children, and that at least one female teacher had to be present in the room whenever he was. He was forbidden to assist any of the children with their toileting needs.

It was recently announced that for the 29th year in succession exam grades across the country have improved. This 'grade inflation' reflects a concerted campaign by Leftie teachers, often feminists, and Leftie government ministers, to continually minimise the grade differences between able and less able pupils. When everyone gets 'A' grades then, arguably, nobody does. It's got so bad that some leading universities are setting their own exams in order to identify the most able candidates.

The bestselling English author Vernon Coleman in his latest book *Diary of a Disgruntled Man* relates the following tale of a walk in a town centre accompanied by his wife:

'We passed a black woman and a small black girl, about three or four years old. The girl was pulling a huge wooden duck on a piece of string. She looked up at me and smiled. I smiled back at the girl and was about to congratulate her on her wonderful toy when the mother grabbed the little girl's hand and pulled her away. What a sad world we have created for ourselves.'

I was planning to make this a lengthy chapter, but after typing out the extract from Vernon Coleman's book I lost the heart to carry on. It's just too depressing. Hopefully you get the picture. 'What a sad world we have created for ourselves'. Indeed.

32 | THE FEMINIST ASSAULT ON MEN

I do a lot of reading about serial killers, mostly *How To* books.
Roseanne Barr 1952- American actress, comedienne, writer, television producer, director

In 1993 the Child Support Agency (CSA) was launched with responsibility for implementing the 1991 Child Support Act and subsequent legislation, in some cases collecting the money it passed to the parent with primary care responsibilities (usually the mother) directly from the bank accounts of the other parent (usually the father). From the beginning it was widely criticised for the inaccuracy of its assessments and for its bullying tactics towards men. The press reported a number of suicides of men directly attributable to pressures placed on them by the CSA.

In 1994 my first marriage came to an end, and my children carried on living with their mother. The CSA made their financial assessment and throughout the years that my children were living with their mother I made payments to her promptly and in full. The payments came to an end in 2002.

By the autumn of 2009 my financial situation was becoming difficult because the market for the service I provided – procurement consultancy – had collapsed. I hadn't worked for six months. Early one morning in the autumn of 2009 I took a phone call. The woman caller explained she worked for the CSA, and the following is as close as I can recall to the conversation which followed:

> 'Mr Buchanan, our records show that there is a sum of £2,382.51 still owing to your ex-wife at the point in time that you ceased payments. You have 28 days to settle this sum. How would you like to pay? Cheque? Credit card?'

'You have to be joking. I finished the payments seven or eight years ago, and now you tell me out of the blue that I owe you money? What proof do you have?'

'We have a record that this is the sum you owe.'

'Well, it's nonsense. Do you have supporting information?'

'No, but that's not important.'

'Call my ex-wife. She'll tell you I paid every penny I owed her, and more besides.'

'Unfortunately we've been unable to track her down.'

'This is obviously a hoax. P*** off and stop wasting my time.'

I angrily slammed the phone down and went about my day. But the call hadn't been a hoax. The next morning a letter arrived from the CSA explaining that if the sum was not paid within 28 days, legal action would be taken against me, and if necessary I would be forced to sell my house in order to settle the debt. I called the CSA and spoke to the woman who'd written the letter.

'If I give you my ex-wife's phone number and she says the sum *is* outstanding, what will you do?'

'We'll continue to seek the money from you, sir.'

'And if she says I've paid in full...?'

'Then we'll drop the matter and apologise for having wasted your time, sir.'

'So this all hinges on the word of my ex-wife who might have malicious intent towards me, seven or eight years after the payments came to an end?'

'I wouldn't put it like that, sir. We shall consider what she has to say and then make a judgement.'

I gave them my ex-wife's phone number. I happened to know she was in a difficult financial situation herself, but trusted her not to take advantage of this ludicrous situation. Ten minutes later the woman at the CSA called back.

'Hello, Mr Buchanan, I'm pleased to say Mrs Buchanan confirmed there were never any arrears, so we shall drop the case.'

'And if my ex-wife had been vindictive towards me, and wanted to make over two thousand pounds at my expense by claiming she was still owed the money, you'd have pursued me for it even if it meant I lost the roof over my head?'

'We look at every case on its merits, sir.'

'Yeah… *right!*'

I slammed the phone down for a second time and heard no more on the matter. I had been presumed guilty until proved innocent, and there had been no way to prove my innocence. I felt – not for the first time – that the state had tried to mug me.

Steve Moxon in his book *The Woman Racket* has a lot to say about the hostility of the justice system towards men in general, and fathers in particular. The following is an extract:

'How parliament was undermined: The disaster of the Child Support Act
Shared parenting… was the express intention of parliament when the Children Act was passed in 1989. Supposedly, out went the notion of 'custody' with one parent, and in came the 'parental responsibility' of both; promoted through 'residence orders' to get rid of the assumption that only the mother was fit, good, and responsible. It was to mimic, we were told, the success of 'joint custody' schemes in California, New Zealand

and Australia. These schemes turned out to have a common flaw in being open to hijacking by those politically motivated to bring about the reverse of what was intended; not least governments, which have a major fiscal reason to insist that shared/equal parenting should not be the norm. In the UK version, it was all for nothing in any case, because the Act contained fatal internal contradictions that actually made matters worse in forcing former partners apart by calling one the 'parent with care' and the other the 'absent parent', thereby destroying the child's right to two parents. This was in order to suit the purposes of the Child Support Agency (CSA). The collection of money from fathers, to offset the rapidly-escalating costs to the state of single parenthood, would have been hindered if it wasn't easy to distinguish between the cash cow and the cow, as it were.

So the Children Act, in being made to fit the purposes of not just the family court but also the CSA, was a hopeless compromise (ditto the subsequent 1991 Child Support Act). The entire purpose of the Act was then comprehensively undermined by the legislation's 'guidance notes'. As at other government departments, officers at the CSA consult day-to-day not the legislation, but the notes produced to interpret it. One sentence proved key: 'It is not expected that (a residence order) will become a common form of order because most children will need the stability of a single home.'

This one line meant that men were once again relegated from the status of parent to visitor; the very state of affairs that the Children Act was passed in order to counter. The intention may well have been merely to clarify that a 50/50 sharing of residence was not an objective but a symbolic starting point. But it was a Trojan horse that allowed an interpretation that was the very opposite of the thinking behind the Act: that any sort of significant residence with the father was to be rare. At one stroke the Children Act turned into an instrument to deprive fathers, on any pretext or none, of the bulk of contact they would normally enjoy with their own children whenever a dispute over contact arose.

For a long time everyone thought that the 1989 Children Act was fine, and it was regularly cited as what everyone should be reminded of to counter the increasing bias against fathers. Without being able to see the guidance notes, people missed that the Act had been retrospectively nobbled. The penny had still to drop outside fathers' activist groups, and was only dawning on sections of the government itself in late 2005, as I will explain. People also still didn't see that the Children Act was the basis of the CSA as well as contact disputes…

It's worth going back a decade and examining the CSA and how it operated, because the CSA being bound up with the family court means that only by viewing the two as part of the same government project can the debacle as a whole be explained.

The abolition of the CSA was announced in 2006, but this is merely the body, not the principles. The principles remain in the 'Child Maintenance and Enforcement Commission' that will replace it, eventually. Of course, the never-ending poor performance in not getting support payments to mothers was and is always in the news; never the greater injustice of a high volume of unreasonable, inflexible, unjustifiable or mistaken payment demands to men, who are at the same time being denied any meaningful contact with the very children the CSA demands that they pay for. If the issue of child contact does surface in the news, then it's often one of the ten percent of cases where the mother is the 'absent parent'.

The appalling impact of the CSA was brought to light in 1996 by Professor Jonathan Bradshaw, director of social policy research at the University of York. The Act betrays a straight absence of morality, as Bradshaw protested to the Commons all-party select committee on the Child Support Act:

> 'The attempt in the Act to separate the whole issue of contact from that of financial support is doomed to failure. Fathers just cannot understand why one agency of government insists that they pay child support when another agency of government fails to protect their rights to have contact with their children.'

This is of course a core reason why millions of fathers are angry. Second:

> 'While (fathers) agree that they have a financial obligation to their children, their understanding of fairness leaves them outraged at the spousal (carer's) element in the formula, particularly if they think that

the caring parent was responsible for the breakdown of the relationship.'

Even more fundamentally there was:

> 'an increasing proportion of fathers who had never been in a 'living together relationship' when they conceived a child. Some of these relationships were very casual, or at least tenuous. The obligation of fatherhood in these circumstances is, to say the least, contentious. The assertion of biological liability in the Child Support Act, in the absence of any social relationship, has created some fundamental problems that we are only beginning to consider. Getting a girl pregnant can now be a form of entrapment.'

Clear cases of entrapment are now showing up, so that in the USA there is a major political movement concerning 'paternity fraud', and a battle between an intransigent Supreme Court and state jurisdictions. Bradshaw's conclusion is that, as with its sisters across the world that have superseded a system of decision between ex-partners at some form of adjudication, the Act is literally unenforceable. Like the poll tax, it jeopardises the consent people give to be ruled.

It's hard to imagine how a report could be more critical of government legislation. Any one of Bradshaw's three moral objections was by itself an infringement of men's basic civil rights. Taken together they are almost incredible. Of course, apart from those men who become an actual CSA case, all men are at risk of becoming subject to the CSA. The legislation is an immoral interference with men's right to pursue happiness and to enjoy family life, by usurping it in favour of forcing his support of what could not be considered any kind of intention to begin family life.

The problem created by ignoring the casualness of a relationship is the most insidious, and Bradshaw draws particular attention to it.

> 'Young men are, as ever, becoming fathers without their knowledge and – if they did know – without any rights to influence whether a pregnancy is aborted. Many very young men are being locked into a financial relationship, often without any prospect of a social

one, for up to 16 years – 16 years during which they might otherwise have become effective social and biological fathers; socially useful rather than disenfranchised and bloody-minded men... The behavioural consequences of the Act have been quite extraordinary: fewer fathers in employment, many more 'absent and untraceable', fewer in contact with their children, less informal financial support of children, fewer taking on new partners, more new partnerships breaking down, and so on...'

Reproductive rights only when it's not through sex: prejudice exposed by crazy law

The ludicrous line that men must carry the financial burden entirely regardless of the circumstances, even runs to compassionate sperm donation, as Andy Bathie (and some years before, a Manchester man) found out when he helped a lesbian couple he knew to start a family. Presumably, the same would apply to a man who visits a prostitute, in the event of the prostitute deciding to conceive and have his baby. Even though the very purpose of prostitution is explicitly to substitute payment for any subsequent liability, the state, in cahoots with the prostitute, could exact ongoing payment through entrapping a client. It's only a matter of time before a case arises. Of those men who take a CSA DNA test, one in six are found not to be the father (on figures up to 2005). This is most probably the tip of the iceberg, because most men who had suspicions will have already tested their child privately, and a result proving non-paternity would enable them to confront the mother, who would then not have the option of subsequently naming him to the CSA. Also, most of those women whose paternity fraud was still unknown to their ex-partner would not name them to the CSA, because this would reveal the secret and entail loss of any informal support they could otherwise expect. CSA rules make it easy for a woman to avoid naming a father in such circumstances; by simply falsely citing threat of violence. Couples with any sense make private arrangements and avoid entanglement with the CSA. This is not least because women are often better off accepting informal support from their ex-partners than receiving CSA payment, only for it to be offset against benefits.

Women trick men into becoming fathers all the time. A 2004 poll for *That's Life!* magazine showed that 42% of women say they would lie about contraception so as to get pregnant, no matter what they knew their partner would feel; and US research estimates that a million American men annually are saddled with fathering babies they did not want. In 1972, Elliott Philip looked at several hundred families in South-East England and concluded that a staggering 30% of the children could not have been fathered by the mother's husband. British medical students are taught that the 'non-paternity' rate is 10-15%. The Family Planning Association and others have researched the deliberate (or absent-mindedly unconsciously-on-purpose) ineffective use of contraception – colloquially known as 'oopsing' – and shown that women use contraceptives less reliably the more casual the sexual encounter (Eisenman, 2003). This is through an unconscious psychology to try to conceive in those circumstances rather than in the context of the stable relationship. There are also the very many cases where women have intentionally deceived.

'Paternity fraud' has become a hot topic in the US, where court cases have been hitting the news for several years. The 'best interests of the child' test was still resulting in men being told by judges they must continue to pay child support, even in the most bizarre cases. The classic paternity fraud case is that of a woman taking the semen from a condom a man used for sex with her, and then inserting it into herself to get pregnant. Far from an 'urban myth', this is an actual scenario that has faced US courts, and the men have lost! There has even been a case where the condom used for impregnation was from sex between the man and another woman. Women who conceal pregnancy to deny paternal rights and then sue for child support a decade later, or women who statutorily rape boys, or women who con their husbands that a baby is his when it is not: all real cases where child support was determined still to be payable. So men are replying by suing, and in 2005 courts began to allow men to do this and to appeal against previously-lost cases.'

We come to the topic of physical violence. Feminists have long cited physical violence used by men against women in the home, or the threat of it, as being a central pillar of patriarchy.

In my limited personal experience, and knowledge of a number of couples, violence in the home was *on every occasion* used by the female partner against the male partner. I know of two cases where women have stabbed their male partners; in one case, the man was stabbed in the chest with a carving knife as he slept. In the other, kitchen scissors were sunk into the man's back and had to be removed in hospital. Sometimes the violence was fuelled by alcohol, but given that drunkenness isn't accepted as an excuse for violence by men against women – quite rightly – nor should it be accepted as an excuse for violence by woman against men.

I've never struck a woman, despite being provoked on a number of occasions. Most men, like myself, have a very deep-seated aversion to physically hurting women. All the same, I had always assumed that my personal experience of violence in the home was untypical until I read a chapter in *The Woman Racket* titled, 'Home Lies: Violence between partners is *not* mostly by men'. The start of the chapter:

> 'Of the various ways that men are supposed to have 'power' over women, perhaps most people would say that domestic or intimate partner violence is the clearest. A key phenomenon of the late twentieth / early twenty-first century is the complete blindness to the truth that domestic violence (henceforth DV), or 'intimate partner violence' is not a male-on-female issue, but is *non*-'gendered'. That is, it's perpetrated by both sexes. In fact, it's predominantly a *female-on-male* phenomenon. If it is 'gendered', then it's not a male crime but a female one.
>
> This general conclusion is one of the most emphatic in all social science. Comprehensive overviews are provided by the leading UK experts, Dr Malcolm George and Professor John Archer, as well as many of the leading US researchers, such as Murray Straus. Most damning of all for the feminist advocacy position is that published in 2005 by Donald Dutton and Tonia Nicholls (*The Gender Paradigm in Domestic Violence*

Research and Theory). But my role here is not to produce a deluge of citations. It's to cut through to the main points, and examine why 'advocacy' retorts are empty.

Quite apart from a simple comparison of the incidence or prevalence of DV according to sex, there is another way of looking at DV that is illuminating. This is to look at the violence of each sex against the other as a proportion of all of the violence that each sex engages in. A very small fraction of violent acts by men are against women, whereas women are violent towards men at twice the rate that they are to their fellow women. (Though when women are on their own, in prison, in almost ubiquitous homosexual relationships, then they tend to be considerably more violent even than their male counterparts.) In this sense, DV is indeed 'gendered'. It's the most common mode of violence by women, but the least common by men.

The collapse of the idea of 'gendered' violence

The root of the popular misapprehension that DV is a women's issue is very simple. If you only look at those in (women's) refuges or in criminal proceedings; or if you only ask women, or both men and women but only about DV as a *crime*: then unsurprisingly you will find that there are few male victims compared to female. It can appear to be 'gender neutral' to ask men whether they have themselves been on the receiving end of the crime of DV, but they will often or usually answer 'no', even if they have been persistently and seriously assaulted by their women partners. This is because men don't usually regard physical assault against them by their partner as criminal, no matter how serious.

To get the real picture of what is going on violence-wise between the sexes in *both* directions, all you have to do is to remove the 'demand characteristic' that responses are about crime per se, and instead to make a list of kinds of aggressive actions, and hand them out to people of both sexes, reassuring them that it is an anonymous social survey about violence in the home. Then men will reply far more honestly, and the real extent of women's DV is revealed. This is then corroborated by asking questions using the same graded list not just about sustaining DV but also perpetration, and again by both sexes. To provide still further confidence in the findings, both men and women partners in the same couples are studied. Such a graded list has been devised, and then refined to put the specific violent acts in context to get a better handle on their actual seriousness. This is the Conflict Tactics Scale (CTS). For upwards of twenty-five years, studies using this have bulked into a body of data where female-on-male DV can be compared with male-on-female.

Professor Martin Fiebert has compiled a regularly-updated reference list with abstracts of *all* studies – not a cherry-picked subset – where male- and female-perpetrated DV are compared (Fiebert, 2007). Of the now over 200 studies and overviews, *not a single one* shows significantly more aggression in the male-to-female direction. Some of the studies show a roughly equal perpetration, but most show either a significant or a considerable preponderance of aggression female-on-male.

They provide a comprehensive picture of the variety of DV. The great majority of it is low-level and tit-for-tat, that most people would hesitate to describe as violence. Even if they did, they would regard it as trivial. Most of this is female-on-male. At the other extreme, where there is no doubt that serious and/or serial violence is being used against the other partner, again women predominate as perpetrators. Where women most outdo men in perpetration is actually for the *more serious* as well as the least serious violence.

Seeing as only a very small proportion of couples experience severe DV, and as DV is not 'gendered', then DV is not the social problem that feminist advocates would have us believe. It's not even remotely on the scale or direction required by a theory based on supposed 'patriarchy'. And male-on-female DV has fallen dramatically in recent years.'

33 | THE FEMINIST ASSAULT ON WOMEN

You don't lead by hitting people over the head – that's assault, not leadership.
Dwight D Eisenhower 1890-1969 five-star general, Supreme Commander of the Allied forces in Europe during World War II, President of the United States (1953-61)

I've long been a fan of guitar-based live music and it happens that my adopted home town, the throbbing metropolis of Bedford, England, has long had a thriving live music scene. In 2008 I published an account of the lives of eight local guitarists, *Guitar Gods in Beds. (Bedfordshire: a heavenly county)*. All eight were men between 53 and 66 years of age, and six of them were from solidly working-class backgrounds.

All eight of them would have been ten-year-olds between 1958-1965, and I mention this because almost all of them had mothers at that time who weren't engaged in paid employment, but were 'stay-at-home Moms', to use the American phrase. From most of the men's accounts I gained the sense that their mothers had led happy and fulfilled lives.

Half a century later we have somehow arrived at a situation where living standards have improved considerably, yet most working class women and many middle class women *have* to work for financial reasons. Now this may be partly to finance higher standards of living, but many of these women work to help pay for the necessities of life, not for luxuries. What might account for this astonishing turn of events? In the course of half a century we've moved from a situation in which most working-class women could afford not to work, to a situation where many middle-class women *must* work.

When Betty Friedan wrote of the lack of fulfilment of women as mothers and housewives in *The Feminine Mystique* (1963) she was relating the perspectives of a minority of women. When a number of women started exerting their right to undertake paid employment they inevitably fuelled house price inflation; and so it was that increasing numbers of women then *had* to work, to help raise the household income to the levels required to pay higher housing costs. This would proportionately have affected younger couples more than older couples, and with ever more women working, house price inflation was boosted yet further. It's been a vicious cycle.

This is an example of the Law of Unintended Consequences which often applies in the area of gender relations. A minority of women chose to take up paid employment which over time has led to a situation where a majority of women *have* to work. This suits feminists fine, of course. In their ideal world all women would be engaged in paid employment. It's just the majority of women who aren't suited to this state of affairs.

In the current era many women are, of course, financially independent, particularly those who are single. While this is to be applauded, there's a flip side to the matter, namely the risk that periods of unemployment – even, in some cases, of a short duration – may have catastrophic consequences for women. There's little doubt that the correlation between unemployment and suicide risk among women at least partly reflects this issue, and markedly higher consumption of alcohol by women in modern times adds to the suicide risk.

I'm reminded of a couple of paragraphs from Professor Louann Brizendine's *The Female Brain* in the earlier chapter on human nature:

'Almost every woman I have seen in my office, when asked what would be her top three wishes if her fairy godmother could wave her magic wand and grant them, says, 'Joy in my life, a fulfilling relationship, and less stress with more personal time.'

Our modern life – the double shift of career and primary responsibility for the household and family – has made these goals particularly difficult to achieve. We are stressed out by this arrangement, and our leading cause of anxiety and depression is stress. One of the great mysteries of our lives is why we as women are so devoted to this current social contract *which often operates against the natural wiring of our female brains and biological reality* [Author's italics].'

I'm not so sure that women *are* so devoted to that social contract. If we take women in executive positions, for example, in my experience most would happily exchange the jobs for a less stressful existence. For many of them it simply isn't a viable option – their financial commitments force them to keep on their treadmills. But let's not delude ourselves this is a choice women make happily.

Opponents of feminism have had minimal impact on the feminist mission. They've focussed on the impact of feminism on men, yet men in general remain peculiarly unaware of how much feminists both hate them and have systematically been harming their interests for *decades*.

But not only men are being assaulted by feminism: the majority of women are, too. One striking thing about feminists is how *unrepresentative* of women they are – ironically – in so many respects. These include:

- feminists have an extreme left-wing philosophy, a dualistic one: 'women good, men bad'
- they're manipulative and aggressive bullies, forcing their will on government and the public and private sectors,

controlling major media outlets (having journalists who are critical of feminism fired), heavily influencing publishers' choices of writers and book topics, and denying their opponents the right to be heard

- they prioritise the search for power over the search for personal happiness
- they revel in hating men, and spreading misandry is their prime strategy to attract support
- they're hostile to women exercising freedom of choice, e.g. choosing 'female typical' lines of employment, choosing to work part-time, or not at all…
- they believe that in *all* fields (other than some involving brute physical strength) women are at least the equals of men, and in many fields innately superior to men
- they're hostile to the concept of the two-parent family, seeing such families as prime examples of male oppression
- they deny men possess any good qualities as parents
- they're hostile to the notions of femininity and attractiveness
- they deny the natures of 'gender-typical' men and women are different, the differences stemming at least in part from brain differences. These brain differences have long been accepted by neuroscientists, and been reported in popular science books
- they see men as the cause of all women's problems – no woman need ever feel responsible for her problems in the feminist utopia

Men would be up in arms if a small band of extreme left-wing men claimed to speak for all men, to represent them, and campaigned on their behalf. Why, then, are women not up in arms about feminists? I think it's partly attributable to female solidarity; many women who don't share the feminists' philosophy still believe that men exert power over women, even in the developed world in the modern era. Phenomena like 'gender imbalance in the boardroom' and the 'gender pay gap' are believed by many women to reflect male oppression of women, although in reality they reflect men's and women's life choices, as many writers and independent academics have conclusively demonstrated. And decades of well-documented feminist lies, distortions and exaggerations of the incidence of rape, and domestic violence by men against women, have done their work to make women fearful and angry.

Despite all this, I see reasons to be optimistic that women will one day rise up against the feminists. The majority of women – in common with the majority of men – don't *want* to hate the opposite sex. Life is richer and altogether happier when individual men and women make their own nuanced accommodations with one another.

Men's chivalry towards women is a good example of a nuanced accommodation between the genders, so it follows that feminists *must* be opposed to it. An article from *The Daily Telegraph* edition of 15 June 2011 titled, 'Chivalry is actually "benevolent sexism", feminists conclude':

> 'If the age of chivalry is dead, it appears a group of feminists psychologists are trying to ensure it is never revived, concluding that a man who helps his wife with her heavy shopping is actually guilty of 'benevolent sexism'.
>
> The researchers created a list of such damaging acts as helping a woman to choose the right computer, calling a group of both men and women 'guys', and offering to do the driving on a long distance journey.
>
> Even men who think they are expressing affection might be guilty – the scientists said calling a woman a 'chick', showering her with unwanted affection, or saying that you cannot live without her could also be sexist.

The researchers, from the feminist Society for the Psychology of Women, which is based in Washington DC, said there were many acts of unnoticed sexism taking place every day through acts or comments that suggested women could not cope without men's help.

They said the victims might be unaware of the damage but the acts were helping to create a culture of women being seen as the vulnerable sex and encouraging inequality and injustice. The study concluded that both men and women were 'not aware of the overall prevalence and extent of sexism in their personal lives'.

However, they recognised that women could also be guilty.

The study was conducted among workers of both sexes in America and Germany and volunteers were asked to keep diaries in which they were asked to note when they encountered examples from a long list of both sexist and non-sexist incidents, without being told what the study was for.

Writing for the *Psychology of Women Quarterly*, co-authors Julia Becker and Janet Swim said: 'Many men not only lack attention to such incidents but also are less likely to perceive sexist incidents as being discriminatory and potentially harmful for women. Women endorse sexist beliefs, at least in part, because they do not attend to subtle, aggregate forms of sexism in their personal lives.'

They said making people aware of the sexism would help to change attitudes and help men feel 'empathy' for the women who are the victims of 'benevolent sexism'.

Psychology of Women Quarterly is the official publication of the Society for the Psychology of Women and is described as a 'feminist, scientific peer-reviewed' journal.'

The next time I stop my car with a view to helping a woman stranded at the roadside, maybe because her car has a flat tyre, I'll ask her whether she's a feminist, and only help her if she isn't one. But of course if she *is* a feminist she'll probably lie, and deny it. How might we get round the tricky problem of feminists benefiting from 'benevolent sexism'? Maybe it's time we demanded that feminists identify themselves with a big red letter 'F' tattooed on their foreheads. They always claim to be proud of being feminists, so how could they possibly object?

We can reasonably assume that feminists are aware of what impact killing off chivalry will have. It will turn one of the more traditionally-minded groups of women against men: women who enjoy the benefits of men's chivalry. All it would take for such women to turn against men in general would be to be left standing by a broken-down car at the side of the road, while a succession of male drivers drove past, ignoring the signs of their distress. After a while the women would surely start to think, 'It's true what they say. All men *are* bastards!' They wouldn't make the connection that the men's behaviour was the result of a climate created by feminist campaigning.

34| THE LESBIAN FEMINIST
ASSAULT ON HETEROSEXUALITY

No woman needs intercourse; few women escape it.
Andrea Dworkin 1946-2005 American radical feminist: *Right-Wing Women* (1978)

Perhaps it's an indication of the political correctness which blights the modern world, but few writers who are critical of feminism have commented on the disproportionate influence of lesbian feminists in the feminist movement. A notable exception is Swayne O'Pie, whose *Why Britain Hates Men: Exposing Feminism* (2011) covers the topic at length in a chapter titled, 'The Power of Lesbian Feminism'. The remainder of this chapter is drawn from the book, with the author's permission:

> A Feminist belief system that is held by a number of Feminists and is politically powerful is Lesbian Feminism. This chapter is not an attack on lesbianism. I have no personal difficulty with lesbians or lesbianism as a sexual orientation. But if I am to be consistently honest in my analysis and show how and why Britain hates men by exposing Feminism then I cannot avoid the political lesbian dimension. So to put it in context, although I have no issue with lesbianism itself I *do* have an issue with politically driven man-hating Lesbian Feminism. This faction has an inordinate amount of cultural, political and policy-making power, and as we shall see, approximately one third of Feminists are lesbians. The post-1997 Labour governments were particularly active in promoting Lesbian Feminists into positions of policy-making power...
>
> Sheila Jeffreys, author, lecturer and Lesbian Feminist, comments:
>
>> 'Every woman who lives with or fucks a man helps to maintain the oppression of her sisters and hinders our struggle.' [1]

---

[1] Quoted in Angela Neustatter: *Hyenas in Petticoats* (1998), p70, Harrap.

Adrienne Rich, lecturer, author and Feminist:

> 'Woman-identification is a source of energy, a potential spring-board of female power, violently curtailed and wasted under the institution of heterosexuality.' [1]

The influential Lesbian Feminists Beatrix Campbell and Anna Coote:

> 'They (British Radical Feminists) insisted that women's personal and political autonomy could be safeguarded only if women's relationships with men were severely curtailed: "As long as women's sights are fixed on closeness to men, the ideology of male supremacy is safe". As for sex, they concluded that, 'liberation for women is not possible as long as vaginal sex is accepted as the norm rather than as a possible variation'.[2]

Anna Coote was employed as a Feminist adviser to the Labour Party's Minister for Women immediately it gained power in 1997. Coote's partner, Beatrix Campbell, is a Professor at Newcastle University, and has been for many years. She has the opportunity to influence generations of students (who generally believe what their lecturers tell them) into the Feminist ideology – including, one supposes, that part of it which advocates hating men. There are literally thousands of Feminists teaching in British universities. I have spoken to very many students over the years, asking them about their university experience; the vast majority agreed that their universities were 'Feminist'…

Lesbian Feminism has a great deal of cultural, academic and political power. One Equality Feminist admits:

> 'Small though they are in number, the convert lesbians, with what seemed a holier-than-though brand of feminism, exerted a powerful influence.' [3]

---

[1] Adrienne Rich: 'Compulsory Heterosexuality and Lesbian Existence' (1980) Signs, Vol 4, No.4, p687.

[2] Anna Coote and Beatrix Campbell: *Sweet Freedom: The Struggle for Women's Liberation* (1982), p29, Picador.

[3] Quoted in Angela Neustatter: *Hyenas in Petticoats* (1998), p69, Harrap.

Campbell and Coote again:

'A precept which unites all radical feminists is that the
fight for women's liberation is primarily against men:
they see it as overriding all other struggles and are
deeply suspicious of any attempt to link it to a wider
political strategy. The question then is whether one is
fighting in order to destroy masculinity as a social
construct, and so transform men as human beings,
with a view to developing a harmonious relationship in
which they wield no power over women; or whether
one seeks to end the necessity of the biological
distinction by establishing ways of living and
reproduction which are entirely independent of men.' [1]

Here we encounter again the Feminist belief in 'sameness'. These
feminists are suggesting that 'maleness' could be 'socialised out'
of men, that 'masculinity could be destroyed' by a social and
cultural revolution.

An unpleasant and condescending view of half the population:
'problematic men need to be "transformed as human beings" '.
Again we see Feminists flirting with eugenics and the social
engineering usually only associated with communist and fascist
regimes. These malicious feminists wouldn't dare make such a
vile comment about any other group in society, for example the
disabled, black people or Jews. And would they advocate that
'gayness' (their own brand of sexuality) should be 'destroyed' or
'transformed' as some far-Right Christians have done? Again we
notice Feminist irrationality, hypocrisy and double standards.

Sheila Jeffreys again:

'Our definition of a political lesbian is a woman-
identified woman who does not fuck men... men are
the enemy.'[2]

Most of the seminal Ideological Feminist authors are lesbian.
Their texts are noted for their anti-male virulence. As an exercise,
I invite the reader to check the truth of this. It is an important
point when answering the question 'why Britain hates men'
because their misandric message carries into British policy-

---

[1] Coote and Campbell p29.
[2] Neustatter p70.

making in the form of advantaging women (mainly Feminists themselves) whilst demonising and blatantly discriminating against men.

I'm not suggesting that *all* lesbians are Feminists, they certainly are not. But what I am suggesting, on the evidence of my reading and personal experience, is that those Feminists who *are* lesbian appear to be the most *aggressively misandric*, and tend to hold leading roles in women's groups and organisations...

Lesbian women have always been at the forefront of the Feminist movement, driving misandry side by side with their Socialist Sisters, and both belief systems denounce marriage. The Leeds Revolutionary Feminist Group in a paper entitled, 'Political Lesbianism: The Case Against Heterosexuality' states, with regards to heterosexual intercourse:

> 'Only in the system of oppression that is male supremacy does the oppressor actually invade and colonise the interior of the body of the oppressed... Penetration is an act of great symbolic significance in which the oppressor enters the body of the oppressed... its function and effect is the punishment and control of women... every act of penetration for a woman is an invasion which undermines her confidence and saps her strength.' [1]

The authors of *Reclaiming the F Word: The New Feminist Movement* – published in 2010 – undertook a survey of over 1,000 Feminists. One of their findings was that 37 percent were lesbian, bisexual or 'other'.[2] This is a large percentage and explains, along with a seriously misandric attitude, why Lesbian Feminism is so powerful a force in the Feminist movement; it is one explanation why this movement has man-hating at its core and why Britain hates men.

---

[1] Valerie Bryson: *Feminist Political Theory* (1992), p214, Paragon House.
[2] Catherine Redfern and Kristin Aune: *Reclaiming the F Word: The New Feminist Movement* (2010), p223, Zed Books.

35 | THE FEMINIST ASSAULT ON MARRIAGE

Marriage as an institution developed from rape as a practice. Rape, originally defined as abduction, became marriage by capture. Marriage meant the taking was to extend in time, to be not only use of but possession of, or ownership.

Pornography (1981)
Andrea Dworkin 1946-2005 American radical feminist

In long-term intimate heterosexual relationships, including marriage, if one or both partners hold views amounting to hatred of their partner's gender, that *must* be damaging to the relationship. In *The Fraud of the Rings* I related what a then recently-divorced acquaintance had told me about his ex-wife, who'd been respectful towards him *before* their marriage:

> 'I thought I'd married a pleasant and kind woman. How wrong I was. It turned out I'd married the military wing of the women's movement. Every day was a battle, a request for a cup of tea an assault against all women over the millennia.'

His ex-wife walked away from the marriage with a good deal of her husband's family's long-accumulated wealth in the divorce settlement, and he was left a bitter man. The justice system effectively mugged the man on behalf of the woman.

We see in societies where feminism isn't an influential belief system that husbands and wives eventually come to a settlement – amicable or otherwise – about how they relate to one another. Failing which, they divorce. Weak women are inclined to employ feminism as a weapon with which to assault their partners relentlessly. A feminist wife is, by definition, an unhappy wife. And she'll do all in her power to make her husband unhappy too.

The modern fashion for women to denigrate men finds its way into marriages, of course. For many husbands, especially those who work hard to support a family where the wife is not in paid employment (or is in part-time employment) the respect of a wife is one of the subtle elements which can help make the effort of making a marriage work worthwhile. Without that respect, marriage can feel like a poor contract from a husband's perspective.

Swayne O'Pie's *Why Britain Hates Men: Exposing Feminism* (2011) has some interesting material on feminist attitudes towards marriage, extracts from which take up the remainder of this chapter:

> Apparently, men make women marry them so that they can then subjugate and enslave them:
>
> > 'Marriage is imposed upon women for the benefit of men, as a means of dividing and controlling women and ensuring that they serve men domestically and emotionally as well as sexually… the rejection of heterosexuality is therefore a political act that strikes at the very heart of patriarchy.' [1]   [1]
>
> Lesbian Feminism seriously dislikes the institution of marriage; so much so that it advocates women living apart from men – the Feminist belief system of 'separatism'. In 1998 Janet Dixon's *Radical Records: Perspectives on Thirty Years of Lesbian and Gay History* was published. Dixon states:
>
> > 'It is my belief that without us, feminism would never have been more than a caucus of the broad Left. Separatism was right there in the middle, influencing all women… What we separatists did was to reduce the very complex set of circumstances which combine to oppress women, to a single uncluttered issue. That

---

[1] Adrienne Rich: 'Compulsory Heterosexuality and Lesbian Existence' (1980), p21.

is the stark injustice of the total humiliation of women on all levels by men.' [1]

[1] Quoted in Angela Neustatter: *Hyenas in Petticoats* (1998), p226, Harrap.

36 | THE FEMINIST ASSAULT ON THE NUCLEAR FAMILY

The problem lay buried, unspoken for many years in the minds of American women. It was a strange stirring, a sense of dissatisfaction, a yearning that women suffered in the middle of the twentieth century in the United States. Each suburban housewife struggled with it alone. As she made the beds, shopped for groceries, matched slipcover material, ate peanut butter sandwiches with her children, chauffeured Cub Scouts and Brownies, lay beside her husband at night, she was afraid to ask even of herself the silent question: 'Is this all?'
Betty Friedan 1921-2006 *The Feminine Mystique* (1963)

Feminists are hostile to the idea of marriage because they see it as the submission of a wife to her husband, and they regard caring for children as variously boring, stressful, and unfulfilling (compared with paid employment). So it should come as no surprise that feminists are hostile to the idea of the nuclear family, and women's traditional roles within it, in particular.

From Wikipedia:

> 'Harriet Harman has received criticism from the right wing and conservative press for her perceived views on families. Erin Pizzey criticised the views expressed by Harman and other leading female Labour figures in the 1990 IPPR report 'The Family Way'. Writing in the *Daily Mail*, Pizzey accused the report of being a 'staggering attack on men and their role in modern life' as a result of its stating, 'it cannot be assumed that men are bound to be an asset to family life or that the presence of fathers in families is necessarily a means to social cohesion'. In May 2008, in an interview she gave to think tank Civitas, Harman stated that marriage was irrelevant to government policy and that there was 'no ideal type of household in which to bring up children'.'

An article by veteran campaigner Erin Pizzey in the *Mail Online* edition of 22 January 2007, 'How feminists tried to destroy the family':

'During 1970, I was a young housewife with a husband, two children, two dogs and a cat. We lived in Hammersmith, West London, and I didn't see much of my husband because he worked for TV's *Nationwide*. I was lonely and isolated, and longed for something other than the usual cooking, cleaning and housework to enter my life.

By the early Seventies, a new movement for women – demanding equality and rights – began to make headlines in the daily newspapers. Among the jargon, I read the words 'solidarity' and 'support'. I passionately believed that women would no longer find themselves isolated from each other, and in the future could unite to change our society for the better.

Within a few days I had the address of a local group in Chiswick, and I was on my way to join the Women's Liberation Movement. I was asked to pay £3 and ten shillings as a joining fee, told to call other women 'sisters' and that our meetings were to be called 'collectives'. My fascination with this new movement lasted only a few months. At the huge 'collectives' I heard shrill women preaching hatred of the family. They said the family was not a safe place for women and children. I was horrified at their virulence and violent tendencies. I stood on the same platforms trying to reason with the leading lights of this new organisation.

I ended up being thrown out by the movement. My crime was to warn some of the women working in the Women's Liberation Movement office off Shaftesbury Avenue that if it persisted in cooperating with a plan to bomb Biba, a fashionable clothes shop in Kensington, I would call the police. Biba was bombed because the women's movement thought it was a capitalist enterprise devoted to sexualising women's bodies. I decided that I was wasting my time trying to influence what, to my mind, was a Marxist/feminist movement touting for money from gullible women like myself.

By that time, I'd met a small group of women in my area who agreed with me. We persuaded Hounslow council to give us a tiny house in Belmont Terrace in Chiswick. We had two rooms upstairs, two rooms downstairs, a kitchen and an outside lavatory. We installed a telephone and typewriter, and we were in business. Every day after dropping my children at school, I went to our little house, which we called the Women's Aid. Soon women from all over Chiswick were coming to ask for help. At last we had somewhere women could meet each other and bring their children. My long, lonely days were over.

But then something happened that made me understand that our role was going to be more than just a forum where women could exchange ideas. One day, a lady came in to see us. She took off her jersey, and we saw that she was bruised and swollen across her breasts and back. Her husband had taken a chair leg to her. She looked at me and said: 'No one will help me.' For a moment I was somersaulted back in time. I was six years old, standing in front of a teacher at school. My legs were striped and bleeding from a whipping I had received from an ironing cord. 'My mother did this to me last night,' I said. 'No wonder,' replied the teacher. 'You're a dreadful child.'

No one would help me then and nobody would ever imagine that my beautiful, rich mother – who was married to a diplomat – could be a violent abuser. Until that moment 35 years later, I had buried my past and assumed that because we had social workers, probation officers, doctors, hospitals and solicitors, victims of violence had enough help. I quickly discovered, as battered women with their children poured into the house, that whatever was going on behind other people's front doors was seen as nobody else's business.

If someone was beaten up on the street, it was a criminal offence; the same beating behind a closed door was called 'a domestic' and the police had no rights or power to interfere. The shocking fact for me was that there had been a deafening silence on the subject of domestic violence. All the social agencies knew about domestic violence, but nobody talked about it. I searched for literature to help me understand this epidemic, but there was nothing to read except a few articles on child abuse in medical journals.

So in 1974 I decided to write *Scream Quietly Or The Neighbours Will Hear*, the first book in the world on domestic violence. I revealed that women and children were being abused in their own homes and they couldn't escape because the law wouldn't protect them. If a husband claimed he would have his wife back, she couldn't claim any money from the Department of Health and Social Security, and social services could only offer to take the children into care.

Meanwhile, our little house was packed with women fleeing their violent partners – sometimes as many as 56 mothers and children in four rooms. All had terrible stories, but I recognised almost immediately that not all the women were innocent. Some were as violent as the men, and violent towards their children. The social workers involved with these women told me I was wasting my time because the women would only return to their partners.

I was determined to try to break the chain of violence. But as the local newspaper picked up the story of our house, I grew worried about a very different threat. I knew that the radical feminist movement was running out of national support because more sensible women had shunned their anti-male, anti-family agenda. Not only were they looking for a cause, they also wanted money. In 1974, the women living in my refuge organised a meeting in our local church hall to encourage other groups to open refuges across the country.

We were astonished and frightened that many of the radical lesbian and feminist activists that I had seen in the collectives attended. They began to vote themselves into a national movement across the country. After a stormy argument, I left the hall with my abused mothers – and what I had most feared happened. In a matter of months, the feminist movement hijacked the domestic violence movement, not just in Britain, but internationally. Our grant was given to them[1] and they had a legitimate reason to hate and blame all men. They came out with sweeping statements which were as biased as they were ignorant. 'All women are innocent victims of men's violence,' they declared.

They opened most of the refuges in the country and banned men from working in them or sitting on their governing committees. Women with alcohol or drug problems were refused admittance, as were boys over 12 years old. Refuges that let men work there were refused affiliation. Our group in Chiswick worked with as many refuges as we could. Good, caring women still work in refuges across the country, but many women working in the feminist refuges, about 350, admit they are failing women who most need them.

---

[1] The organization became Refuge http://refuge.org.uk

With the first donation we received in 1972, we employed a male playgroup leader because we felt our children needed the experience of good, gentle men. We devised a treatment programme for women who recognised that they, too, were violent and dysfunctional. And we concentrated on children hurt by violence and sexual abuse.

Yet the feminist refuges continued to create training programmes that described only male violence against women. Slowly, the police and other organisations were brainwashed into ignoring the research that was proving men could also be victims. Despite attacks in the Press from feminist journalists and threatening anonymous telephone calls, I continued to argue that violence was a learned pattern of behaviour from early childhood.

When, in the mid-Eighties, I published *Prone To Violence*, about my work with violence-prone women and their children, I was picketed by hundreds of women from feminist refuges, holding placards which read: 'All men are bastards' and 'All men are rapists'. Because of violent threats, I had to have a police escort around the country.

It was bad enough that this relatively small group of women was influencing social workers and police. But I became aware of a far more insidious development in the form of public policy-making by powerful women, which was creating a poisonous attitude towards men.

In 1990, Harriet Harman (who became a Cabinet minister), Anna Coote (who became an adviser to Labour's Minister for Women) and Patricia Hewitt (yes, she's in the Labour Cabinet, too!) expressed their beliefs in a social policy paper called 'The Family Way'. It said: 'It cannot be assumed that men are bound to be an asset to family life, or that the presence of fathers in families is necessarily a means to social harmony and cohesion.' It was a staggering attack on men and their role in modern life.

Hewitt, in a book by Geoff Dench called *Transforming Men* published in 1995, said: 'If we want fathers to play a full role in their children's lives, then we need to bring men into the playgroups and nurseries and the schools. And here, of course, we hit the immediate difficulty of whether we can trust men with children.' In 1998, however, the Home Office published a historic study which stipulated that men as well as women could be victims of domestic violence.

With that report in my hand, I tried to reason with Joan Ruddock, who was then Minister for Women. The figures for battered men were 'minuscule' she insisted, and she continued to refer to men only as 'perpetrators'. For nearly four decades, these pernicious attitudes towards family life, fathers and boys have permeated the thinking of our society to such an extent that male teachers and carers are now afraid to touch or cuddle children.

Men can be accused of violence towards their partners and sexual abuse without evidence. Courts discriminate against fathers and refuse to allow them access to their children on the whims of vicious partners. Of course, there are dangerous men who manipulate the court systems and social services to persecute their partners and children. But by blaming all men, we have diluted the focus on this minority of men and pushed aside the many men who would be willing to work with women towards solutions.

I believe that the feminist movement envisaged a new Utopia that depended upon destroying family life. In the new century, so their credo ran, the family unit will consist of only women and their children. Fathers are dispensable. And all that was yoked – unforgivably – to the debate about domestic violence. To my mind, it has never been a gender issue – those exposed to violence in early childhood often grow up to repeat what they have learned, regardless of whether they are girls or boys.

I look back with sadness to my young self and my vision that there could be places where people – men, women and children who have suffered physical and sexual abuse – could find help, and if they were violent could be given a second chance to learn to live peacefully. I believe that vision was hijacked by vengeful women who have ghettoised the refuge movement and used it to persecute men. Surely the time has come to challenge this evil ideology and insist that men take their rightful place in the refuge movement. We need an inclusive movement that offers support to everyone that needs it. As for me, I will always continue to work with *anyone* who needs my help or can help others; and yes, that includes men.'

In a manner that reminds us of Soviet-era manipulation of the media, feminists seek to deny Erin Pizzey's existence. She's not even mentioned on Refuge's website. [Update: Erin Pizzey remains a heroine to men's human rights advocates (MRAs) around the world. She runs a website dedicated to revealing the truth about domestic violence.[1]]

Throughout the years 1997 to 2010 the government of the United Kingdom, the Labour administrations in which Harman played senior roles, was determinedly anti-men and anti-family. Through its welfare policies it actively encouraged single motherhood. In August 2011 London a number of other major English cities were rocked with the worst riots in living memory. Most of the rioters were young and most of their lives would have been lived during the Labour administration of 1997-2010. A reputable broadsheet later reported that the majority of convicted rioters and looters had been, or were being, brought up in single-parent households, almost all by single mothers. A number of cases emerged of children as young as 10 years of age found looting in the early hours of the morning, *their mothers being unaware of their absence from their homes.*

A substantial proportion of daughters of single mothers go on to become single mothers in their own right. What a dysfunctional cycle we have created through the benefits system. Harriet Harman should hang her head in shame, but needless to say she's in denial about the connection between her administration's policies and social breakdown.

Some people have concluded from the title of my book *The Fraud of the Rings* that I must be anti-marriage and possibly anti-family as well. Neither is true, but we have to recognize that for several decades (in the UK and across much of the developed world) marriage has been a highly toxic institution for men. Over 50 per cent of marriages end in divorce, and women file

---

[1] http://whiteribbon.org

for 75 per cent of divorces. [Update: my thoughts on marriage in the modern era are on one of my websites.[1]]

One of the conclusions of my book was that most people in the developed world in the modern era are unsuited to traditional marriage. But I know some happily married people and some close families and, truth be told, I envy them. Such couples and families clearly form the centre of ordered, civilised societies, and the children raised within such families are more likely to become well-adjusted adults than children raised in other circumstances.

In September 2011 I received an email from a feminist who was intrigued by my thesis that most people in the developed world in the modern era are unsuited to marriage. She proceeded to give me her views on marriage and the family:

> 'I may have got you wrong (haven't read your book yet) but you seem to me to be a male-supremicist (sic) maybe even a bit of a misogynist, and very right wing, whereas I am very left wing and have been a radical feminist and critic of patriarchal system all my life. And yet, strangely, we end up in agreement about marriage. Probably got there from different directions, but we got there.
>
> I was very disappointed when my niece got married recently. She is a privately-schooled, university-educated career woman in her early thirties and she posted on Facebook 'Oooh, only a week to go, I cannot WAIT to become Mrs Johnson!' I could not believe she was going to lose (to my mind) everything she'd achieved just to lose her very identity and have it subsumed under that of a bloke who mends bicycles for a living.
>
> Sorry if that sounds snobby but maybe if she was marrying an earl I might think it worth losing her name to become a duchess, just as men lose their names when they become Lord so and so of somewhere rather than Jack Smith. I could not believe she was prepared to change her name on everything – her mortgage, car insurance, library ticket, passport, house

---

[1] http://menshouldntmarry.wordpress.com

utilities, work-related documents and passes, even the name plate on her office door! Especially as we had both watched her cousin, my nephew's marriage, after a wedding which cost about £20,000, go down the pan in just two years! She might have to change them all back again soon!

I do agree with you that our society is only interested in self-help on a superficial scale such as *Ten Secrets of Happy Marriages* rather than analysing what is wrong with the whole set-up of marriage in the first place, isn't that something to do with wanting a 'quick fix' and also wanting to continue with the romantic delusion sold to us by advertising? In a way your book (though I have not yet read it) is a kind of self-help because you are proposing change – more like self-help for society?

I'm in my fifties and when I look at the problems associated with marriage I think the whole thing needs a radical re-think. Very few people seem to be suited to it, yet 90% do it. That's mad. I keep thinking we'd all be happier if women and children comprised the family group, and all men were bachelors, roaming about shagging and impregnating women who want to be impregnated and playing snooker with the boys the rest of the time LOL. If nothing was expected of men, commitment-wise, then they wouldn't disappoint.

But of course where this all falls down is in the area of economics. If women are at home with children and no husband, how can they go out to work? Who is going to support them? I suppose state nurseries could raise them, allowing mothers to get paid employment. They (and the single men) could then pay taxes which would pay the nursery staff. But then this all smacks of communism. And what about women who believe their children will be psychologically affected by being brought up in nurseries rather than by their own mothers?

The current economic unit is husband, wife, kids. Both adults work until reproduction takes women out of paid employment, forcing them into dependence upon men. Then they return to work as soon as the children start to become more self-sufficient, perhaps part-time at first, then back to full-time till retirement. In fairyland, this works rather well. Where it all goes wrong is that 50% of couples split up at some point during this sequence.'

From *The Daily Telegraph* of 2 October 2011, an article titled, 'Fathers denied right to see children':

'Divorced fathers are to be denied a legal right to a relationship with their children in a review of family law due to be published tomorrow. Plans to enshrine in law the principle that a child has a 'meaningful relationship with both parents' are likely to be dropped, *The Daily Telegraph* has learnt.

The proposal would have proved too disruptive to children and would have made it necessary for judges to allocate time that parents each had to spend with their offspring, according to Whitehall sources.

The recommendation is understood to have been left out of a report on family justice by David Norgrove, the former pensions regulator and civil servant. It is likely to anger fathers' groups that have pushed for a legal right to retain access to children after a divorce.

Figures show that eight per cent of single parents are fathers, meaning there are 200,000 single fathers in the country bringing up 300,000 children.

Courts decide to leave children with their mothers in the vast majority of cases. Mr Norgrove's interim report in March recommended that there should be a 'statement in legislation to reinforce the importance of the child continuing to have a meaningful relationship with both parents, alongside the need to protect the child from harm'. This fell short of fathers' groups demands for a right to equally shared parenting, but was seen as an important step forward.

However, Mr Norgrove is thought to have ruled out making this a legal principle. A Whitehall source said, 'If you put a statement to this effect into legislation there is evidence that this would risk creating confusion, misinterpretation, false expectations and would also lead to more litigation. This risks undermining the fundamental principle of the Children Act 1989 that the welfare of the child must be paramount in guiding these types of decisions and risks harming children instead.' The source said that the proposals still emphasised the importance of involving both parents in the upbringing of their children after separation.

Mr Norgrove's interim report recognised that this area of family law was a 'particularly emotive issue'. He refused to comment last night.'

This sordid treatment of fathers by the justice system in the United Kingdom will come as no surprise to anyone with an interest in the topic. The remainder of this chapter is drawn from a chapter titled 'Excluding the Family: The state as the real absent father' in Steve Moxon's *The Woman Racket*:

> The separate worlds of men and women are starkly apparent in so many ways, but nowhere more so than in the determination to keep men out of the family. Here follows an astounding tale of intransigence and deception that is impossible to explain without what we know of the evolved differences between the sexes and what they entail. More superficially, sense can be made of this only in terms of an entirely woman-centred, anti-male and anti-family politics that stems from 'cultural Marxism' underpinned by evolved 'folk prejudice' against (lower-status) men.
>
> The family and the domestic sphere around it is regarded as being firmly within woman's separate world, even more – much more – strongly than the workplace is regarded as the separate world of men. Of all the rights abuses systematically directed against men, the worst is the unwarranted obstruction from playing their natural part in the lives of their biological children, by denying the basic human and civil right to contact (apart for the barest minimum). This is at root justified through refusing to recognise that men have a strong affiliation to and bond with their own children which a step-father does not have. This most blatant denial of human nature lasts only until the issue of money arises. Entirely regardless of circumstances, it's the biological father and not the 'social' male parent who must support the child financially.
>
> Imposed on men are non-negotiable and often unreasonable financial demands for child support, even in respect of a child that resulted from a one-night-stand when, more than ever, fertility is controlled by women. (The man very likely will have no knowledge of the woman's contraceptive use, and may well not be told the truth if he asks; and the passion of the encounter is likely to mean that the issue of condom use is waived or not even broached.) There is also the unfairness to men of divorce settlements, and the policies of the government that actively encourage the

dissolution of relationships. This is in not so much by financially penalising couples as encouraging single parenthood with huge subsidies.

This is all in the face of overwhelming evidence of the positive social outcomes of marriage for children and the negative outcomes on average for any other arrangement, with a single-parent household shown to be the worst possible milieu of all for a child to start in life (even controlling for income and other variables concerned with disadvantage). The evidence for this is so readily available that it is unnecessary for me to set it out here, though I will be dealing with an aspect that has had little discussion. Despite repeated requests to various government departments and agencies for any research to show that a non-shared parenting model is in any way preferable, none has ever been forthcoming. This is because there isn't any. Sometimes it's claimed that marriage merely correlates with positive outcomes – ignoring the fact that other variables that could have produced positive outcomes have been controlled for.

As much as destroying the family is central to PC politics, it will never succeed because the family is the natural social unit we have evolved live within. Three in four children remain in intact families even today...

There is no longer any dispute that Britain is the lone-parent capital of the world, partly – if not largely – because of government bribes for women to eschew having a partner. With a six-fold multiplier of effective net earnings to £30 an hour, the sums at stake are so huge that this anti-social engineering must be a main or the main factor in the decision not to start or to continue living together for hundreds of thousands of people. Single parenthood is now a major career option for *any* woman, let alone just for the underclass.

The issue of heavy financial discrimination against fathers and the two-parent family was put into stark relief by a 2007 report by the former Labour minister for welfare reform, Frank Field. He did the following calculations: In 2007, a single parent with two children under eleven, working part-time (sixteen hours a week) on the minimum wage, receives in total after tax credits, £487 per week net. For this same single parent to re-couple or revert to the status quo ante and have a man living with her, she and her man between them would have to work 116 hours a week to achieve the same income. That is the equivalent of both of them working a full-time job plus more than three days a week of a second job. This is not only impossible but illegal under the working time directive.

This tax-credit subsidy of single parenthood was introduced in 1998, making a single parent who had never worked as well-off, to the nearest pound per person, as married or co-habiting couples on average earnings (as was pointed out in the Centre for Policy Studies report, *The Price of Parenting*). Tax credits are massive welfare benefits in disguise, and the very reverse of Bill Clinton's reforms of time-limiting benefits that have so successfully cut US welfare dependency (literally in half)...

The mess we are in arises from a wilful blindness to the most basic reality that it takes both a mother and a father to raise children; and not just the one to provide most of the care, the other most of the resources. Both are needed to provide complementary but very different parenting to produce a well-adjusted child who will grow into a responsible adult with a window on the separate worlds of the sexes. A father is the conduit to the wider world, and the domain of men, and of how reliable it is. Without a father, the government has to step in to pay enormous sums to deal with the long-term consequences (children growing into dysfunctional adults), but more immediately to pay benefits and/or tax credits. All out of the pockets primarily of the fathers who properly planned to provide for their own children through households supported by working...

The one thing the world does not lack is people. Women need no encouragement to have children, and the less encouragement they're given then the more likely are the children they have to be wanted, loved, and well-adjusted as adults – so that they are not actually deleterious to society. Population, even leaving out the consequences of direct immigration, is still increasing: the supposed decline in birth rate is an illusion caused by the ongoing shift to later childbearing by an entire age cohort of women. Using the measure of 'cohort fertility', fertility in the UK is at near replacement level. Population decline would be of enormous benefit to all those millions who are currently deprived of work merely because they are over-fifty or even over-forty, and would make it easier to force into work the large numbers of idle younger people. The children of single parents – as research overwhelmingly demonstrates – are much more likely to be social problems and cost the taxpayer further expense; not least when they perpetuate the cycle and become single mothers or feckless fathers who in turn themselves become strangers to their own children.

Why continue to pay women to create social breakdown? It makes less sense than it would to pay men to visit prostitutes to further their corresponding natural inclinations. Nobody in their right mind would suggest such a thing, of course; but the social implications would be incomparably more benign than subsidising women to have children.

Having children is the most obvious personal asset anyone could have; and those who are childless, and especially those who are single and who may be unable to form a partnership, are the truly disadvantaged in any society. The principal attraction that women feel for men is status, and this most easily translates into earnings. Men who earn so little that they are unattractive to most or to nearly all women, form the most disadvantaged subgroup in our own, as in any, society. Yet as a proportion of their income, they more than anyone are forced to pay taxes to provide for single parenthood. They are literally bankrolling a lifestyle for the very women who would not have them in the first place.

37 | THE FEMINIST ASSAULT
ON CAPITALISM

Few trends could so thoroughly undermine the very foundations of our free society as the acceptance by corporate officials of a social responsibility other than to make as much money for their shareholders as possible.
Milton Friedman 1912-2006 American economist and statistician: *Capitalism and Freedom* (1962)

In the chapter 'Caution: Women at Work' I provided a précis of the material in my book *The Glass Ceiling Delusion* which covered issues relating to women and men in the world of work. In the modern era we are seeing more 'gender balance initiatives' aimed at 'improving' the proportion of women in senior positions. In the public sector these initiatives will lead to even poorer performance and higher costs to the taxpayer, but who will notice in the grand scheme of things?

I turn now to the matter of gender balance initiatives in the private sector, up to and including boardrooms. Shortly after the publication of *The Glass Ceiling Delusion* an interesting article appeared in *The Economist*. From the edition of 23rd of July 2011 an article titled, 'Women in business: Still lonely at the top':

> 'These days no one doubts that women can run companies: think of Indra Nooyi at PepsiCo, Carol Bartz at Yahoo! or Ursula Burns at Xerox. Sheryl Sandberg, the number two at Facebook, is more widely applauded than her young male boss, Mark Zuckerberg.
>
> Yet the number of female bosses remains stubbornly small. Not a single one on France's CAC 40 share index is run by a woman. In America, only 15 chief executives of Fortune 500 companies are women. Britain does better, but not much: five of the FTSE-100 firms have female bosses.

Several governments, especially in Europe, have decided that radical action is required to increase the number of women in the executive suite. Norway passed a law in 2003 that obliged all publicly listed firms to reserve 40% of the seats on their boards for women by 2008. Spain passed a similar law in 2007; France earlier this year. The Netherlands is working on one.

On July 6th the European Parliament passed a resolution calling for EU-wide legislation stipulating that at least 40% of seats on listed companies' supervisory boards will be reserved for women by 2020. This does not oblige member states to do anything, but it reflects a spreading mood. The German government is considering whether to impose quotas. America is not, but new rules from the Securities and Exchange Commission will require firms to reveal what, if anything, they are doing to increase diversity at the top table. [Author's note: the expression 'the thin end of the wedge' comes to mind….]

Viviane Reding, the EU commissioner for justice, argues that compulsion is the only way to overcome entrenched discrimination. For a whole year she has tried to cajole companies to take voluntary measures to promote more women. In March, she posted a 'Women on the Board Pledge for Europe' on her website. This allows companies to promise that women will make up 30% of their boards by 2015 and 40% by 2020. Only seven companies have signed up so far. Moët Hennessy Louis Vuitton (LVMH), a French luxury-goods maker, added itself rather ostentatiously on July 12th. But cynics doubt that this owed much to the commissioner's powers of persuasion. LVMH was only pledging itself to do what the new French law already obliges it to.

There is a powerful business case for hiring more women to run companies. They are more likely to understand the tastes and aspirations of the largest group of consumers in the world, namely women. They represent an underfished pool of talent. And there is evidence that companies with more women in top jobs perform better than those run by men only. [Author's note: if the assertions in this paragraph had any validity then men – rather than women – would by now be in a small minority on company boards. Two of the most dynamic and successful economies of the second half of the

20th century, Germany and Japan, had very small numbers of women in senior positions by international standards.]

McKinsey, a consultancy, recently looked at 89 listed companies with a very high proportion of women in senior management posts and compared their financial performance with the average for firms in the same industry. It found that these firms enjoyed a higher rate of return on equity, fatter operating profits and a more buoyant share price. The authors described the correlation between promoting women and doing well as 'striking', though they admitted that they could not prove what was causing what. It is possible that firms that are already doing well tend to hire more female directors. [Author's note: the latter explanation is surely more credible. Talented women will naturally be attracted to the firms which offer the best remuneration packages, which will invariably be the more profitable ones.]

Proponents of quotas cite the superior performance of firms with female directors as evidence that quotas will benefit companies and their shareholders. Sceptics doubt this. The women that companies voluntarily appoint to boards are mostly excellent (indeed, they may have had to be particularly talented to overcome the barriers in their way). The effect of quotas, however, will be to elevate women who would not otherwise get onto the board. It would be surprising if they proved as able as those appointed without such help.

The evidence from Norway, the first European country to impose strict quotas, suggests that compulsion has been bad for business. Norwegian boards, which were 9% female in 2003, were ordered to become 40% female within five years. Many reached that target by window-dressing. The proportion of board members in Norway who are female is nearly three times greater than the proportion of executive directors [Author's note: for the reader unfamiliar with corporate governance, this means that most female directors in Norway are non-executive directors. Relatively speaking a cushy job, and some women – as well as some men – hold down several such positions simultaneously.]

To obey the law, Norwegian firms promoted many women who were less experienced than the directors they had before. These new hires appear to have done a poor job. A study by Amy Dittmar and Kenneth Ahern at the Ross School of Business at the University of Michigan found that firms that were forced to increase the share of women on their boards by more than ten percentage points saw one measure of corporate value (the ratio of market capitalisation to the replacement value of assets, known as Tobin's Q) fall by 18%...'

At the very least, then, the eventual outcome of the social engineering experiment of increasing the proportion of women on corporate boards is uncertain, and it could quite possibly be negative. The inevitable result is to put the capitalist model at risk. It's scarcely imaginable that even if it were proved beyond all doubt that increasing female representation on company boards was harming companies' viability, the legislation requiring higher female representation would be repealed given feminist politicians, spineless male politicians, and universal suffrage.

There is a real risk of 'death by a thousand cuts'. Is this a reasonable risk to suffer in the name of gender equality? In my opinion, it's not. But I'll never enjoy the opportunity to give expression to that opinion at the ballot box, and nor will you. I'm not aware of a single country where the intention to increase the proportion of women on company boards has been presented to the citizens in a party manifesto.

In common with followers of other faiths, feminists have a ready answer for any evidence that conflicts with their faith. They even have one to explain the failure rate of women in senior positions: the phenomenon of women who, having shattered the 'glass ceiling', proceed to fall off the 'glass cliff'. From Wikipedia:

'A glass cliff is a term coined by Prof Michelle Ryan and Prof Alex Haslam of University of Exeter, United Kingdom, in 2004. Their research demonstrates that once women break through the glass ceiling and take on positions of leadership they often have experiences that are different from those of their male counterparts. More specifically, women are more likely to occupy positions that are precarious and thus have a higher risk of failure – either because they are appointed to lead organizational units that are in crisis or because they are not given the resources and support needed for success. Extending the metaphor of the glass ceiling, Ryan and Haslam evoke the notion of the 'glass cliff' to refer to a danger which involves exposure to risk of failing but which is not readily apparent. 'It therefore appears that after having broken through a glass ceiling women are actually more likely than men to find themselves on a "glass cliff", meaning their positions of leadership are risky or precarious.'

Michelle Ryan is a Professor of Social and Organisational Psychology in the College of Life Sciences at the University of Exeter. Alex Haslam is a Professor of Psychology at University of Exeter and former editor of the European Journal of Social Psychology. Their research into the glass cliff has been funded by the Leverhulme Trust, the European Social Fund and the Economic and Social Research Council.'

Any experienced business person could tell you the idea of the glass cliff is absurd; left to their own devices, businesses would never operate in such a manner. Women sometimes fail at a senior level for precisely the same reasons that men sometimes do; it takes an academic not to grasp that obvious reality. Why can women not simply fail at challenges and learn from the experience, as men are expected to?

The funding for research into the 'glass cliff' comes from the left-leaning Economic and Social Research Council. The same band of intellectual giants which was behind the 'Experiencing and Celebrating Fatness' seminar we'll be considering in a later chapter. Isn't it good to see our taxes put to such productive use in these straitened times?

Evidence of feminists' anti-capitalism isn't hard to find. From Wikipedia's entry on Germaine Greer:

'Over the years Greer has continued to self-identify as an anarchist or Marxist. In her books she has dealt very little with political labels of this type, but has reaffirmed her position in interviews. She stated on ABC Television in 2008 that 'I ought to confess I suppose that I'm a Marxist. I think that reality comes first and ideology comes second,' and elaborated later in the program to a question on whether feminism was the only successful revolution of the 20th century saying, 'The difficulty for me is that I believe in permanent revolution. I believe that once you change the power structure and you get an oligarchy that is trying to keep itself in power, you have all the illiberal features of the previous regime. What has to keep on happening is a constant process of criticism, renewal, protest and so forth.

Speaking on an interview for 3CR (an Australian community radio station), also in 2008, she described herself as 'an old anarchist' and reaffirmed that opposition to 'hierarchy and capitalism' were at the centre of her politics.'

[Update: I launched Campaign for Merit in Business[1] in May 2012, three months after the ebook edition of this book was published. I launched it to challenge the government over its bullying of FTSE companies into increasing the representation of women on their boards. To the best of my knowledge, it remains the only organization in the world challenging a government in this area.

Later in 2012 I engaged with House of Commons and House of Lords select committees, and a video of me giving verbal testimony to the former – 'Women in the Workplace' – is on our YouTube channel.[2] I presented evidence from five longitudinal studies of a causal link between increasing female representation on corporate boards, and financial decline.[3]

---

[1] http://c4mb.wordpress.com
[2] http://tinyurl.com/c4mbhoc
[3] http://tinyurl.com/c4mbstudies

Not one of our public challenges of proponents of 'more women on boards' to provide evidence of a beneficial impact on corporate results has been met with a substantive response.[1]

Professor Susan Vinnicombe leads the Cranfield International Centre for Women Leaders, and for many years has been the foremost academic proponent in the world for 'more women on boards'. In her testimony to the aforementioned House of Lords inquiry, she admitted she had no evidence of a causal link between more women on boards, and enhanced financial performance.[2]

The government continues to bully FTSE companies into appointing more female directors. The Conservative-led coalition which was in power over 2010-15 bullied FTSE100 companies into doubling the proportion of women on their boards from 12.5% in 2011 to 25.0% in 2015. Virtually all the newly-appointed female directors had something in common with virtually all the existing ones. They were appointed as non-executive directors, illustrating the shortage of well-qualified women for FTSE100 board positions.

The government is currently (November 2015) bullying FTSE350 companies into ensuring a third of their directors will be women by 2020. It won't stop there, of course. It is known the government's longer-term goal is gender parity on FTSE350 boards, and this social engineering initiative will be extended in time to ever smaller companies, which are less able to bear the negative consequences than larger companies.]

---

[1] http://tinyurl.com/c4mbpublicchallenges
[2] http://tinyurl.com/c4mbsusanvinnicombe

38 | THE FEMINIST ASSAULT ON DEMOCRACY

A democracy cannot exist as a permanent form of government. It can only exist until the voters discover that they can vote themselves largesse from the public treasury. From that moment on, the majority always votes for the candidates promising the most benefits from the public treasury with the result that a democracy always collapses over lousy fiscal policy, always followed by a dictatorship. The average of the world's great civilizations before they decline has been 200 years. These nations have progressed in this sequence: From bondage to spiritual faith; from faith to great courage; from courage to liberty; from liberty to abundance; from abundance to selfishness; from selfishness to complacency; from complacency to apathy; from apathy to dependency; from dependency back again to bondage.
Alexander Fraser Tytler, Lord Woodhouselee 1747-1813 British lawyer and writer: 'Cycle of Democracy' (1770)

One of my motivations behind writing *David and Goliatha* and *The Glass Ceiling Delusion* was that feminists were (and are) clearly exerting enormous influence in a number of areas, but I'd never knowingly met a militant feminist. Nor had the people I spoke to about this: friends, family, work associates.

How could it possibly be, in a modern democracy, that such a small number of people wield such disproportionate influence? John Strafford, Chairman of the Conservative Campaign for Democracy, posted the following review for *David and Goliatha* on Amazon's British website:

'A Refreshing Antidote to the Radical Feminists
8 Dec 2010

At long last Mike Buchanan has courageously taken on the radical feminists. For too long this group has dominated the public policy agenda. Pay equality, gender balance in the boardroom, all women short lists have been given far too much prominence in public life. We needed the other side to be put and in his book Mike Buchanan does just this. His description of the Prime Minister having a 'female-pattern brain' is an interesting aspect of David Cameron. Without being insulting it explains some of the current direction of Conservative policy.

The book calls for a fight back against the radical feminists. It deserves to succeed. Women had a long hard justifiable fight to obtain the vote in our democracy (see my book *Our Fight for Democracy: A History of Democracy in the United Kingdom*), but now they have it the radical feminists want special treatment. This isn't acceptable, each person's vote should have an equal value regardless of gender. Manipulating Parliamentary candidate short lists to give preference to women is a distortion of democracy and anyone who believes in democracy should oppose it.'

We encounter fewer feminist spokeswomen in our mass media than historically, and I think there's an obvious reason for this. Feminists have recognised that their views are deemed absurd by the vast majority of the population. It follows that by stating their opinions publicly, they will only stimulate opposition to their cause. So they lurk in the shadows and refuse to engage with people who might be critical of their activities, such as myself.

This approach is not limited to feminists but is common to their supporters, who are invariably Lefties. As we have seen, most of the women who run taxpayer-funded Women's Studies and Gender Studies courses in British universities were unwilling to provide me with course details or recommended reading lists. Most did not even reply to my letters and emails.

In *The Glass Ceiling Delusion* I included the text of letters I wrote to four prominent individuals seeking audio interviews about the specific matter of the then forthcoming proposed change in British law (finally enshrined in The Equality Act 2010), moving public sector bodies from a requirement to have equality of opportunities towards having equality of outcomes of race, gender etc. The individuals were:

- The Rt Hon Harriet Harman MP
- Lord Davies of Abersoch
- Ceri Goddard, the Chief Executive of The Fawcett Society
- Trevor Phillips, the Chair of the Equality and Human Rights Commission ('EHRC')

I received an email from Harriet Harman's deputy diary secretary – Ms Harman was evidently so busy that just one diary secretary was insufficient – stating that, 'Unfortunately the Minister will not be able to grant your request due to heavy diary commitments at the time.' I hadn't specified a 'time' I wished to meet Ms Harman, and I should have been perfectly happy to wait for as long as required. But at least Hattie was courteous enough to respond. I'm assuming, of course – perhaps naively – that her various diary secretaries didn't simply and automatically refuse meetings with undesirable elements such as myself. I didn't even receive acknowledgements of my letters from the other three people.

The Glass Ceiling Delusion contains a lengthy critique of the downloadable 750-page EHRC triennial report published on 11 October 2010, 'How Fair is Britain? Equality, Human Rights and Good Relations in 2010'. The report states that one of six organisations which 'provided invaluable assistance as we developed our research' was The Fawcett Society. From their website:[1]

> 'Fawcett is the UK's leading campaign for equality between women and men. Where there's an inequality gap between women and men we're working to close it.'

---

[1] http://fawcettsociety.org.uk

No mention there, you'll notice, of the possibility that women (and men, for that matter) might make life choices which lead to 'inequality gaps' in the first place. No, gaps are unfair, and all of them must be closed. The Fawcett Society is, of course, only interested in inequality gaps which they believe disadvantage women, not those that disadvantage men. You don't have to spend too long scanning their website to have your intelligence insulted:

> 'Women working full-time are paid on average 17.1% less an hour than men for doing work of equivalent value.'

I emailed The Fawcett Society to enquire what 'equivalent value' meant in the above context. In the absence of a response a month later I could only conclude that 'equivalent value' was a wholly subjective value judgment not reflecting supply and demand of suitably qualified workers in the workplace. I wasn't surprised at the lack of response to my email, as I hadn't received a response to a letter written to Ceri Goddard six weeks earlier. I still haven't received a response to that letter, 17 months after writing it.

The Fawcett Society is a feminist campaigning organisation. The fact that the Conservative / Liberal Democrat Coalition introduced 90% of Labour's 2010 Equality Bill – the remaining 10% being under consideration – wasn't enough for these strident ladies. From an article on their website, 'Coalition plans around Equality Act "Endorse Pay Gap" ':

'Rendering the Equality Act virtually toothless undermines every speech Coalition ministers ever gave endorsing the notion of a fairer Britain. The Fawcett Society has today warned that the Coalition's failure to implement the Equalities Act 2010 in full risks not just endorsing but widening the gender pay gap in the current and foreseeable economic climate.

The government has stated that it is now 'reviewing' several sections of the Act that was passed by Parliament in April 2010. All of the sections under review were opposed by the Conservatives in opposition but supported by the Liberal Democrats. Among these are the provisions that would give government the power to require big business – private sector companies with over 250 employees – to establish whether they have a pay gap between men and women, and publish their findings if they do not make enough voluntary progress in the next three years. Ceri Goddard, Chief Executive of The Fawcett Society, said:

> 40 years after the Dagenham machinists first striked (sic) for equal pay, women working in Dagenham earn an average 30 per cent less than men and nationally the gap between the average man and women's pay is a staggering 16.4 per cent [Author's note: feminists are an excitable lot, aren't they? A surprisingly large number of things appear to them to be staggering, shocking, utterly nonsensical...]
>
> It's ironic that the film charting their struggle hit cinemas the same day that the key equal pay measures in the Equality Act 2010 are being held back by government. Rowing back on the requirement for big business to publish and take action on any differences in pay between men and women employees – so to conduct gender pay audits – is tantamount to endorsing the shocking gender pay gap.
>
> All our research and experience shows that gender pay audits are key to shrinking the persistent gap in pay between women and men – it's utterly nonsensical to suggest we can tackle pay differences between men and women if we can't see where they are – more transparency is key. While banning secrecy clauses will go some way to creating a more transparent discussion around pay, it's not nearly enough to ensure real progress. Done right, conducting a pay audit is a simple and inexpensive process that can happen alongside annual accounts...
>
> The Equalities Act 2010 is a litmus test of the government's commitment to fairness. Failing to implement

it in full sends out a clear signal that creating a more equal society is a low priority for the Coalition.

Alongside concerns around measures to combat the pay gap, we are also worried that government plans to review the mechanism that allows those who may face 'double discrimination' – black women for example – to bring just the one claim means making it harder for some of those most at risk of discrimination to defend themselves.

Scrapping the Positive Action clause that would allow organisations to better address under-representation of people with protected characteristics would also be a backwards step – especially at a time of rising unemployment.

People at risk of discrimination face even tougher times than the rest during periods of financial unrest; watering down equality law during a recession weakens what little protection some of the most marginalised in our society have.

Rendering the Equality Act virtually toothless undermines every speech Coalition ministers ever gave endorsing the notion of a fairer Britain. The Act isn't perfect, but the government seems determined to implement it in name only.

Following an emergency budget that is seeing over 70 per cent of public spending cuts being borne by women this adds insult to injury, and joins the increasing battery of anti equality measures emanating from the Coalition that is far outweighing its positive actions.'

How, precisely, do feminists manage to wield such influence, other than through the unfortunately energetic ladies at the Fawcett Society? In the remainder of this chapter I speculate on the matter.

Men don't campaign for their collective interests: they have no interest in gender politics

Men have perfectly legitimate collective interests, but because they don't act collectively and campaign for them to be recognised, politicians can safely ignore them. Politicians legislate against men's collective interests in the knowledge that men will just put up with it. To be discriminated against is the lot of men in the modern era; to complain about the situation remains unmanly. So women are free to carry on collectively manipulating men. They can rely on men of all political persuasions to support them, or at the very least not challenge them.

Men are starting to recognise that they are being discriminated against in terms of job recruitment and promotion. My hope is that this will, in time, make them interested in gender politics, and a long overdue backlash will finally begin.

Political correctness has triumphed

For all the criticism levelled against political correctness, you might have expected it to wither away and die. But you'd be wrong; it's alive and well and controlling the thinking of many British citizens, and most politicians, on a daily basis. Maybe it's partly the result of 13 years of a dismal Labour administration with the likes of Harriet Harman in senior positions.

The first rule of political correctness is that women – as a class, and individually – are beyond criticism. The second is that their interests must be furthered by any means: given the nature of the perceived injustice, either equality or special treatment will usually suffice.

Men and women are delusional; business people aren't immune

Whilst researching for this book I spoke to a number of former business associates and colleagues, both men and women, who had worked for many years at senior levels in the business world. Without telling them the theses I planned to put forward in the book, I asked them for their general thoughts about the genders at senior levels in business. Talking as if on some form of mental auto-pilot, most said that women were as capable as men of succeeding in senior positions, and they were confident that over time the number of women in Britain's boardrooms would rise inexorably, leading to gender balance in Britain's boardrooms in the fullness of time.

Then I asked them for their *personal* experiences of men and women in business. It turned out, to my surprise, that almost all of them shared my own experience, including:

- women are more interested in work-life balance than men, so they're less interested in competing for senior positions
- women find it more difficult than men to make the tough decisions required in senior-level positions, especially with respect to firing people
- women are more likely than men to suffer adverse reactions to the stress which inevitably accompanies senior roles
- women are more likely than men to bail out of senior positions, partly because they're more likely than men to have the option of doing so, due to their partners being willing to finance the option
- women are highly risk-averse and loathe to make decisions which might be criticised

I then asked my former colleagues how they might explain the discrepancies between the views they'd earlier expressed about men and women in the workplace, and their personal experience. After considering the question for a time, most of the men said they had assumed their personal experience was untypical. The women said it was an unspoken rule for women to point out and criticise the common failings of men, but not those of women. In the business world this translated into a tendency to claim that women's failings, if and when noticed, were *not* characteristic of women. An example of any 'female typical' characteristic could always be found among some men, thereby neutralising the claim.

Big business has no representation against militant feminism

One organisation above all represents big business in Britain, and has long been considered 'the voice of business' in its dealings with politicians: the CBI, the Confederation of British Industries. It has a President – Helen Alexander – who had a successful career in business. A good start, but then one notes on their website, a lady Director whose biography runs as follows:[1]

> '[Name supplied] is responsible for leading the CBI's work on employment, employee relations, pensions and diversity. She was previously Head of Employee Relations and Diversity, responsible for the CBI's work on trade union issues, dispute resolution, working time, diversity and family-friendly policies. Prior to this, [name supplied] worked in employee relations and HR Policy at the BBC and as head of Employee Resourcing at the CBI, covering pay and pensions, labour market flexibility, welfare reform and sickness absence.
>
> [Name supplied] is a member of the Ethnic Minority Employment Taskforce, the Fair Employment Enforcement Board and the Employment Tribunal Steering Board. She is also a member of the Social Affairs Committee of BUSINESSEUROPE, the European Employers' Organisation and chairs its Employment and Skills Working Group.'

Diversity… family-friendly policies… ethnic minorities… fair employment enforcement… How can an employers' organisation both campaign in these areas and also represent its membership, which will surely be in firm opposition to social engineering agendas such as increasing boardroom diversity and eliminating the gender pay gap? It can't, of course. In this

[1] http://cbi.org.uk

area, at least, the CBI is not representing but campaigning; which might be fine for the women in the organisations they represent, but what about the men?

No organisations exist to counter the arguments of feminist campaigning organisations

In the absence of such organisations the militant feminists have an open goal to kick into. Woe betide any politician who dared to publicly criticise organisations such as the Fawcett Society. The simple fact is, however, that such organisations *have no democratic mandate*. Why, then, are they permitted – encouraged, even – to wield such influence on our political processes?

Men are more reasonable than women

Men are by nature more reasonable than women; they know a working balance has to be struck between opposing interests. Women don't have this sense of a need for balance. Their instinct is always to want more: more money, more clothes, more free time, more everything. In the political field, feminist politicians relentlessly seek more power. They will *never* be content.

Harriet Harman exhausted her colleagues

How did Harriet Harman manage to exert so much woeful influence over Labour administrations' gender agendas between 1997 and 2010? I suspect it was largely a matter of personality. She's a sterling example of the sort of women whose long-suffering husbands mutter in a weary tone, 'Yes, dear'.

I doubt if such women know why they generally get what they want in life. Maybe they flatter themselves that they're 'strong'. But the reality is that when faced with the zeal of such women, most people – and almost all men – rapidly lose the will to live, and will say or do *anything* to stop the relentless torrent of words. 'What's that, Harriet? The boards of Britain's major companies should better reflect the diversity of British citizens in terms of weight, height, eye colour, and IQ? Another brilliant idea! How do you keep thinking of them?'

39 | THE FEMINIST ASSAULT ON
THE ENGLISH LANGUAGE

Don't you see that the whole aim of Newspeak is to narrow the range of thought? In the end we shall make thoughtcrime literally impossible, because there will be no words in which to express it.
George Orwell 1903-1950 English novelist, journalist, literary critic and poet: *Nineteen Eighty-Four* (1949)

Feminist thinking impacts upon the bedrock of the English language, major dictionaries. Because I like to complete *The Daily Telegraph* cryptic crosswords and I'm fond of the odd game of Scrabble, I own *The Chambers Dictionary*, more specifically the 1993 edition. I see the 12th edition has recently been published (August 2011). I wonder if it's the testament to political correctness that the 1993 edition is.

The Managing Editor of the 1993 edition is Catherine S. The Chambers lexicographers are named as George D, Elaine H, Susan R, Mairi R and Anne S, while the 'external lexicographers' are named as Kay C (and The Sunshine Band, presumably), Virginia K, Ruth M and Howard S. So that's eight women and two men, which must put the dictionary's publisher in line for a Harriet Harman Award for Gender Balance in the Workplace.

Catherine S and most of her colleagues are editresses. Rowan Pelling, the former editress of *The Erotic Review*, used to term herself an editrix. The good ladies of *The Chambers Dictionary* (1993) sniffily dismiss the term 'editress' as 'archaic', and don't even recognise the word 'editrix'.

40| EQUALITY, HAPPINESS, PHYSICAL AND MENTAL HEALTH

What makes equality such a difficult business is that we only want it with our superiors.
Henry Becque 1837-99 French dramatist and critic: *Querelles littéraires* (1890)

March 2009 must have been a happy month to be a Leftie, for that was the month in which a book was published comparing countries around the world and concluding there were strong causal links between inequality and a host of undesirable societal outcomes such as increased physical and mental health problems, crime etc. The book, co-authored by two British epidemiologists, Richard Wilkinson and Kate Pickett, was *The Spirit Level: Why More Equal Societies Almost Always Do Better*. It was published as a paperback in February 2010 with the slightly more confident title *The Spirit Level: Why Equality is Better for Everyone*.

The book called for a radical shift in power from the individual to the state based on the supposedly devastating effects of wealth, economic growth and inequality. Predictably, the book was seized upon by prominent Lefties as providing empirical proof of what they'd been asserting for many years.

In April 2010 a critique of the book's arguments was published by the Democracy Institute, *The Spirit Level Delusion: Fact-Checking the Left's New Theory of Everything*. The book was written by Christopher Snowdon, a British history graduate and author. The book's Introduction ends with the following:

> '*The Spirit Level* offered a whole new way of looking at politics. Almost by accident, it seemed, two sober and disinterested scientists had proven beyond reasonable doubt that narrowing the wealth gap and restricting economic growth

was the panacea for all social ills. The implications could scarcely be exaggerated and its authors had no intention of playing them down. Comparing their findings to those of Louis Pasteur and Joseph Lister, they wrote: 'Understanding the effects of inequality means that we suddenly have a policy handle on the wellbeing of whole societies.'

There was just one problem. In political terms it wasn't a huge problem. Greater obstacles had been overcome in the past and yet, for sticklers and pedants, it remained a problem. It wasn't true.'

The book is an intriguing read and I urge you to buy it. The author successfully demonstrates that the apparently scientific conclusions of *The Spirit Level* largely rely on ignoring sources of data which conflict with the conclusions of the book, and ignoring a range of explanations which are more plausible than inequality for the different outcomes in different countries. In almost all areas *The Spirit Level Delusion* indicates an inverse correlation between greater equality and health and other outcomes, although it's careful not to claim a causal relationship. From the final chapter:

'In the case of life expectancy, homicide, 'happiness', mental illness and obesity, there is no association with inequality whatsoever. In terms of divorce, crime, alcohol consumption, smoking, single-parent households and suicide, the more equal countries appear to do worse.'

The writers of *The Spirit Level* believe that high income differentials drive 'status anxiety', although a more obvious cause of that anxiety might arguably be the envy that is central to Leftie thinking, and would therefore be expected to be restricted to Lefties. Snowdon makes an interesting point:

'The anti-consumerists and the inequality theorists, I would suggest, vastly exaggerate the psychological damage of these normal human emotions. In doing so, they patronise and infantilise the people they purport to be defending. Most of us come to terms with the fact that some people have more money than us at a young age, just as most teenagers come to terms with the fact that they will never be professional footballers or supermodels.'

A nuance that seems to have evaded the numerous – and generally prosperous – Leftie writers of books on happiness and the modern capitalist world, is that for one group in society at least there *is* a relationship between inequality and unhappiness: Lefties themselves. Why should we be concerned with that? Inequality isn't a problem for normal people.

The parallels with feminism are obvious. Feminists are fond of asserting that increasing the power wielded by women will result in their becoming happier. Women as a group have undoubtedly been wielding ever more power – especially economic power – with each passing decade, for perhaps the past five decades in much of the developed world. I know of no study that suggests women over this period have become happier, and most studies indicate that women have become *less* happy.

It's long been known that women are more prone to depression than men, and in an earlier chapter we read Professor Louann Brizendine's biological explanation for this fact. It appears that the differential in depression rates between men and women has remained fairly constant despite so many women in the developed world having left the home for paid employment, which Betty Friedan and others of her outlook would presumably have expected to result in *less* unhappiness.

Medical researchers have accumulated a good deal of data on the incidence of depression over the past few decades and there is a general consensus that it hasn't reduced over that time; most researchers maintain that it has increased markedly. Some writers – including the British clinical psychologist and Oliver James – maintain that depression is far more common in the modern era than, say, in the 1950s.

The extent to which diagnosis plays a part in this is uncertain. It could be that a person who would have been regarded as sad half a century ago – and possibly sad for perfectly understandable reasons – and expected to 'pull themselves together', might today be regarded as depressed and in need of medical intervention. There's a school of thought that says the high levels of diagnosis of depression in the modern era are very convenient for the manufacturers of anti-depressants, as the English author Dr Vernon Coleman pointed out in his bestselling book *How To Stop Your Doctor Killing You.*

But shouldn't more equality lead to more happiness, as argued in *The Spirit Level?* Almost all the popular writers on the topic of happiness are Lefties. Is it not reasonable to assume that some of the things that make people of one political persuasion happy, may make people of a different persuasion unhappy?

Divorce is, of course, markedly more common in the modern era than in previous eras. Might this have at least something to do with feminist outlooks on the relations between the genders? An interesting account of the possible relationships between depression, 'gender rancour', and divorce was put forward by English author Oliver James in his book *Britain on the Couch: Treating a Low Serotonin Society* (1998):

> 'DEPRESSION AND GENDER RANCOUR
> There are sound scientific, as well as anecdotal, grounds for supposing that the increases in depression and aggression since 1950 have resulted in a rancorous disharmony between the sexes. That there is so much more recorded violent crime

is a self-evident indication that aggression has increased. The role of increased depression is a less commonsensical indicator of increased rancour.

DEPRESSED PEOPLE MAKE DEPRESSING, HOSTILE PARTNERS

Until the publication of Myrna Weissman's classic 1974 account (co-authored with Eugene Paykel) of *The Depressed Woman*, it was widely assumed that depressed people were passive and withdrawn (it should be stressed that most of Weissman's findings probably apply to depressed men as well). Their aggression was turned against themselves, as was evident in the savage negativity they displayed towards themselves mentally, and at its most extreme, in the physical attacks they made against their bodies, not just in suicide attempts, but in such self-destructive illnesses as the eating disorders bulimia and anorexia nervosa, both of which are more common among the depressed.

The assumption was that outwardly directed hostility must be reduced since it is all turned against the self. However, this view had to be modified after Weissman's careful comparison of 40 depressed women with 40 nondepressed ones. It showed that depressed women are anything but unaggressive in intimate relationships. They displayed 'significantly more overt interpersonal hostility in most relationships, and the intensity of these feelings ranged from resentment, general irritability, through arguments of increasing intensity, to physical encounters.'

The brunt of this hostility was borne by their children, with whom they had twice as much friction as their spouses. However, they were also significantly more hostile to their spouses than to their extended family members, friends and professional colleagues: 'Marital relationships become an arena for the depression and are characterised by friction, poor communication, dependency and diminished sexual satisfaction. The depressed woman feels a lack of affection towards her husband together with guilt and resentment. Communication is poor and hostility overt.'

That this marked viciousness was confined to intimates explained why researchers had not noticed the pattern before. Not being intimates, the researchers doing the studies did not evoke it: 'The depressed patient's behaviour at interview is a poor sample of her actual behaviour outside. In the initial psychiatric interview she is cooperative, compliant and not hostile.'

Given that depressives are like this, the finding that depressives create unhappiness in their intimates is no surprise. Partners of depressives are themselves more likely to be depressed, to get ill, to abuse alcohol and to commit both suicide and homicide. The relationship suffers. Compared with couples where neither party is depressed, in couples with one depressive, the depressed one is more likely to be domineering and overbearingly insistent in solving disputes. The couple are likely to use destructive methods for doing so, to feel miserable about their relationship, be secretive and uncommunicative and provide little support to each other.

This miserable list could double up as a fair definition of the word 'rancour'. Given that there has been a large increase in the number of such depressed adults, it is almost certain that there has been a concomitant increase in the number of disharmonious couples and therefore, in the amount of gender rancour.

DOES DEPRESSION CAUSE DIVORCE, OR VICE VERSA?

An important effect of such increased rancour may be on the divorce rate – itself an important cause of the increase in depression since 1950. One study of 56 married depressives followed over a two-year period found they were nine times more likely to have divorced than the general population. Not only do couples with a depressive member show more disharmony, they are more at risk of divorce. This is not surprising if depression is such a powerful cause of gender rancour. At the same time, as noted above, other studies show that marital disharmony and divorce are a cause as well as an effect of depression. Disentangling them is not done easily and there are two very different theories.

The first, which became extremely fashionable during the 1960s and 1970s and remains dominant today, is the 'marital compatibility' view. Troubled marriages are seen as the product of ineffectual communication patterns resulting from personal incompatibility. John Gottman, for example, asked over 100 newly-wed couples to pick a perennial bone of contention between them and videotaped the ensuing discussion. How they dealt with the problem predicted whether they were still together four years later. In this view, successful marriage is a case of finding the right person for you and making sure that destructive patterns of problem-solving do not develop – unsuccessful marriages cause depression.

That this perspective became so popular during a period (after 1960) when millions of dissatisfied husbands and wives were asking themselves if they were with the right partner may be no coincidence. The perspective is also supported by considerable evidence and there is little doubt that unhappy marriages can cause previously stable and well-adjusted individuals to develop depression and other problems. However, this view has become so dominant that the alternative has been almost totally forgotten: that emotional problems, often dating back to childhood, in one or both of the partners could cause the marital problems. In this view, there are people whose personalities would have put them at high risk of divorce whoever they had married.

As one author bluntly put it back in 1935, 'One would hardly expect a man and a woman, both highly neurotic, to achieve a very high order of marital happiness.' In order to test this theory properly a study would ideally have followed a large sample from childhood to late adulthood. Only then would it be clear how much any emotional problems during marriage preceded the union. No studies have gone as far back as that, but there are no fewer than seven which tested the personalities of couples before they married and followed up what happened to them subsequently. In all of these, 'neuroticism' (in these studies, 'neuroticism' includes mild or more severe depression as part of its definition) and lack of 'impulse control' (in the male partner) predicted subsequent disharmony and divorce compared with people without these traits before marriage.

There are also several other studies suggesting that males with poor impulse control are more likely to have marital problems (it may be recalled that low impulse control correlates strongly with low levels of serotonin). To this can be added a British study which found that high neuroticism among girls at age 16 predicted subsequent increased risk of divorce. . .

To some, the idea that depressed, neurotic and impulsive people are more at risk of divorce might seem to be plain old-fashioned common sense. But so deep rooted is our reluctance to 'stigmatise' individuals that we dare not suggest that one individual has got a problem. Rather, we blame it on The Relationship. Others might also feel that it may be true but best left unsaid since it seems very negative. Yet many marriages might be greatly helped by this understanding. Where one individual is clearly suffering from depression, rather than encouraging both to agonise over their compatibility, it can be extremely helpful for the disturbed person to seek treatment for their individual angst. It is particularly so with depressives, who (as Weissman's and subsequent studies prove) are especially liable to be paranoid and to blame everything on their intimates and then to launch a barrage of hostility and aggression towards them. The 'personal incompatibility' model is very convenient for such people but they may find the same problems recurring with subsequent partners – divorcees are more likely to divorce if they remarry than first-time unions.

This is not to say that incompatibility never happens or that there are not men and women who treat each other intolerably badly and for whom divorce is the only sane response. Both statements are true, and incompatibility and poor communication skills remain well-established causes of divorce. It is simply that the emphasis on relationship rather than individual pathology has been so all-consuming in recent years that it is important to redress the balance in explaining divorce.

RELATING THE INDIVIDUAL TRAIT PERSPECTIVE TO THE RISE IN DEPRESSION, RANCOUR AND DIVORCE SINCE 1950

The Individual Trait approach helps a great deal in explaining this rise.

Firstly, given that there has been a large increase in depression since 1950 and given that we know depressives are hostile and aggressive partners and that they have higher rates of divorce, it could be that the increase in depressed people has partly directly caused the increase in divorce.

Secondly, we saw in the last chapter that the divorce increase is also due to a significant extent to changes in values, especially to changing sex roles, increased individualism and increased expectations of relationships as a source of gratification. It seems highly probable that the new freedoms and accompanying values will not have affected everyone in the same way.

Neurotic and impulsive people may always have had a greater risk of unhappy marriages but in the past have been protected by social pressures from expressing them in ultimately self-destructive attacks on their marriages. Furthermore, such people may have been made even more neurotic and impulsive by the excitement and overheated expectations of the prevailing *zeitgeist*. This might have caused their marriages to become even unhappier and increased the likelihood of divorce in an era when it was fashionable to believe the relationship was to blame and there was a better partner somewhere out there just waiting to meet you.

Thus, the rise in depression, the increase in gender rancour and the ascending divorce rate may have all impacted on each other to create a firestorm of rage and despair.'

41 | MEN'S DEFERENCE
TOWARDS WOMEN

Arguments out of a pretty mouth are unanswerable.
Joseph Addison 1672 - 1719 English essayist, poet, playwright and politician: 'Women and Liberty'

Most men have an innate deference towards women, and this is a tricky area for feminists. On the one hand they maintain that men are hard-wired to be aggressive towards women so as to exert power over them, and to be prone to hurting them (or at least to threaten to). The reality is that female-on-male domestic violence is at least as common as male-on-female domestic violence for all degrees of severity, as we saw in an earlier chapter.

On the other hand, feminists cannot deny the reality they see all about them, as men open doors for women and engage in countless acts of kindness towards them.

As with everything else which poses a difficulty for their ugly creed, feminists – who see all gender relations in terms of exerting power – have a pat explanation for men's deference towards women, calling it 'benevolent sexism'. Men are evil if they're threatening towards women, and also evil if they're… er… kind towards them.

For years some women were cross when men used the terms 'Miss' or 'Mrs' to denote a woman's marital status, so feminists came up with the useful term 'Ms', possibly the one intelligent idea feminists have ever came up with. Needless to say, some women objected to the term 'Ms'. So now you're likely to upset a woman if you use the terms Miss, Mrs or Ms. Maybe men should just refer to women as 'Sweetheart' when talking to them, though doubtless feminists would find something to object to even then.

For many years women in the United Kingdom retired five years earlier than men despite women having a markedly longer life expectancy than men, and men being more likely than women to be engaged in heavy physical work. So a secretary could retire at 60 while a man digging the roads would have to work until he reached 65.

At the time of writing the government has recently introduced sizeable tuition fees for university students, which will be paid for by government loans repayable by deductions from salaries when the individuals start to earn over £21,000 p.a. After 30 years any outstanding sums will be written off. Government estimates based on current employment statistics suggest that more than twice as many women as men will have at least part of their debts written off in this way. Who'll pay the balance? The taxpayer, which means mainly men, given women's relatively greater propensity either to work part-time or not to undertake paid employment.

If anyone should be campaigning for more equality it should be men, not women. Feminists say they want equality when what they *really* want is ever more special treatment.

42| WERE THE SUFFRAGETTES SILLY?

The argument of the broken pane of glass is the most valuable argument in modern politics.
Emmeline Pankhurst 1858-1928 English suffragette leader: George Dangerfield *The Strange Death of Liberal England* (1936)

I'm informed that one of the words applied to some women, which most annoys feminists, is 'silly'. Could it be that women find the word offensive precisely *because* they're only too painfully aware that a proportion of women *are* silly? In the interest of balance, I must concede that silly men exist too; but the proportion of men who are silly is substantially smaller than the proportion of women who are silly, as recent research carried out by a team of psychologists at the University of Wakefield has convincingly demonstrated.

Only silly people could believe in astrology, for example, and *all* the people I know who believe in it are women. Even my mother believes in astrology – albeit 'not the daily paper variety', she asks me to point out – despite being perfectly sane in other respects. I've a strong hunch that male astrologers, male psychics, male spiritualists and all the other male charlatans are only in it for the money, and they laugh all the way to the bank. *Literally* at the expense of women.

In former times people in positions of power – men, obviously – were less reticent about recognising the silliness of some women, and their lack of interest in politics in particular. When did the pretence that women have any interest in politics (beyond "women's issues") begin? Political movement towards women's suffrage in the United Kingdom began before the First World War, and in 1918 Parliament passed an act (the Representation of the People Act) granting the vote to women over the age of 30 who were householders, the wives of householders, occupiers of property with an annual rent of £5 or more, and graduates of British universities. Women in the United Kingdom finally achieved suffrage on the same terms as men in 1928. [Update: William Collins, an important British blogger on gender issues, published an insightful piece on this subject, 'Universal Suffrage in the UK'.[1]]

The suffragettes are among the great icons of feminism, so I was interested to learn more about their movement in Steve Moxon's *The Woman Racket*:

> 'The cry of 'votes for women', in great contrast to the brutal suppression of various movements through history which could be characterised as 'votes for ordinary men' (notably the Chartists, little more than half a century before), was a push at an open door. Parliament had been long persuaded of the case, despite the lack of popular demand for female suffrage. The tactic of the suffragettes was counter-productively to try to kick the door in. What is not appreciated today is that it was directly as a result of suffragette militancy that legislation for universal suffrage was not hastened but *delayed*, and introduced not in full but in two stages.
>
> The female suffragist cause was an extremely well-to-do affair generally: not middle- but *upper*-class. The only places in the country where there was any significant involvement by working-class women were some of the Lancashire textile towns. Everywhere else it was characterised by the absence of a working-class or of even a middle-class element, in contrast to other political movements at the time. Very well politically-connected, wealthy, and titled women made up the Women's Social & Political Union. Far from being the case that ordinary women were clamouring for the vote, there was general indifference, as Gladstone, prime minister at the time, remarked.
>
> Militancy confirmed the one fear the general population had about the female franchise – irresponsible behaviour by those who would be newly enfranchised. The twin concerns that the movement needed to address – being unrepresentative and

---

[1] http://mra-uk.co.uk/?p=271

irresponsible – were exactly the concerns that the suffragettes haplessly highlighted and confirmed.

This was of little if any consequence to the suffragettes, because through their connections they well knew they were nonetheless secure in that parliamentary opinion was substantially in favour of women getting the vote, despite MPs knowing that there was little support in the country. They were simply playing at politics, and managed to turn newspapers from offering almost uniform open support to being obliged to attack their methods.

The onset of militancy in 1908 spawned The Ladies League for Opposing Women's Suffrage, which by 1914 boasted 42,000 members. They appealed over the heads of the politicians by canvassing female local government electors, whom they found *consistently opposed to female suffrage by a factor of four to one* [Author's italics], but this had no impact on MPs.

As women, and even more so as well-to-do women, the suffragettes knew full well that they were immune from physical harm, regardless of what they did. The sole fatality in the campaign, Emily Davison, was a well-to-do woman too out of touch with the real world to know that the King's racehorse would not be made to stop simply by jumping out from the rail and standing in front of it. Suicide it was not, it is now known. Suffragettes, unlike Chartists and their ilk, never needed to be brave. They never needed even to fear loss of any reputation. A night or more in the cells was generally seen as a badge of honour, as suffragettes had *carte blanche* to be shameless.

Unabashed by the fact that men were dying in huge numbers in a war over which half of all men had been denied the expression of any opinion whatsoever; throughout World War I, Sylvia Pankhurst campaigned undaunted, along with The Women's Freedom League. Pankhurst set up a 'League of Rights for Soldiers' and Sailors' Wives and Relatives'. This focus away from those who were the real sufferers, is exemplified in an absurd statement by Isabella Ford, writing in 1915: 'Women have more to lose in the horrible business than some men have; for they often lose more than life itself when their men are killed.'

Two leading suffragette organisations did agree to suspend their window breaking, arson, policemen-hitting and the like, right from the start of WWI, when they realised that their campaign would be seen to be a disgrace. The leader of the whole movement, Emmeline Pankhurst, with her daughter Christabel, toured the country speaking at meetings to recruit young men into the army. Christabel wrote of her mother: 'She called for wartime conscription for men, believing that this was democratic and equitable'.

Did she also think it democratic that her supporters handed white feathers to every young man they encountered wearing civilian dress? These would be those reserved for essential heavy industrial work, government employees, those too unfit for service, boys too young to enlist, and convalescents from physical or psychological wounding, as well as those very few men who had indeed taken the sure route to total social ostracism and punishment beatings by declaring themselves conscientious objectors.

These last would not include Emmeline's daughter, Sylvia, because being a woman she was free to actively campaign against the war effort with impunity. But her mother's white feather brigade contributed to so many children lying about their age in order to enlist, making them even more likely to be killed than the average soldier, on account of the extra vulnerability of their impetuous youth.

It cannot have been unknown to Emmeline, the foremost and most well-known suffragette of all, that even by 1914 and the start of World War One, half of adult men were still not entitled to vote; and that therefore they had no say in the political process that brought about Britain's involvement in the war.

For the first part of the war, soldiers were not called up but volunteered, albeit under massive social pressure. Conscription would mean that all men below a certain age could be forced into a situation where they could be ordered to take part in attacks in which they faced a very good chance of being killed or seriously wounded, in a war which overall they stood a high chance of not surviving, and an even better chance of being maimed and so unable to live a normal life afterwards. This would apply disproportionately to those men without the vote, because conscription had an upper age limit of forty-five.

The subset of younger men aged 21 – 45 was made up of those within the electorate less likely to have established themselves in terms of tenancy, property ownership or residence – the very criteria by which many would have failed to be enfranchised. How could Emmeline Pankhurst of all people have had the hypocrisy to actively campaign for conscription at a time when the majority of those who would be conscripted did not have the vote?

Militancy was not the women suffragists' worst blunder. This was that they saw themselves as quite separate from, and unhelped or even hindered by, progressive male enfranchisement. They repeatedly demanded that the next step should be purely in regard to women. The root of their difficulties was a false belief that there was no clamour amongst the working classes for extending the male vote.

They could not have been more wrong. Presumably, they must have falsely extrapolated from the indifference of working-class women for votes for themselves to imagine that enfranchisement was generally not an issue for the whole working class. In fact, the male franchise was a big issue for working men, and their women supported them. This delusion was motivated by something worse than that the women suffragists simply did not care about the extent of adult male suffrage.

A common theme in the movement, on both sides of the Atlantic, was that the vote initially should be extended to women through an education qualification. The converse of this was also argued, and quite openly: that *uneducated men should be denied the vote.*

The suffragettes wanted first and foremost an elitist enfranchisement of themselves to join the men of their own upper- and upper-middle classes, and only argued for universal *female* suffrage because it was more politically expedient. Their second preferred option was to give way and allow the vote for the entire 'sisterhood', but only if there was qualified voting for men. The sentiment was here perhaps a little less elitist but decidedly separatist, betraying the common attitude of women of being not only anti-male per se, but just against the majority of lower-status men. This is why women prominent in the Labour movement at the time were not persuaded by the suffragettes and stuck to campaigning for adult suffrage and not for a separate bill for women.

The wider perception was that the suffragettes created a needless divide between the sexes, and in the years before politicians were fully persuaded the tactic of an initial partial extension of franchise for women backfired. It alerted politicians that gallantry could be aroused to concede the vote to a section of the female population, and this would then act as a Trojan horse for a complete capitulation to democratic rule by the masses.

The elitism of the suffragettes' demands is even more apparent when you consider that these privileged women were married to men who often already provided *two* votes for the household in having a business as well as a residence qualification. Upper-class or upper-middle-class women felt aggrieved not so much that their husbands or the husbands of friends (if they were in business or academia) could command two votes to their none, but that the vote had been accorded to other men beneath their social milieu. This is the reason for campaigning for a male educational qualification. Ladies of leisure received an education (falsely) regarded as superior to the technical education of upper-working-class men, so this was a ticket with which to maintain social differentials.

After 1918 the observation was made by one politician that full male suffrage had taken 600 years to achieve, so why should female suffrage take only ten? But the overriding male deference to women as ever ruled the day. Influential men joined in the women's campaign, and the wider 'chivalrous' principle was allowed to overcome what in any other matter considered by government would have been continuing inertia. Yet this issue concerned the very survival of the elected members of political parties themselves. Any proposed changes to the electoral system make political parties extremely wary. Albeit that the Rubicon had been crossed in 1918; with politics in some turmoil the unpredictable effect of the entire mass of young women suddenly joining the electoral roll must have given politicians of all parties some worry. The underlying reason for the short delay, was to see what the great change in the franchise of 1918 would lead to. After being sure that the destabilisation was containable, only then could MPs responsibly proceed further. Ten years, and just a couple of elections, would have been a minimum period to assess this.'

I urge you to buy *The Woman Racket* but before you start reading it – if you're a man, anyway – stock up well with anti-depressants or whisky, whichever of the two helps get you through this vale of tears the feminists have created.

43 | WOULD PATRIARCHAL HEGEMONY BE SUCH A BAD THING?

Women's suffrage will, I believe, be the ruin of our Western civilisation. It will destroy the home, challenging the headship of men laid down by God. It may come in your time – I hope not in mine.
John Dillon 1851-1927 Irish nationalist politician c.1912, to a deputation led by Hanna Sheehy Skeffington: Diana Norman *Terrible Beauty* (1987)

Given that we appear to be rushing headlong towards a grim future of matriarchal hegemony, we can all agree at least that patriarchal hegemony would be the lesser of two evils, can't we? Can you imagine living in a country where Harriet Harman is the prime minister? Nor I. A friend once had a nightmare which involved her. It took three months of therapy before he could function normally, and he's still not quite right. His head twitches at the mere mention of her name.

My friend dreamed he was a Cabinet minister and Harman was chairing a Cabinet meeting, the first in her new role as prime minister. The meeting took place in the context of a national emergency, and the atmosphere was tense. As the meeting was about to begin, in an effort to lighten the mood, a fellow minister remarked out loud to Ms Harman, 'Harriet, may I kick off proceedings by remarking on how very *pretty* you're looking this morning?' Whereupon she frowned and drew a .44 Magnum revolver [Author's note: The gun used by Clint Eastwood in *Dirty Harry*] from her handbag, slowly took aim, and shot his right arm off at the shoulder. She then glared around the table at the other ministers and growled, 'Does anyone *else* think I'm looking pretty this morning?' They stared glumly at their papers and mumbled, 'No, prime minister.'

44 | THE DREADED 'C' WORD

How important it is for us to recognize and celebrate our heroes and she-roes!
Maya Angelou (1928 -) American authoress and poet

While I was carrying out research for *The Glass Ceiling Delusion* I encountered the website of the Feminist and Women's Studies Association:[1]

> 'The FWSA is a UK-based network promoting feminist research and teaching, and women's studies nationally and internationally. Through its elected executive committee, the FWSA is involved in developing policy on issues of central importance to feminist scholars in further and higher education, supporting postgraduate events and enabling feminist research. Committed to raising awareness of women's studies, feminist research and women-related issues in secondary and tertiary education, the FWSA liaises regularly with other gender-related research and community networks as well as with policy groups.'

The website was promoting two seminars, one of which is relevant to this chapter:

'**Experiencing and Celebrating Fatness**
Bigness Beyond Obesity: Seminar 3

ESRC seminar series: Fat Studies and HAES

18th-19th November 2010, London (The Hopkins Room, Stratford Library, 3 The Grove, Stratford, London E15 1EL).

This seminar will address the intersection between Fat Studies, Health At Every Size and fat activism. It will explore individuals' experiences of activism, sites for intervention, and

---

[1] http://fwsa.wordpress.com

the possibilities for fat activism in relation to health and beyond. There will be a combination of presentations and workshop activities.'

Beneath the details of the seminar were a number of relevant Google advertisements. My eye was caught by one with the title, 'Lose 7lbs of ugly body fat every week!' Another was for gastric bands.

The seminar was sponsored by the ESRC, the Economic and Social Research Council, which derives most of its funding from the Department for Business, Innovation and Skills, which in turn derives its funding from long-suffering British taxpayers. What seminars might logically follow on from 'Experiencing and Celebrating Fatness'? Obvious contenders include 'Experiencing and Celebrating Ugliness' and 'Experiencing and Celebrating Stupidity'.

It doesn't take a leap of imagination to suppose that every one of the women 'celebrating fatness' would give their back teeth to be slim; they simply aren't prepared to do what it takes to become slim.

For a time I planned to title this book *Feminism: Crones' Disease*. We should perhaps not be surprised that some women celebrate being crones, and a Google search using the word 'crone' led me to the 'Triple Goddess' philosophy wherein – if I have this right – women are a combination of the three different forms of the Goddess at different points in their lives, namely Maiden, Mother, and Wise Woman. The Wise Woman is sometimes referred to as the 'Hag' or 'Crone', and the general idea seems to be that women acquire wisdom with age. I suppose to an extent all people acquire *some* wisdom with age, but wisdom is of course a very slippery attribute, easy to apply to oneself. It's seemingly being used by some women to bring comfort in the light of their physical unattractiveness.

A number of websites clearly make an association between being a feminist and being a crone, in an admiring way, and some of the ladies in question proudly put their photographs on their websites, to dispel any possibility of argument. So might there be an association between unattractiveness and wisdom? Unfortunately for these ladies, evolutionary theory suggests otherwise. There are a number of attributes deemed attractive by men in addition to facial attractiveness, and they include height and intelligence, both indicators of evolutionary 'fitness'. Studies have shown a positive correlation between IQ and height. It's not looking good for the crones.

A number of books cover the issue of crones, and *Maiden, Mother, Crone* – written by Deanna 'DJ' Conway – was published in 1984. From Amazon.com:

> 'Deanna Conway (born 1939) is a non-fiction author of books in the field of magic, Wicca, Druidism, shamanism, metaphysics and the occult, and the author of three fantasy novels. Born in Hood River, Oregon to a family of Irish, North Germanic, and Native North American descent, she has been studying the occult and Pagan religion for over thirty years. In 1998 she was voted Best Wiccan and New Age author by Silver Chalice, a Neo-Pagan magazine. She is an ordained minister in two New Age churches and holder of a Doctor of Divinity degree. Several of her stories have been published in magazines, such as the science fantasy publication *Encounters*, and she has been interviewed in magazines and appeared on such television shows as Journey with Brenda Roberts. She has also designed Tarot decks, in collaboration with fellow author Sirona Knight and illustrator Lisa Hunt.
>
> The Triple Goddess is with every one of us [Author's note: Possibly not *every* one of us] each day of our lives. In our inner journeys toward spiritual evolution, each woman and man goes through the stages of Maiden (infant to puberty), Mother (adult and parent), and Crone (aging elder)…
>
> *Maiden, Mother, Crone* reveals the vital interconnections of all the diverse and glorious myths and archetypes of the

Goddess. In this book you'll meet Siren, Ceres, Freyja, and a host of others. You'll learn to interpret the symbolism of their myths as models that you can follow to develop your inner strength, spiritual growth, and understanding in twentieth-century life.

Maiden, Mother, Crone introduces the concept of the Labyrinth, a journey where you learn to face past emotional upheavals, become responsible for your actions and reactions, and accept all aspects of the cycle of life. The Labyrinth can be traversed with the knowledge and balance provided by the Goddess. This book shares the rituals, meditations, and techniques that will make the journey possible.

Maiden, Mother, Crone also helps you use the Goddess for guidance in day-to-day experiences. You'll discover the meanings of hundreds of symbols that occur in myths, legends, and your own dreams, allowing you to identify symbolic messages that the Goddess wants you to know.

Maiden, Mother, Crone provides a full explanation of the myths of the Triple Goddess from around the world, making this the most complete book on the subject ever. Get it today for a more beautiful tomorrow. [Author's note: I *shall*.]'

In my forties I slept regularly with a priest over the course of a couple of years. Now that may not be an admission you'd be shocked to find coming from a man who was schooled by priests in single-sex Roman Catholic boarding schools in England between the ages of seven and sixteen, as I was, but I have an innocent explanation. In my mid-forties, as a divorced man, I had a relationship with a Scottish woman who was a priest' in a California-based New Age 'church'. The 'church' didn't permit its priests to divulge anything about the organisation, but from the little I gathered, it charged for courses all aimed at achieving states of spiritual enlightenment. The 'highest' spiritual state – said to be equivalent to that achieved by Jesus Christ and Buddha – had been achieved by only the three people running the organisation and all three of them were men. It rankled with the lady that no women had yet achieved the highest spiritual state in her church.

It struck me at the time that becoming a priest in a New Age church was an exercise in self-aggrandisement, and making such positions available at a price was a lucrative business for those at the top of the organisation.

There seems little that some women won't celebrate but the idea of celebrating crones surprised even me. A Google search led me quickly to numerous websites with references to crones.[1, 2, 3]

---

[1] http://spiralgoddess.com/CroneMoon.html
[2] http://women-at-heart.com/crone-story.html
[3] http://tinyurl.com/maidenmothercrone

45 | THE DREADED 'S' WORD

When we are capable of living in the moment free from the tyranny of 'shoulds', free from the nagging sensation that this moment isn't right, we will have peaceful hearts.
Joan Borysenko American writer: *A Woman's Book of Life* (1998)

If I encounter one more whiny feminist who thinks that employing the word 'should' somehow adds substance to an otherwise fatuous argument – including the current feminist favourite, '50% of corporate board directors should be female' – I shall again consider emigrating to the still largely feminist-free paradise that is France. Feminists will be happier, I'll be happier…

46 | THE DREADED 'F' WORD

A fair society is one in which some people fail – and they may fail in
something other than precise, demographically representative
proportions.
William A Henry III 1950-1994 American cultural critic and author: *In Defence of Elitism*
(1994)

If a single word can be said to represent the acceptable face of
militant feminism, it would surely be 'fairness'. What
reasonable person wouldn't want more fairness in society?
Politicians use the term all the time, and infantilise voters in the
process. From *The Economist* of 3 July 2010, an article titled,
'Against fairness: what's wrong with the British coalition
government's favourite word':

> 'How could anyone dislike the notion of fairness? Everything
> is better when it is fair: a share, a fight, a maiden, a game and
> (for those who think blondes have more fun) hair. Even
> defeat sounds more attractive when it is fair and square.
>
> A sense of fairness, as any parent knows, develops
> irritatingly early. A wail of, 'It's not fair!' is usually the first
> normative statement to come out of the mouths of babes and
> sucklings. People seem to be hard-wired to demand fairness.
> Studies in which people are offered deals that they regard as
> fair and unfair show that the former stimulate the reward
> centres in the brain; the latter stimulate areas associated with
> disgust.
>
> For the British, fair play is especially important; without it,
> life isn't cricket (especially when you score a perfectly good
> goal against the Germans and it is unfairly disallowed). Their
> country becomes quite pleasant when the weather is fair,
> though unfortunately it rarely is. And these days fair-trade
> goods crowd their supermarket shelves.
>
> Fairness is not only good, but also moderate, which is
> another characteristic that the British approve of. It does not
> claim too much for itself. Those who, on inquiry, admit that
> their health and fortunes are fair-to-middling navigate
> carefully between the twin dangers of boastfulness and

curmudgeonliness, while gesturing in a chin-up sort of way towards the possibility of future improvement.

The French have taken to using *le fair-play* in sport, presumably because (as their coach's refusal to shake hands with his opposite number after losing to South Africa suggested) their own culture finds the concept rather difficult. When talking politics, however, the French, like the Americans, tend to go for the more formal notion of justice. But fairness appeals to the British political class, for it has a common sense down-to-earthiness which avoids the grandiosity of American and continental European political discourse while aspiring to do its best for all men – and of course for all maidens too, fair and otherwise, for one of its virtues is that it does not discriminate on grounds of either gender or skin colour.

Not surprising, then, that Britain's government should grab hold of the word and cling to it in the buffeting the coalition has had since the budget on 22 June proposed higher taxes and even sharper spending cuts. 'Tough but fair' is what George Osborne, the Conservative chancellor of the exchequer, called the cuts he announced. 'It is going to be tough, but it is also very fair,' said Vince Cable, the Liberal Democrat business secretary. At last, something they could agree on.

Yet the fact that everyone believes in fairness is a clue to what's wrong with the notion. Like that other warm-blanket word, 'community', it signals limp thinking. What exactly is 'fair' about restricting trade, for example? Or 'unfair' about letting successful people in business or other fields enjoy the fruits of their enterprise without punitive taxes?

'Fairness' suits Britain's coalition government so well not just because its meanings are all positive, but also because – like views within the coalition – they are wide-ranging. To one lot of people, fairness means establishing the same rules for everyone, playing by them, and letting the best man win and the winner take all. To another, it means making sure that everybody gets equal shares.

These two meanings are not just different: they are opposites. They represent a choice that has to be made between freedom and equality. Yet so slippery – and thus convenient to politicians – is the English language that a single word encompasses both, and in doing so loses any claim to meaning.

Fairness is fudge. This newspaper will have none of it. We reject the wide, woolly notion of fairness in favour of sharper, narrower words that mean what they say, like just or cruel. Sadly, British politicians are unlikely to follow our lead. They will continue to paper over their cracks with fairness. Which, given how handy the word is, is probably fair enough.'

I was a subscriber to *The Economist* for many years, but cancelled my subscription when it started to publish nonsense on gender issues.

47 | THE VILIFICATION OF MEN

What an absurd thing it is to pass over all the valuable parts of a man, and fix our attention on his infirmities.
Joseph Addison 1672-1719 English essayist, poet, playwright and politician

It might be 'an absurd thing... to pass over all the valuable parts of a man', but dualism *requires* that it be done. The problem for feminists is that most women's experiences tell them that men are generally *not* the demons the feminists portray them to be. With few exceptions they're not raped by their partners and they're not abused by their fathers, brothers, or sons. And over time this realisation can only gather pace, making feminist arguments based on vilifying men appear increasingly ridiculous.

There's little doubt that the vilification of men by feminists over maybe 40 years of more – and here I'm referring to both gender and equity feminists – has had an unfortunate effect on men. Men have used it as an escape clause from life's responsibilities – 'Yes, I'm feckless and unreliable, but what can you expect of me? I'm only a man!' And who have suffered the most from men exercising this option? Women and children.

48 | THE SELF-GLORIFICATION OF WOMEN, AND THE TROOP NUMBERS PROBLEM

Any effort that has self-glorification as its final endpoint is bound to end in disaster.
Robert M Pirsig 1928- American writer, philosopher and author

The dualism model requires not only that men are vilified, but that women are glorified. Now men are accustomed to glorifying women, it's the beating heart of chivalry.

Which leads us on to the feminists' main problem, one which is becoming increasingly evident over time. Feminists don't have enough troops – angry men-hating women willing to devote their lives to the war against men – to prevail in the long term. In the business context, for example, many women – after experiencing the stresses of senior positions – 'jump ship' and won't be persuaded back on board again. So the drive to increase the number of women in senior positions necessarily means that ever weaker candidates must be advanced, and this naturally builds up resentment among men, who find themselves reporting to less qualified women. And the gap between those men and women is only going to increase over time.

It is already becoming common knowledge that the problem with initiatives designed to advance women into senior positions isn't that the initiatives are being scuppered by men, but that there simply aren't enough women able and willing to take on the positions. The root cause of the 'problem' is the basic natures of men and women, and they're not going to change any time soon, no matter how much feminists may screech and stamp their feet.

What of the future? How does popular culture aimed at the young feed into their images of the genders? For some insights into this we turn to a perceptive article from *The Daily Telegraph* edition of 8 October 2011, titled 'Feisty girls, feckless boys', penned by the authoress Eleanor Updale:

'As a judge in this year's Costa Book Awards, I have spent the summer with the cream of fiction for children and young adults. Although such intensive reading reveals some writing of breathtaking quality, it also exposes the fashions of our times. There are words I never want to see again. 'Amulet' is top of the list, closely followed by 'portal', 'orphan' and 'stepmother'. But more worrying is the fact that the same lead character turns up time and again.

Whether we meet her in a world of dragons and trolls, a Victorian slum, a medieval market or a modern schoolroom, she's a feisty female with a bag of chips on her shoulder. She doesn't suffer fools gladly (in fact she doesn't suffer anyone gladly). She perceives herself, and is apparently perceived by the author, as inherently in the right; the victim of a society determined to do her down. Even if she has magical powers, she employs them with a supercilious smirk.

Irritating though it is to encounter this girl repeatedly, it's even more alarming to see how the menfolk in her world are portrayed. If she has a father, he's likely to be a self-indulgent idiot, preoccupied with his work, with sport or with drink and his mates. More likely, he is completely absent, having selfishly lunged into the arms of a glamorous airhead far away. He doesn't understand our girl as she battles to overcome a disability, prejudice, bullying or the sheer grinding awfulness of having been spawned by such an inadequate man.

If our girl has male siblings or classmates, they are apprentice losers, already on the way to a witless future. They are lazy oafs or violent thugs. When our heroine kicks against convention, she is showing insight and determination. When they do it, it is through some uncontrollable spasm of testosterone that has somehow numbed the brain.

While the plots woven around these characters may be entertaining, and even funny, it's the cliché at their heart that grates. And though some of the books I read were written with male readers in mind and males at the heart of the story, it's remarkable how often the key characters were the same sneering, violent underachievers I'd met in the girl-based books.

Even in the spy and war books, adult males are hard to find. When they do turn up, they are witless drones. There's no one to admire, and hardly anyone even to like. Masculinity emerges as a redundant quality, a burden on males and females alike, and an automatic bar to cleverness and compassion.

It's such a narrow focus that books cease to perform one of their major functions: to provide a place to experiment safely with other lifestyles, and to see the world through unfamiliar eyes. Far from being helped to walk in other people's shoes, readers are being invited only to stamp on their feet of clay.

Why does this matter? It's hard not to be concerned by the recent National Literacy Trust survey which suggests that reading has become a largely female occupation. If these are the books boys are being given, I'm not surprised. Even those who do read will find that the stories collude with a long-established playground pressure not to seem too clever. School is a place where 'boffin' is one of the most shameful labels to earn.

How has the bias against males come about? No doubt there was once a need to promote girls. Many well-known women who started writing at the turn of the century say they did it because as adolescent girls they had found no books reflecting the world they knew. Their sales figures suggest they were right, but I doubt whether they intended to found a new orthodoxy or to leave boys unprovided for.

Meanwhile publishing, with its potent mix of low salaries and enlightened employment practices, has become a deeply feminised industry (I sometimes think that the collective noun should be a 'maternity leave' of publishers). Most of these women are clever enough not to fall into the stereotype trap, but increasingly they are servicing a retail trade dominated by marketers who are less interested in editorial content than in replicating things that have sold well before. This inevitably leads to the mimicking which has landed us in this very disconcerting place. Add to that the view that girls and their mothers are the people most likely to purchase books, and the cycle spins ever faster.

And, of course, in many ways the literary scene is only reflecting the state of things in the outside world. The violence of video games is hardly a celebration of the many forms masculinity can take. Anyone who has visited a school staff room recently will know how scarce male teachers have become. In schools, years of redressing a perceived bias against girls have perhaps proved too successful. My son was advised on tactics for answering multiple-choice GCSE questions such as 'Mary thinks water boils at 100C, John says 200C – who is correct?' 'If you don't know,' said the teacher, 'choose the girl. The examiners won't let the boy be right.'

Experience shows that fashions don't last. Let's hope that boys and men can be rehabilitated soon, without sending girls back into a world of pink and glitter. And take heart, there are still plenty of good books out there. It's no surprise to find that most of the candidates for the Costa prize display writing skills of which many authors of 'adult' fiction should be jealous; not least control of plot, and respect for the demands of the most critical audience in the world (unlike some pretentious grown-ups, young people who find a book boring never think it's their own fault.)

So we judges will find it as difficult as ever to whittle down the submissions to a shortlist, let alone to choose a winner. But maybe you know of new books that show boys and men in an engaging, realistic and positive light.'

49 | DO FEMINISTS SUFFER FROM PENIS ENVY?

Envy is the ulcer of the soul.
Socrates 469BC - 399BC Greek philosopher, one of the founders of Western philosophy

A phenomenon which is more common among feminists than normal women is a fondness for converting their first names into men's names, or at least into names that *sound* like men's names:

- Christine > Chris
- Josephine > Jo
- Samantha > Sam
- Jacqueline > Jack
- Frances > Frankie
- Alexandra > Alex etc.

Some of these women style themselves on men. A favourite look appears to be a hungover Johnny Cash, for some reason.

There's no male equivalent to this curious phenomenon, so what might account for it? Might it be good old penis envy? As the owner of a good old penis myself, I appreciate that the ladies have something to be envious about. But is the lack of this organ sufficient justification for them to assault everything we hold dear? I think not. Let's have a vote on that.

Male to female sexual reassignment surgery is far more common than its female to male equivalent. While feminists might want a penis, they're not prepared to put up with some minor discomfort to acquire one. Typical.

I'm no fan of Sigmund Freud – as a fully qualified amateur psychologist, I lean more towards Carl Jung – but I think Freud may have been onto something with regards to penis envy. It was only when I read the Wikipedia entry on the matter that I concluded feminists are *clearly* suffering from it. The clincher was the last section, 'Feminist criticisms' which, as we would expect, are absurd. The entry:

'Penis envy in Freudian psychoanalysis refers to the theorized reaction of a girl during her psychosexual development to the realization that she does not have a penis.

Freud considered this realization a defining moment in the development of gender and sexual identity for women. According to Freud, the parallel reaction in boys to the realization that girls do not have a penis is castration anxiety. In contemporary culture, the term sometimes refers inexactly or metaphorically to women who are presumed to wish they were men. [Author's note: 'inexactly'? This is the sort of thing that happens when feminists are allowed to edit entries in online encyclopaedias. It shouldn't be allowed. I'm planning to have a word with Jimmy Wales on the matter.]

The psychoanalytical concept of penis envy is unrelated to the 'small penis syndrome' which is the anxiety of thinking one's penis is too small.

Freud's theory
Sigmund Freud introduced the concept of interest in – and envy of – the penis in his 1908 article 'On the Sexual Theories of Children', but did not fully develop the idea until 1914 when his work *On Narcissism* was published. It wasn't mentioned in the first edition of Freud's earlier *Three Contributions to the Theory of Sex* (1905). The term came to significance as Freud gradually refined his views of sexuality, coming to describe a mental process he believed occurred as one went from the phallic stage to the latency stage.

In Freud's psychosexual development theory, the phallic stage (approximately between the ages of 3.5 and 6) is the first period of development in which the libidinal focus is primarily on the genital area. Prior to this stage, the libido (broadly defined by Freud as the primary motivating energy force within the mind) focuses on other physiological areas. For instance, in the *oral stage*, in the first 12 to 18 months of life, libidinal needs concentrate on the desire to eat, sleep, suck and bite. The theory suggests that the penis becomes the organ of principal interest to *both* sexes in the phallic stage. This becomes the catalyst for a series of pivotal events in psychosexual development. These events, known as the Oedipus complex for boys, and the Electra complex for girls, result in significantly different outcomes for each gender because of differences in anatomy.

For *girls*:
- Soon after the libidinal shift to the penis, the child develops her first sexual impulses towards her mother.
- The girl realizes that she is not physically equipped to have a heterosexual relationship with her mother, since she does not have a penis.
- She desires a penis, and the power that it represents. This is described as penis envy. She sees the solution as obtaining her father's penis.
- She develops a sexual desire for her father.
- The girl blames her mother for her apparent castration (what *she* sees as punishment by the mother for being attracted to the father) assisting a shift in the focus of her sexual impulses from her mother to her father.
- Sexual desire for her father leads to the desire to replace and eliminate her mother.
- The girl identifies with her mother so that she might learn to mimic her, and thus replace her.
- The child anticipates that both aforementioned desires will incur punishment (by the principle of *lex talionis*)
- The girl employs the defence mechanism of displacement to shift the object of her sexual desires from her father to men in general.

For boys

A similar process occurs in boys of the same age as they pass through the phallic stage of development; the key differences being that the focus of sexual impulses need not switch from mother to father, and that the fear of castration (castration anxiety) remains. The boy desires his mother, and identifies with his father, whom he sees as having the object of his sexual impulses. Furthermore, the boy's father, being the powerful aggressor of the family unit, is sufficiently menacing that the boy employs the defence mechanism of displacement to shift the object of his sexual desires from his mother to women in general.

Freud thought this series of events occurred prior to the development of a wider sense of sexual identity, and was required for an individual to continue to enter into his or her gender role.

Criticisms of Freud's theory within psychoanalytic circles

Although Freud's theories regarding psychosexual development (in particular the *phallic stage* and the Oedipal crisis) were popular in the early twentieth century when the theory was initially floated, theories by other influential psychoanalysts such as Erik Erikson and Jean Piaget have challenged the Freudian perception of child psychological development. Nevertheless, Freud's theory continues to be relevant in theoretical circumstances, and is of such historical significance that it continues to find its way into psychoanalytical teachings. Most of Freud's theories are discussed as part of curriculum in many universities and academic circles, but not necessarily endorsed.

Feminist criticisms

A significant number of critics, activists and feminists, have been highly critical of penis envy as a concept and psychoanalysis as a discipline, arguing that the assumptions and approaches of the psychoanalytic project are profoundly patriarchal, anti-feminist, and misogynistic and represent women as broken or deficient men. Karen Horney – a German psychoanalyst who also placed great emphasis on childhood experiences in psychological development – was a particular advocate of this view. She asserted the concept of 'womb envy' as an emotional reaction to the idea of penis envy. [Author's note: yeah, *right*. A leading feminist has expressed the view that male to female transsexuals should be denied places in women-only university colleges until they've had wombs implanted. Surprisingly, not a single male to female transsexual is on record as having done so.]

A small but influential number of Feminist philosophers have worked within Psychoanalysis including Luce Irigaray, Julia Kristeva and Hélène Cixous who operate within a Post-Structuralist Feminist tradition [Author's note: I imagine they get invited to lots of dinner parties...] inspired by Jacques Lacan and Jacques Derrida. Juliet Mitchell – another Feminist theorist – attempted to reconcile Freud's thoughts on psychosexual development with Feminism and Marxism by declaring his theories to be simply observations of gender identity under capitalism. She proposed a shift to Marxist models of rearing children [Author's note: that was a resounding success in the Soviet Union...] which would result in the dismantling of the Electra complex and the Oedipus complex and the avoidance of penis envy.'

So the answer to the question, 'Do feminists suffer from penis envy?' is clear. Yes, of course they do.

One of the most remarkable things about feminism is not so much its disproportionate influence on all our lives, but the absence of a backlash from men, given how feminists damage men's interests in particular, and even put their lives at risk. It begs the question, why aren't men revolting? It's a matter we turn to now.

50| WHY AREN'T MEN REVOLTING?

The average man's a coward.
Mark Twain 1835-1910 American author & humorist: *Adventures of Huckleberry Finn* (1884)

It's said that if a frog is placed in a pan of cold water, and the pan placed above a heat source, the frog will make no attempt to jump out of the water, but remain in the pan until it dies. I can't think of a more fitting metaphor for how men have responded to their interests being progressively assaulted by feminists over many years. In short, why aren't men revolting?

Even today few men have an active interest in gender politics, but with each year that passes their number increases, and the number of anti-feminist organisations, articles, books, websites and blogs rises. Examples of men's rights activism are becoming more common and more visible. About damned time, you might reasonably think, as I do.

The media is increasingly noticing (and reporting on) male rights activism. A good example of such activism at a local level is 'The Men's Network' in Brighton & Hove.[1] It was through this organisation that I first learned of a Conference held in Brighton in November 2011:

> 'On Tuesday 1st November 2011 hundreds of experts and professionals from across the UK will gather in Brighton & Hove to take part in the UK's FIRST NATIONAL CONFERENCE FOR MEN & BOYS.
> The event aims to be the biggest gathering of people committed to improving the lives of men and boys ever seen in the UK and will provide a unique opportunity to:
>
> - Meet some of the country's leading specialists working with men and boys in the UK

---

[1] http://brightonmanplan.wordpress.com

- Find out about some of the most innovative men and boys projects in the UK today
- Take part in a series of great debates on issues that really matter to men and boys
- Hear what actions the experts think are needed to help all men and boys in the UK to fulfill their potential
- Help us create a national action plan for men and boys
- Make new contacts and connections to help you in your specialist field
- Get inspired and motivated with new ideas for improving the lives of men and boys

The day long National Conference For Men and Boys will feature:

A BIG DEBATE: Where some of the country's leading thinkers debate a series of big questions including:

- Do We Need A National Strategy For Men & Boys?
- Were the riots a Men's issue?
- Is Fatherlessness worth fighting?
- Are schools failing Boys?
- How do we stop Violence Against Men and Boys?
- Do we need a Big Male Society?
- Is it time we had a Minister for Men and Boys?

FOUR ROLLING ACTION WORKSHOPS: Where all delegates get the opportunity to take part in an interactive workshop on one of four themes:

- Helping Men Live Longer, Happier, Healthier Lives
- Giving Every Boy The Best Possible Start In Life
- Helping Every Dad To Be A Great Dad
- Making Communities Safe By Keeping Men and Boys Safe

A PROJECT SHOWCASE: Where you can meet the people behind some of the top examples of innovative ways to work effectively with men and boys in areas such as:

- Tackling male suicide
- Improving boys' literacy
- Working with excluded fathers

- Mentoring young men and boys
- Beating male cancer in the community
- Tackling drug, alcohol and substance abuse in men
- Working with men to end domestic violence
- Helping men who have been raped and sexually abused
- Working with men and boys to promote healthy sex lives
- Promoting emotional and mental wellbeing in men and boys
- Engaging men and boys in community and voluntary action
- Tackling the isolation of men in later life

A SECTOR MARKETPLACE: Where you can find out about a whole range of different organisations, projects and initiatives for men and boys from across the UK.

AN ACTIVIST'S SOAPBOX: Where we give passionate people who are committed to improving the lives of men and boys in the UK a platform to share and debate their views.

CAMPAIGN CORNER: Where you can find out about some of the different issues that people across the country are campaigning for on behalf of men and boys.

MEET THE EXPERTS: Where you can take part in a series of mini masterclasses in an informal environment with a range of sector experts.

A BIG PLAN: Where you can contribute to the creation of a national action plan for men and boys.'

The scope and content of the conference is both impressive and encouraging – but where's the challenging of feminism?

In evolutionary terms the feminist threat to men's welfare is a recent phenomenon; maybe it's simply a matter of time before men become more conscious of the threat, and formulate more robust responses.

Male writers in the modern era have been shamefully quiet with respect to feminism. Some critique feminist activities, it's true, but generally within a humorous context which softens the impact of their messages. Their readers tend not to recognise the dangers posed by feminism. Notable exceptions to the rule about male writers are Steve Moxon (*The Woman Racket*) and Swayne O'Pie (*Why Britain Hates Men: Exposing Feminism*).

Perceptive warnings about feminist excesses tend to come from such estimable women as the campaigner Erin Pizzey. She struggled to find a publisher for her latest book *This Way to the Revolution: A Memoir* (2011). In the next chapter I explain why – quite apart from there being few writers interested in opposing feminism – there aren't more such titles published.

We've just passed the fortieth anniversary of the publication of a book written by Esther Vilar, a German-Argentinean writer who originally trained as a doctor. She's best known for her 1971 book *The Manipulated Man* and its various follow-ups which argue that contrary to common feminist and women's rights rhetoric, women in industrialised cultures aren't oppressed, but rather exploit a well-established system of manipulating men. A revised edition appeared in 2008. From its back cover:

> 'Esther Vilar's classic polemic about the relationship between the sexes caused a sensation on its first publication. In her introduction to this revised edition, Vilar maintains that very little has changed. A man is a human being who works, while a woman chooses to let a man provide for her and her children in return for carefully dispensed praise and sex.
>
> Vilar's perceptive, thought-provoking and often very funny look at the battle between the sexes has earned her severe criticism and even death threats. But Vilar's intention is not misogynistic: she maintains that only if women and men look at their place in society with honesty, will there be any hope for change.'

In a new introduction for the 2008 edition Vilar stated that, 'if anything, the female position of power has only consolidated… now, as before, it does not occur to the underprivileged (men) to fight against this grotesque state of affairs.' The book starts with a short chapter, 'The Slave's Happiness':

> 'The lemon-coloured MG skids across the road and the woman driver brings it to a somewhat uncertain halt. She gets out and finds her left front tyre flat. Without wasting a moment she prepares to fix it: she looks towards the passing cars as if expecting someone. Recognizing this standard international sign of woman in distress ('weak female let down by male technology'), a station wagon draws up. The driver sees what is wrong at a glance and says comfortingly, 'Don't worry. We'll fix that in a jiffy.' To prove his determination, he asks for her jack. He does not ask if she is capable of changing the tire herself because he knows – she is about thirty, smartly dressed and made-up – that she is not.
>
> Since she cannot find a jack, he fetches his own, together with his other tools. Five minutes later the job is done and the punctured tire properly stowed. His hands are covered with grease. She offers him an embroidered handkerchief, which he politely refuses. He has a rag for such occasions in his tool box. The woman thanks him profusely, apologizing for her 'typically feminine' helplessness. She might have been there till dusk, she says, had he not stopped. He makes no reply and, as she gets back into the car, gallantly shuts the door for her. Through the wound-up window he advises her to have her tire patched at once and she promises to get her garage man to see to it that very evening. Then she drives off.
>
> As the man collects his tools and goes back to his own car, he wishes he could wash his hands. His shoes – he has been standing in the mud while changing the tire – are not as clean as they should be (he is a salesman). What is more, he will have to hurry to keep his next appointment. As he starts the engine he thinks, 'Women! One's more stupid than the next.' He wonders what she would have done if he had not been there to help. He puts his foot on the accelerator and drives off – faster than usual. There is the delay to make up. After a while he starts to hum to himself. In a way, he is happy.

Almost any man would have behaved in the same manner – and so would most women. Without thinking, simply because men are men and women so different from them, a woman will make use of a man whenever there is an opportunity. What else could the woman have done when her car broke down? She has been taught to get a man to help. Thanks to his knowledge he was able to change her tire quickly – and at no cost to herself. True, he ruined his clothes, put his business in jeopardy, and endangered his own life by driving too fast afterwards. Had he found something else wrong with the car, he would have repaired that, too. That is what his knowledge of cars is for. Why should a woman learn to change a flat when the opposite sex (half the world's population) is able and willing to do it for her?

Women let men work, think for them and take on their responsibilities – in fact, they exploit them. Yet, since men are strong, intelligent and imaginative, while women are weak, unimaginative, and stupid, why isn't it men who exploit women?

Could it be that strength, intelligence, and imagination are not prerequisites for power but merely qualifications for slavery? Could it be that the world is not being ruled by experts but by beings who are not fit for anything else – by women? And if this is so, how do women manage it so that their victims do not feel themselves cheated and humiliated, but rather believe themselves to be what they are least of all – masters of the universe? How do women manage to instil in men this sense of pride and superiority that inspires them to ever greater achievements?

Why are women never unmasked?'

To return to the question posed by this chapter, why aren't men revolting? I'm increasingly convinced that there's an ever-growing anger among men which *will* find means of expression. As more men become more conscious of the feminist threat, they *will* revolt. They'll do this in a variety of ways, and some of those ways will come as a surprise to our politicians, accustomed as they are to think of men as a group not prepared to fight for its perfectly legitimate interests.

51 | THE DIRE STATE OF THE MAINSTREAM MEDIA

It is inexcusable for scientists to torture animals; let them make their experiments on journalists and politicians.
Henrik Ibsen 1826-1906 Norwegian playwright and theatre director

Anyone who relies solely on the mainstream media to inform them about men's issues will be woefully ignorant about them, although the print media is starting to improve, albeit never or almost never making the point that radical feminists are to account for so many of the problems facing men and boys.

I'm not generally one for conspiracy theories, but I believe the silence of the mainstream media is largely attributable to feminists working in the sector, as well as advertisers' reluctance to be associated with anything that might be considered critical of women as a class.

Over the course of 2011 I was contacted by a number of writers expressing support for the theses put forward in *David and Goliatha* and *The Glass Ceiling Delusion*. One was a well-known 50-something authoress who for some years has been critical of feminism and feminists. I'd speculated in an email that the small number of articles and books attacking feminism might be attributable to the preponderance of women in key positions in the newspaper and publishing sectors. She replied:

> 'The few male journalists I have known who have tried to write anti-feminist articles were banned by (you are right) a whole phalanx of women editors who are gender feminists. So are publishing women editors. I had an appalling time with a succession of women editors who were militant lesbians…'

Feminists now control the content of our newspapers and decide which books are going to be published by the major publishers.

[Update: Globally, mainstream radio and television are almost silent on men's issues. The British state is hostile to men and boys, as we've seen, so we shouldn't be surprised that the BBC, the state broadcaster, is too.

100+ of our appearances on BBC radio and television are on our YouTube channel,[1] but we are very rarely given any significant time to expound on our analysis of gender-related matters, or talk about our proposals.

From time to time we post examples of outrageous BBC anti-male bias on our website.[2] At the time of writing, they include:

- 10 stories the BBC considers more notable than male suicides resulting from false rape allegations.
- A debate on sexism, broadcast live, is limited to anti-female sexism, which is... er... sexist. Special Snowflake (Laura Bates) lies AGAIN, after being publicly exposed as a liar by a student in the studio audience.
- Andrew Marr fails to challenge Jess Phillips, a Labour MP, over her denial of an application by Philip Davies, a Conservative MP, for a debate on men's issues on International Men's Day.
- Andrew Neil refuses to engage with Philip Davies MP over his request for a debate on men's issues on International Men's Day.
- BBC anti-male bias – in a fishing competition!

---

[1] http://tinyurl.com/j4mbyoutube
[2] https://j4mb.wordpress.com/key-posts/

- The BBC has never reported a case of male suicide occasioned by false rape allegations.
- Manipulation of pre-election hustings, 2015 general election. Mike Buchanan and other Ashfield candidates (including Gloria De Piero, Shadow Minister for Women & Equalities) are asked questions about women's issues by an all-women audience.
- *Newsnight* piece on domestic violence breached 50+ of their editorial guidelines. Our complaint was rejected.
- *Newsnight* piece on women-only railway carriages, studio discussion with feminists only.
- Simon Schama should hang his head in shame, for comparing 'heroic' Suffragettes with the 'patriotic' men who fought in WW1.
- The BBC is a job creation scheme for women, run by women.
- *Tyger Takes On...* Mike Buchanan, Ray Barry, and Josh O'Brien.
- Women's Equality Party spokeswoman Sandy Toksvig appears on *The One Show*, and duly wins the first of her Lying Feminist of the Month awards.
- Women's Equality Party spokeswoman Sandy Toksvig appears on *Question Time*, J4MB not invited to provide balance.
- Women's Equality Party is given considerable (unchallenged) exposure on prime time TV and radio programmes, J4MB is being given almost no exposure on them. An example, a video of Catherine Mayer, WEP president, on *The Andrew Marr Show*.
- Women's Equality Party is given 23 minutes of coverage on BBC Parliament, relating to the launch of the party's policy document.]

52| THE DIRE STATE OF MODERN PUBLISHING

Gentlemen, I agree with you that Napoleon is a tyrant, a monster, the sworn foe of our nation, and if you will, of the whole human race. But, gentlemen, we must not forget that he once shot a publisher.
Thomas Campbell 1777-1844 Scottish poet

Given the damage being wrought by feminism, our bookstores should be displaying many titles analysing the ideology and its impacts on the modern world, but they don't. What might explain this?

Established writers appear unable – or possibly unwilling? – to critique modern feminism, so it's left to little-known and unknown writers to rise to the challenge. However, they face a problem. It's rare in the modern era for a new writer to be directly taken on by a major commercial publisher. Publishers rely on literary agents to filter the output of new writers and to present them with manuscripts having commercial potential.

If you look through publications such as *The Writers' and Artists' Yearbook* and their lists of literary agents, one thing will immediately strike you: the vast majority of literary agents are women. I'm convinced their natural sympathies lie in publishing new female authors, and female-friendly books.

DH Lawrence and many of our greatest writers – George Orwell comes to mind – wouldn't have had a hope of attracting agents in the modern era. Lawrence started off his writing career self-publishing (as have many famous authors) and it's an approach that more and more writers in the modern era have adopted. I'm proud to call myself a self-publisher, and my readers know I'm free to say exactly what I want. Nobody censors even a single word of my output. Self-publishing is booming, and commercial publishers face an increasingly uncertain future.

I've contacted a number of literary agents in the past with respect to my books which are critical of feminism and feminists, but I no longer bother to do so. One prominent (female) literary agent told me candidly that no literary agent (whether male or female) would submit to a major publisher a manuscript which was critical of feminism *regardless of its quality*, because a likely consequence would be that the agency would be blacklisted by the publisher.

I've self-published most of my books, including this one, through my imprint, LPS publishing.[1] In 2010 I published my guide to publishing books and ebooks, *The Joy of Self-Publishing.*

The *doyen* of self-publishers worldwide is the English writer Dr Vernon Coleman, who was the first British 'TV doctor', an 'agony uncle' for many years in tabloid newspapers, and a bestselling author represented in his early writing career by a number of major publishers.

In time he became disenchanted with them and turned to self-publishing, very successfully. His latest book *Diary of a Disgruntled Man* charts his daily life over 2010 and it's a gem, documenting many of the trials and tribulations of self-publishing. It's available along with many of his books by mail order. Details of Vernon Coleman and his books are on his website.[2]

Coleman has been complimentary about my books, and I first encountered him in a curious manner. In 2009 I'd bought the rights to a photograph for use on the cover of a planned book *Harriet Harman Drove Me to France*. Harriet Harman is the most

[1] http://lpspublishing.co.uk/titles.html
[2] http://vernoncoleman.com.

widely recognised and 'successful' radical feminist politician of her generation. The title was inspired by my intention to emigrate to France if the Labour party won a fourth successive term in office at the forthcoming general election, widely expected to be held in 2010. In the event the election *was* held in 2010 and the Labour party duly exited from office, to be replaced by a Conservative / Liberal Democrat coalition.

The cover image for the book was taken with a camera positioned just above the shoulder of a lady looking out of her open doorway during an election campaign. A smiling Harriet Harman was on the doorstep looking up to, and speaking to, the woman. Behind Harriet Harman was Gordon Brown, wearing his infamous forced smile. My idea was to have a speech bubble directed at Harriet Harman and a thought bubble directed at Gordon Brown:

Harman: 'Good morning, Ms Johnson! I hope we can count on your vote once again for the anti-men, anti-family, anti-business, anti-taxpayer and anti-democracy party?'

Brown: 'Dear God. On the campaign trail with Mad Hattie again. Livin' the dream, eh? Roll on the 2010 election and *freedom*.'

I had at one time considered titling the book *Gordon Is a Moron*, the title of a popular music hit in 1978 for English comedy actor and musician Graham Fellows, under the name of his alter ego 'Jilted John'. Fairly confident that nobody would have used the title for a book, I looked on Amazon anyway, and was surprised to find that the title *had* already been used, by Vernon Coleman. From his website:

'Vernon Coleman is the author of 114 books which have sold over 2 million copies in the UK, been translated into 25 languages and now sell in over 50 countries. His non-fiction books include *Bodypower* (voted one of the nation's 100 most popular books by British readers) and *How To Stop Your Doctor Killing You* and his novels include *Mrs Caldicot's Cabbage War* (which has been turned into a major movie starring Pauline Collins) and the Bilbury series of books.

Vernon Coleman has a medical degree and has worked as a General Practitioner and a hospital doctor. Often described as an 'iconoclast' he has organised numerous campaigns for people and for animals. Although he now concentrates on writing books he has in the past presented numerous programmes on television (he was breakfast television's first doctor) and radio and has written over 5,000 columns and articles for over 100 of the world's leading newspapers and magazines.'

The Publishing House, it transpired, sells only books written by Vernon Coleman and his wife. His biography on the website ends with the following gem:

'Vernon Coleman, born in Walsall, Staffordshire, England, is balding and widely disliked by members of the Establishment. He doesn't give a toss about either of these facts. He is married to Donna Antoinette, the totally adorable Welsh Princess, and is very pleased about this.'

Jerome K Jerome, author of the Victorian classic *Three Men in a Boat*, was born in Walsall too. There's obviously something in the local water. I used a quotation from *Gordon Is a Moron* in *Buchanan's Dictionary of Quotations for right-minded people* and sent Vernon Coleman a complimentary copy by way of appreciation. He replied and was very complimentary about the book, which quite made my day. We later corresponded further, from which I learned that he was then working on several titles simultaneously – from his prodigious output, this was clearly his custom – and he employed four members of staff.

The Mission Statement of The Publishing House is as insightful, punchy, and lengthy as we might expect from the good doctor:

The Publishing House Mission Statement
(Why We Believe Small Publishers Are The Only Real Publishers Left)

Compared to the big international conglomerates Publishing House is very definitely a 'small publisher'. We don't have a massive sales force (actually, we don't have a sales force at all). We don't have a board of eminent directors (since we're not a limited company we don't have any directors). We don't have offices in a skyscraper (we do have offices but we just have an upstairs and a downstairs). And we don't have a PR department full of bright young things called Hyacinth and Jacoranda. (We don't have a PR department at all). But we have one enormous advantage over the conglomerates. We care passionately about books.

They have marketing departments which decide which books will sell. They then commission books that the sales force think they will be able to flog. They won't even consider a book until they've done a marketing feasibility study.

We publish books we believe in. We then try to sell them. Naturally, we try to make a profit. If we didn't we wouldn't last long. We have to pay the printing bills, the electricity bills, the phone bills, the rates, the insurance and so on.

But we've been publishing for 15 years. In that time, we've sold over two million books. Our books have been translated into 22 languages and are sold by other publishers (including some big ones) in over 50 countries.

The conglomerates insist that every book should make a profit. We don't. Some of our books make more money than others. But that's fine with us. We don't mind if the better sellers sometimes subsidise the other books. We don't mind if a book is a little slow to sell. Like good parents we love all our children equally – however successful, or unsuccessful, they might be.

Despite all the talk about the need for each book to stand on its own two feet many big publishers make an overall loss. They are kept alive – effectively as vanity publishers – by other parts of the conglomerate. So, for example, the TV division or the magazine division may help to subsidise the book publishing division. We believe that book publishing can, and should, be allowed to stand alone. We believe that small publishers are now the only REAL publishers alive.

The big publishers often accept sponsorship from outside companies. We never do. We rely on the sale of books to earn our living and pay our bills. None of our books are sponsored or carry any advertising. We believe this helps us to remain truly independent. We publish books which international conglomerates wouldn't dare touch.

Big publishers have lost touch with people's needs. They are slow and unwieldy. It can take them two years to turn a typescript into a finished book! (We can, if pushed, get a book out within a month – while the material is still topical.)

They are too market orientated and derivative. They produce more of what other publishers did well with last year. We look forwards not backwards.

They pay huge amounts as advances to film stars, politicians and young hot shot authors. Much of the time they don't earn back those advances. They don't care because the books are just seen as 'tools' to help other parts of the empire. For example, a conglomerate will publish a politician's dull biography as a way of putting money into the politician's pocket.

Despite their huge marketing departments they are often out of touch with people's needs. If we published as many 'turkeys' as they do we'd be out of business.

They worry enormously about upsetting powerful politicians and other corporations. The big conglomerates need to co-operate with the establishment because they are part of the establishment. We stand outside the establishment. They don't like us much at all. They often do their best to shut us down.

But we don't give a fig for what politicians or corporate bosses might (or might not) think of us. We're only interested in publishing books that inform and entertain. When they try to shut us down we fight back.

At big publishers there are loads of men and women in suits who slow things down and interfere with the artistic process. Literary originality and integrity have been replaced by marketing convenience.

We have no men or women in suits to tell us what to do. We do what we believe is right. We publish books the old fashioned way. We're a small, independent publishing house. We publish books we believe in; books we want to publish and which we hope that our readers will want to read.

That's what we think publishing is all about.'

I have a copy of the Mission Statement on the wall above my desk. I should do one thing differently from Dr Coleman, if and when I ever become as successful at self-publishing. I *would* employ bright young things with names like Hyacinth and Jacoranda. I'm sure I could find them *something* to do.

53 | POLITICIANS ARE ~~IMPORTANT~~ IMPOTENT

The word 'politics' is derived from the word 'poly', meaning 'many', and the word 'ticks', meaning 'blood sucking parasites'.
Larry Hardiman

The impotence of politicians when faced with manipulative feminists is a depressing phenomenon. The average jellyfish has more backbone. I can't recall an instance of a British politician in the past 40 years reducing the feminists' influence on public policy agendas and legislative frameworks. It's rare that we hear politicians criticise them although the estimable Conservative MP Dominic Raab memorably noted in an article in January 2011 that 'some feminists are now amongst the most obnoxious bigots'. What an insightful gentleman he is.

In the United Kingdom we've reached the sorry position where the leaders of both the main political parties, David Cameron (Conservative) and Ed Miliband (Labour), are firm supporters of all-women prospective parliamentary candidate ('PPC') shortlists. In March 2008 Harriet Harman introduced legislation enabling political parties to use such shortlists for the ensuing *25 years*.

In the autumn of 2009, while his party was in opposition, Cameron announced his intention to use Harman's legislation to create some all-women shortlists to select candidates for the forthcoming general election. When the move was announced, I resigned my party membership. Not long after, having met with fierce resistance, the plan was shelved.

[Update: Cameron became prime minister in May 2010 at the head of a Conservative-led coalition with the Liberal

Democrats, and again as the head of a majority Conservative government in May 2015.]

Cameron's treacherous and un-Conservative plan to introduce all-women shortlists inspired me to write *David and Goliatha: David Cameron – heir to Harman?* The book argues that a contributory factor to Cameron's feminist tendencies is his female-pattern brain, for which there is considerable evidence.

Ed Miliband's first role in politics was as an aide and handbag carrier to Harriet Harman. He still has something of a haunted look about him at times, which I attribute to him having flashbacks to that presumably traumatic period of his life.

During the Labour party annual conference in Liverpool in late September 2011 – Ed Miliband's first conference as party leader – a rule change was announced to the effect that henceforth either the leadership or deputy leadership positions would always be held by a woman. Harriet Harman called the decision 'historic'. As we know only too well, any change welcomed by Harman as 'historic' must surely be regrettable.

[Update: As expected, Cameron has proved relentlessly anti-male and anti-meritocratic as prime minister. Justice for Men & Boys (and its related organizations) presents Toady awards to men in positions of power and influence, who drive or accede to feminist agendas. Cameron won the Toady of the Year award four years in succession – 2012, 2013, 2014, 2015.[1] The party has stated its intention to field candidates in the top 20 Conservative marginal seats at the 2020 general election. Funding streams are already in place for all 20 £500 deposits. The 2020 election strategy has been published.[2]]

---

[1] http://tinyurl.com/j4mbcamerontoady
[2] http://tinyurl.com/j4mb2020strategy

54| LADIES, WHAT DO YOU WANT? HAPPINESS OR POWER?

There's a rule, I think. You get what you want in life, but not your second choice too.
Alison Lurie 1926- American novelist: *Real People* (1969)

I would have no objection to the notion of equality of gender outcomes – in the boardroom, say – if there was so much as a shred of evidence that as many capable women as capable men were *willing* to take on such positions, to make the effort and sacrifices required, and perform as well. But all my personal experience, and that of former business acquaintances I've consulted, is that the proportion of women with the necessary experience and qualities required for such positions is far exceeded by the proportion of men with them.

In *The Glass Ceiling Delusion* I listed my 'Top 20 reasons why female executives are uncommon in the most senior levels of major businesses'. By seeking equality of outcomes through gender initiatives and the like, women show themselves to be precisely what they seek to deny: manipulative and weak. Talented women with the qualities to reach the boardroom find such initiatives condescending. Only less talented women need them: the very ones who could never reach boardrooms on the grounds of merit, all too often feminists. The last people you'd want in a boardroom.

Are we really prepared to risk the viability of the private sector – the only wealth creating sector – in an effort to appease a band of angry whining Leftie harridans? Surely not.

[Update: The current Conservative government is going further than any of its Labour predecessors in bullying major companies into appointing more women onto their boards.]

55 | WOMEN AGAINST FEMINISM, HONEY BADGERS

Fetter strong madness in a silken thread.
William Shakespeare 1564 - 1616 English poet and playwright: *Much Ado About Nothing* (1598)

We turn now to the group which could – should it so choose – halt and then reverse the influence of feminists: the vast majority of women, who aren't feminists. If more women were more vocal in their opposition to feminism, the feminists' claim to speak on behalf of women – the feminists' only potential source of legitimacy – would be exposed as the fraud it has always been.

These women can, of course, continue their current policy of not dealing with the problems arising from feminism; but over time they will find they have to take on ever more paid employment and watch society become more dysfunctional. The day will surely dawn when a sufficient number of women question why they followed the battle cries of a miniscule band of feminists, or at least turned a deaf ear to them. Women are paying a terrible price for their inaction, as feminists exert ever more influence, and what are they getting in return? Nothing. Absolutely nothing.

From *The Daily Telegraph* of 26 January 2012, an article titled, 'Househusbands triple as wives turn breadwinner':

> 'The number of men living in households while their wives go to work has tripled in 15 years. Last year 62,000 men were classed as economically inactive and looking after their family or home. In 1996, there were only 21,000 men in this category, according to analysis by the Office for National Statistics.

> Anastasia de Waal, head of family policies at the think tank Civitas, said society's attitudes to gender roles had changed, while growing numbers of women were earning more than their partners. 'A few decades ago the idea of the primary carer being a man would have been emasculating.' She said. 'That has changed. Men feel much more comfortable with the idea.'
>
> The true number of stay-at-home fathers could be much higher as the ONS figure does not take account of men who describe themselves as 'artists' or 'writers' who are 'working from home'. A recent survey for the insurance company Aviva suggested that up to 1.4 million men were their children's main carers.'

Anastasia de Waal[1] is talking through her hat. She's a frequent contributor to 'Comment is Free', a comment and political opinion site in the online edition of the left-leaning *Guardian* newspaper. Staff at *The Daily Telegraph*, a historically right-leaning newspaper, now deem a young woman qualified to pronounce on what men find emasculating, and what they don't. Her comments are emasculating in themselves.

De Waal's remarks are an attempt to put a positive spin on the predictable outcome of women gaining employment at the expense of men: widespread male unemployment. I have no doubt that if the 62,000 men were interviewed, a sizeable majority would prefer to be the primary breadwinner.

But what of the men's partners? Are *they* happy with the situation? I have no doubt that the majority – given a free choice – would prefer to be the primary carer rather than the primary breadwinner. But you can rest assured that no taxpayer's money will be spent on finding out what they (or the men) think.

[Update: There's a small but growing number of women in the United Kingdom who are openly critical of feminism, and

---

[1] http://guardian.co.uk/profile/anastasiadewaal

most are social conservatives, as we would expect. To my mind, the most impressive are contributors to The Conservative Woman website,[1] notably Kathy Gyngell and Laura Perrins, the co-founders, and Belinda Brown, a social anthropologist.

Too many women lack their courage, and continue to self-identify as feminists – even when their political instincts aren't left-wing – thereby giving support to the evil ideology.]

A number of women are attempting to re-define the meaning of the word 'feminism' in terms which aren't left-wing. This effort is doomed to failure. Feminism is irredeemably associated in the popular imagination with the small band of whining left-wing ideologues who've controlled the movement for decades.

A new term is clearly required for non-feminists. Some women have started to call themselves 'post-feminists', in the next chapter I provide a guide for women seeking to decide whether to call themselves feminists or post-feminists.

Young women provide a source of hope. I find them markedly less likely to be anti-men than their mothers and grandmothers. Most young women I know have no interest in feminism. The few who have an interest are opposed to it and see what damage it has wrought on the lives of women and children in particular. Is this why feminists campaign with such determination for initiatives such as gender balance in the boardroom? Are they trying to entrench their fantasy in various institutions before the tide of public opinion turns strongly and irreversibly against them?

Herewith a few suggestions as to what normal women should now be campaigning for, or doing:

---

[1] http://conservativewoman.co.uk

- ending taxpayer funding of Women's Studies / Gender Studies 'academics', departments, courses etc.
- ending taxpayer support of single motherhood (for conceptions after a given date, to be widely advertised). If the taxpayer no longer funded this lifestyle choice it would soon stop being an attractive option for so many young women.
- abolishing the Positive Action provisions in the Equality Act 2010 and other legislation aimed at 'improving' gender balances in organisations.
- abolishing gender balance initiatives in the workplace and elsewhere.
- abolishing women-only prospective parliamentary candidate shortlists.
- disbanding the ultra-Leftie Equality and Human Rights Commission.
- making a donation to The Conservative Woman website[1]
- declaring themselves non-feminists or post-feminists, and – in the light of the Fawcett Society T-shirts – wearing T-shirts bearing the slogan, 'This is what a post-feminist looks like'
- staging regular demonstrations outside the offices of the Fawcett Society (Unit 204, Linton House, 164-180 Union Street, London SE1 0LH). Suitable placards might include the words, 'The Fawcett Society doesn't represent women', 'Feminism? Not in my name!', and 'Are feminists barking mad? Woof!'
- calling the Fawcett Society (0203 598 6154) and asking to speak to the Chief Executive. If and when you get through

---

[1] http://www.conservativewoman.co.uk/donate/

to the harridan, ask her for her qualifications, and those of the Fawcett Society, to represent women. Whatever she says in reply will be laughable, so prepare to laugh.
- writing to your Member of Parliament.
- improving state education, starting with the phased sacking of all Leftie teachers and academics, who should then be barred from other public sector positions. To see them seeking work in the private sector should prove an amusing spectacle.

The final action can only be carried out by Conservative MPs. The appointment of a new leader of the party is restricted to them under the party's rules. Unfortunately they made a disastrous decision in 2005 when they picked David Cameron in preference to David Davis. There were a number of Conservative MPs of strong intellect and integrity who campaigned for Davis, but those who campaigned for Cameron, and those who voted for him, should at least now have the decency to admit – with the benefit of hindsight – that they made a serious mistake.

The opportunity to appoint a new leader may come as early as 2015, if the Conservatives lose the next general election. [Update: The Conservatives won the election.] We can but hope that Conservative MPs then appoint to the leadership of the party a new leader with right-of-centre convictions. Possibly a women, given that the only female prime minister in this country's history, Margaret Thatcher, did such a sterling job.

[Update: In recent years, there has been a considerable growth in the number of women publicly self-identifying as non-feminists and anti-feminists. In the last survey I heard about, fewer than 20% of women self-identified as feminists, and the proportion is declining year after year. Feminists never represented women in general, and with each passing year their claim to do so looks ever more ridiculous.

When this book was first published, I was unaware of the term 'Honey Badger', as applied to women who are anti-feminists and/or men's human rights advocates. It's a term of deep admiration, you'll need to watch a hilarious video[1] about Honey Badgers to appreciate why. It was published in 2011 and has since attracted over 76 million views.

Most prominent Honey Badgers are Canadian or American:

- Karen Straughan (Girl Writes What)[2]
- Janet Bloomfield (JudgyBitch)[3]
- Alison Tieman (Typhon Blue)[4]
- Hannah Wallen[5]

Karen, Alison, and Hannah are among the Founding Hosts of the Honey Badger Brigade.[6]

In July 2013 the website Women Against Feminism[7] was launched. Thousands of photographs have been posted, mostly of women holding up signs starting with, 'I don't need feminism because...]

---

[1] https://www.youtube.com/watch?v=4r7wHMg5Yjg
[2] http://youtube.com/user/girlwriteswhat
[3] http://judgybitch.com
[4] https://www.youtube.com/user/Genderratic
[5] http://tinyurl.com/gram7lu
[6] http://honeybadgerbrigade.com/
[7] http://womenagainstfeminism.tumblr.com/

56 | ARE YOU A FEMINIST
OR A POST-FEMINIST? A GUIDE

Parameter	Feminist
Political views	Extreme left-wing
Customary demeanour	Miserable
Optimist or pessimist?	Pessimist
Emotional maturity	Low
Intelligence	Below average
Predominantly emotional or rational?	Emotional
Attractive physically?	Rarely[1]
Attractive personality?	Never
Tone of voice	Whiny[2]
Inclination to wear black clothes	High
Weight	Likely to be obese and blame her hormones
Understanding of business	Nil
Work ethic	Poor
Employed in which sector?	Probably public sector
Opinion of men	They're all bastards
Opinion of women	They're all wonderful and to be celebrated
Opinion of Margaret Thatcher	She was a disaster for the country in general, and for women in particular
Opinion of Harriet Harman MP	She's *amazing* and has strongly promoted women's interests whilst trampling on men's interests – great!

---

[1] Although Harriet Harman MP in her younger days was quite attractive, it has to be said – by feminist standards, anyway.
[2] For example, Laura Bates, Kat Banyard, Laurie Penny, Angela Eagle MP…

Parameter	Post-Feminist
Political views	Variable, but not extreme left-wing
Customary demeanour	Cheerful
Optimist or pessimist?	Optimist
Emotional maturity	High
Intelligence	Above average
Predominantly emotional or rational?	Rational, emotional on occasion (but in a good way)
Attractive physically?	Probably
Attractive personality?	Probably
Tone of voice	Pleasant
Inclination to wear black clothes	Low
Weight	Variable
Understanding of business	Variable
Work ethic	Strong
Employed in which sector?	Probably private sector
Opinion of men	Variable, depends on the man in question
Opinion of women	Variable, depends on the woman in question
Opinion of Margaret Thatcher	She was the finest peacetime prime minister of the 20th century, and remains the ultimate role model for women
Opinion of Harriet Harman MP	She's *awful* and has harmed the interests of the majority of women, and all men

57 | THE TEN CONCLUSIONS

People do not like to think. If one thinks, one must reach conclusions.
Conclusions are not always pleasant.
Helen Keller 1880-1968 American deaf blind author, political activist and lecturer

I present you with not one, not three, not even five
conclusions. Herewith the ten conclusions:

*Conclusion #1 – denying the differences between men and women is
leading to disastrous consequences for both men and women*
Most men and women are by definition gender-typical, and
they generally think and act in gender-typical ways. This hasn't
changed over time, and shows no signs of changing. Initiatives
which deny the gender-typical natures of the majority of men
and women – for example, gender balance initiatives in the
workplace – will be a driver of unhappiness among the majority
of men and women. They will result in individuals, families,
organisations and countries becoming ever more dysfunctional.

Conclusion #2 – men need to organise more effectively to fight feminism
Men need to organise themselves more effectively to campaign
for their legitimate interests. At the moment there are many
men making useful individual efforts, but they don't collectively
amount to anything like the force that will be required to halt
the ever-growing influence of feminists and reduce their
influence over time.

Given how much power is wielded by feminists in a covert
manner, there's a clear need for a substantial organisation to
fight feminism. The organisation's name must be unambiguous
along with its objectives – the Anti-Feminism League,[1] anyone?

---

[1] http://fightingfeminism.wordpress.com

Such an organisation would need to be well-financed for there to be any prospect of having a major impact.

Conclusion #3 – the focus of women's interests tends to differ from men's
Women's main interests in life are their personal relationships, whether with family members, friends, or work colleagues. They're typically less interested than men in the worlds of business and politics.

Conclusion #4 – the people best suited to lead major organisations are mostly men
Only a very small minority of men have the qualities necessary – including an ability to see the 'big picture' – to lead major organisations successfully. But they outnumber the number of women with those qualities, and for this reason alone we must expect men to continue dominating the senior reaches of major organisations. Ambitious men are hard-wired to work hard in pursuit of their work goals, in contrast to ambitious women who are hard-wired (in common with less ambitious women) to seek more 'work/life balance'.

Conclusion #5 – women's natures haven't changed over time
Some women may have changed their rhetoric as part of their effort to gain power in politics, business and other fields, but through their decisions when faced with choices (e.g. seeking high-status men rather than low-status men as partners, or their refusal to support non-working partners) they reveal that women's basic natures remain unchanged.

Conclusion #6 – we need to stop feminists wrecking democracy
Feminists will wreck democracy given the opportunity, through women-only candidate shortlists and the like. Let's not give them that opportunity.

Conclusion #7 – we need to stop feminists wrecking capitalism
Feminists will wreck capitalism given the opportunity, through gender-balanced boardrooms and manipulation of recruitment and promotion processes. Let's not give them that opportunity.

Conclusion #8 – the vast majority of women aren't feminists, and they need to find the courage to admit it to themselves and others
Only a small number of women share the extreme Leftie views of gender feminists, and other women – the vast majority – need to understand that in calling themselves feminists, they give legitimacy to feminists' claims to speak for them, and to represent them. These women need to find the courage to criticise feminism openly, and to declare with pride that they're not feminists themselves. Other women will be inspired by their honesty, and the number of women willing to dissociate themselves from feminism will rise inexorably over time.

Conclusion #9 – feminists aren't the sharpest knives in the rack
It's *always* futile seeking to hold discussions with feminists. Their deep commitment to dualism ('women good, men bad') leads to an utter inability to discuss matters rationally. You'd as usefully seek an intelligent discussion with a goldfish.

Conclusion #10 – feminists are at war against all men and most women, who share a common interest in combining forces to defeat them
Feminism is an ugly totalitarian ideology based upon the hatred of half the people on the planet. Men and women need to join

forces in a war against feminism, using every weapon at their disposal. I invite you to join me in fighting that war.

APPENDIX 1 | QUOTATIONS

Women like silent men. They think they're listening.
Marcel Achard 1899-1974 French playwright and screenwriter

Politics, as a practice, has always been the systematic organization of hatreds.
Henry Adams 1850-1906 American farmer, public official and politician: *The Education of Henry Adams* (1907)

More than any other time in history, mankind faces a crossroads. One path leads to despair and utter hopelessness, the other to total extinction. Let us pray we have the wisdom to choose correctly.

My wife was an immature woman... I would be home in the bathroom, taking a bath, and she would walk in whenever she felt like it and sink my boats.
Woody Allen 1935- American screenwriter, film director, actor, comedian, writer, musician and playwright

Woman is the salvation or the destruction of the family. She carries its destiny in the folds of her mantle.
Henri-Frédéric Amiel 1821-81 Swiss philosopher, poet and critic

If you can't annoy somebody with what you write, I think there's little point in writing.
Sir Kingsley Amis 1922-95 English novelist, poet and critic: *Radio Times* 1 May 1971

The sadness of the women's movement is that they don't allow the necessity of love. See, I don't personally trust any revolution where love is not allowed.
in *California Living* 14 May 1975

We allow our ignorance to prevail upon us and make us think we can survive alone, alone in patches, alone in groups, alone in races, alone even in genders.

If you don't like something, change it. If you can't change it, change your attitude. Don't complain.
Maya Angelou 1928- American authoress and poet

Resolved, that the women of this nation in 1876, have greater cause for discontent, rebellion and revolution than the men of 1776.
Susan B Anthony 1820-1906 American civil rights leader

A man's looks are measured by the depth of his pockets.
Elizabeth Aston *Mr Darcy's Daughters* (2003)

My vigor, vitality, and cheek repel me. I am the kind of woman I would run from.
Nancy Astor 1879-1964 first woman to sit in the British House of Commons as a Member of Parliament

Evil is unspectacular and always human,
And shares our bed and eats at our own table.
WH Auden 1907-1973 Anglo-American poet

A woman should never be trusted with money.
The Watsons (unfinished novel started in 1803)

Where so many hours have been spent in convincing myself that I am right, is there not some reason to fear I may be wrong?
Jane Austen 1775-1817 British novelist

I mean, damn it all, one minute you're having a perfectly good time and the next, you suddenly see them there like – some old sports jacket or something – literally beginning to come apart at the seams.
of women
Alan Ayckbourn 1939- English dramatist: *Absurd Person Singular* (1971)

Going to war without France is like going deer hunting without an accordion. You just leave a lot of useless, noisy baggage behind.
Jed Babbin a born diplomat, former United States Deputy Under Secretary of Defence, author, political commentator, contributing editor to *The American Spectator* and talk radio host

No man has ever yet discovered the way to give friendly advice to any woman, not even to his own wife.
Petite misères de la vie conjugale (1846)

Equality may perhaps be a right, but no power on earth can ever turn it into a fact.
[Author's note: true, but try telling that to Harriet Harman...]

No man should marry before he has studied anatomy and dissected the body of a woman.
Honoré de Balzac 1799-1850 French novelist and playwright

I can win an argument on any topic, against any opponent. People know this, and steer clear of me at parties. Often, as a sign of their great respect, they don't even invite me.
Dave Barry 1947- American author and columnist

The way to fight a woman is with your hat. Grab it and run.
John Barrymore 1882-1942 American actor

It is not necessary to understand things in order to argue about them.
Pierre-Augustin Caron de Beaumarchais 1732-99 French dramatist

It is not in giving life but in risking life that man is raised above the animal; that is why superiority has been accorded in humanity not to the sex that brings forth but to that which kills.
Simone de Beauvoir 1908-86 French philosopher and social theorist: *The Second Sex* (1950)

A great deal of intelligence can be invested in ignorance when the need for illusion is deep.

There is only one way to defeat the enemy, and that is to write as well as one can. The best argument is an undeniably good book.
Saul Bellow 1915-2005 American novelist

One of the few lessons I have learnt in life is that there is invariably something odd about women who wear ankle socks.
Alan Bennett 1934- English actor and playwright: *The Old Country* (1978)

You can't be fuelled by bitterness. It can eat you up, but it cannot drive you.
Benazir Bhutto 1953-2007 Pakistani stateswoman, Prime Minister 1988-90 and 1993-96: *Daughter of Destiny* (1989)

Bride, n. A woman with a fine prospect of happiness behind her.

Cabbage: A familiar kitchen-garden vegetable about as large and wise as a man's head.

Convent, n. A place of retirement for woman who wish for leisure to meditate upon the vice of idleness.

Female, n. One of the opposing, or unfair, sex.

Maiden, n. A young person of the unfair sex addicted to clewless conduct and views that madden to crime. The genus has a wide geographical distribution, being found wherever sought and deplored wherever found. The maiden is not altogether unpleasing to the eye, nor (without her piano and her views) insupportable to the ear, though in respect to comeliness distinctly inferior to the rainbow, and, with regard to the part of her that is audible, beaten out of the field by the canary – which, also, is more portable.

Weaknesses, n.pl. Certain primal powers of Tyrant Woman wherewith she holds dominion over the male of her species, binding him to the service of her will and paralyzing his rebellious energies.

Witch, n. (1) Any ugly and repulsive old woman, in a wicked league with the devil. (2) A beautiful and attractive young woman, in wickedness a league beyond the devil.
Ambrose Bierce 1842-1913 American writer and satirist: *The Devil's Dictionary* (1911)

Silence is one of the great arts of conversation, as allowed by Cicero himself, who says, 'there is not only an art, but an eloquence in it.' A well bred woman may easily and effectually promote the most useful and elegant conversation without speaking a word. The modes of speech are scarcely more variable than the modes of silence.
Tom Blair

Women have no wilderness in them,
They are provident instead,
Content in the tight hot cell of their hearts
To eat dusty bread.
Louise Bogan 1897-1970 American poet: 'Women' (1923)

Humor is by far the most significant activity of the human brain.
Edward De Bono 1933- physician, author, inventor and consultant

All I can say about Gary Cooper is he's hung like a horse and can go all night.
Clara Bow 1905-65 American actress, flapper and sex symbol

Sex is like pizza. Even when it's bad it's good.
Mel Brooks 1926- American film director, screenwriter, composer, lyricist, comedian, actor and producer

My lesbianism is an act of Christian charity. All those women out there praying for a man, and I'm giving them my share.
Rita Mae Brown 1944- American writer

Across much of Britain's public discourse, a reliance on reason has been replaced with a reliance on the emotional appeal of an argument. Parallel to the once-trusted world of empiricism and deductive reasoning, an often overwhelmingly powerful emotional landscape has been created, rewarding people with feelings of virtue for some beliefs, punishing with feelings of guilt for others. It is a belief system that echoes religion in providing ready, emotionally satisfying answers for a world too complex to understand fully, and providing a gratifying sense of righteousness absent in our otherwise secular society.

Anthony Browne 1967- British journalist, think tank director, Policy Director for Economic Development for Boris Johnson, the Mayor of London: *The Retreat of Reason* (2006)

The so-called conservative, uncomfortably disdainful of controversy, seldom has the energy to fight his battles, while the radical, so often a member of the minority, exerts disproportionate influence because of his dedication to his cause.

God and Man at Yale (1951)

Conservatism is the tacit acknowledgement that all that is finally important in human experience is behind us; that the crucial explorations have been undertaken, and that it is given to man to know what are the great truths that emerged from them.

Liberalism cannot sustain our civilization on the little it has to offer. It is sustaining the majority of our intellectuals, but that proves easier than holding together the world.

A marked characteristic of the liberal-in-a-debate-with-a-conservative is the tacit premise that debate is ridiculous because there is nothing whatever to debate about. Arguments based on fact are especially to be avoided.

Up from Liberalism 2nd ed. (1968)

I'd rather entrust the government of the United States to the first 400 people listed in the Boston telephone directory than to the faculty of Harvard University.

I would like to take you seriously but to do so would affront your intelligence.

William F Buckley Jr 1925-2008 American conservative author and commentator

A pretty woman is a welcome guest.

Lord Byron 1788-1824 British poet

What is a rebel? A man who says no.
Albert Camus 1913-1960 French author, journalist, and philosopher: *The Rebel* (1951)

Life's difficult enough without Meryl Streep movies.
Truman Capote 1924-84 American writer

Abstract art is a product of the untalented, sold by the unprincipled to the utterly bewildered.
Al Capp 1909-1979 American cartoonist and humorist

We have given away far too many freedoms in order to be free. Now it's time to take some back.
John Le Carré 1931- British author

Behind every successful man is a woman rolling her eyes.
Jim Carrey 1962- Canadian-American actor, comedian and writer: *Bruce Almighty* (2003)

I visited Karl Marx's tomb in Highgate Cemetery in London last week. It was a communist plot.
Paul Carrington 1950- British martial arts expert, security man, thrice married (to Yugoslavian, Italian and Ugandan women), thrice divorced, single, eternal optimist, singer-songwriter, socialist, the chauffeur in the author's travelogue *Two Men in a Car* and one of eight guitarists – Thunderin' Paul Carrington – whose life stories are related in the author's *Guitar Gods in Beds. (Bedfordshire: a heavenly county).*

Difficulties are meant to rouse, not discourage. The human spirit is to grow strong by conflict.
William Ellery Channing 1780-1842 Unitarian preacher

In all legends men have thought of women as sublime separately but horrible in a herd.
GK Chesterton 1874-1936 English writer: 'What's Wrong With the World' (1910)

To be conservative at 20 is heartless and to be a liberal at 60 is plain idiocy.

You can always trust the Americans. In the end they will do the right thing, after they have eliminated all the other possibilities.

The inherent vice of capitalism is the unequal sharing of blessings. The inherent virtue of socialism is the equal sharing of misery.
Sir Winston Churchill 1874-1965 British Conservative politician, Prime Minister 1940-45, 1951-55, soldier and painter

When you have no basis of argument, abuse the plaintiff.
Cicero 106BC - 43BC Roman orator and statesman

Oh, to be seventy again!
on seeing a pretty girl on his eightieth birthday
Georges Clemenceau 1841-1929 French statesman, physician, journalist, Prime Minister
of France 1906-09, 1917-20

Sensible and responsible women do not want to vote. The relative
positions to be assumed by man and woman in the working out of our
civilization were assigned long ago by a higher intelligence than ours.
Grover Cleveland 1837-1908 President of the United States (1885-9, 1893-7)

A female acquaintance of The Princess [Author's note: The Princess is
Vernon Coleman's wife Donna Antoinette, 26 years his junior, often
referred to in his books as 'the totally adorable Welsh Princess'] came to
lunch today. She believes in equality and the liberation of women and is a
huge fan of Harriet Harman which I personally believe probably makes
her certifiable. She complained bitterly that her new boyfriend always
leaves the toilet seat up. She asked why men do this. I told her that men
are equally upset by the fact that many women leave the toilet seat down.
She tried to comment on this but failed to find anything to say and
managed only to give an excellent impression of a goldfish singing in a
church choir.
Vernon Coleman 1946- English author and former general practitioner: *Diary of a*
Disgruntled Man (2011)

The most happy marriage I can imagine to myself would be the union of
a deaf man to a blind woman.
Samuel Taylor Coleridge 1772-1834 English poet, literary critic and philosopher

Being a woman is a terribly difficult task since it consists principally in
dealing with men.
Joseph Conrad 1857-1924 Polish-born English novelist

Apparently bears are attracted to women in their menstrual cycles. A
1,000lb grizzly against a 120lb woman with cramps. I say fair fight.
Simon Cotter Canadian comedian

I've sometimes thought of marrying, and then I've thought again.

Certain women should be struck regularly, like gongs.
Private Lives (1930)

If you'd been any prettier it would have been 'Florence of Arabia'.
to Peter O'Toole on *Laurence of Arabia* (1962)

I can take any amount of criticism, so long as it is unqualified praise.
quoted in Laurence J Peter, *Quotations for Our Time* (1977)

My dear boy, forget about the motivation. Just say the lines and don't trip over the furniture.
advice to a theatre actor

For God's sake, go and tell that young man to take the Rockingham tea service out of his tights.
to choreographer about male dancer with unsightly bulge

The food was so abominable that I used to cross myself before taking a mouthful... I used to say, 'Ian, it tastes like armpits.'
of Ian Fleming's hospitality

She couldn't get a laugh if she pulled a kipper out of her cunt.
of an actress unable to elicit comedy from his lines

I don't see why not; everyone else has.
passing a Leicester Square movie poster which proclaimed 'Michael Redgrave and Dirk Bogarde in *The Sea Shall Not Have Them*'

Doesn't everyone?
when asked why he drank champagne for breakfast

I was delighted to see that you thought I was as good as I thought I was.
Sir Noël Coward 1899-1973 English entertainer and writer

The strongest possible piece of advice I would give any young woman is: Don't screw around, and don't smoke.
Edwina Currie 1946- British Conservative politician, novelist and broadcaster: *Observer* (1988)

The first man to compare the cheeks of a young woman to a rose was obviously a poet; the first to repeat it was possibly an idiot.
Salvador Dali 1904-1989 Spanish surrealist painter: *Dialogues with Marcel Duchamp* (1987)

Happiness is always a by-product. It is probably a matter of temperament, and for anything I know it may be glandular. But it is not something that can be demanded from life, and if you are not happy you had better stop worrying about it and see what treasures you can pluck from your own brand of unhappiness.

Many a promising career has been wrecked by marrying the wrong sort of woman. The right sort of woman can distinguish between Creative Lassitude and plain shiftlessness.
Robertson Davies 1913-95 Canadian novelist, playwright, critic, journalist and academic

There comes a time in every woman's life when the only thing that helps is a glass of champagne.
Bette Davis 1908-89 American actress of film, television and theatre

The first and great commandment is: Don't let them scare you.
Elmer Davis 1890-1958 American journalist and author

I have long since come to believe that people never mean half of what they say, and that it is best to disregard their talk and judge only their actions.
Dorothy Day 1897-1980 American journalist and social activist

A good psychic would pick up the phone before it rang. My psychic once said to me, 'God Bless you.' I said, 'I didn't sneeze.' She looked deep into my eyes and said, 'You will, eventually.' And damn it if she wasn't right. Two days later I sneezed.
Ellen DeGeneres 1958- American stand-up comedienne, television hostess and actress

The feminist movement seems to have beaten the manners out of men, but I didn't see them put up a lot of resistance.
Clarissa Theresa Philomena Aileen Mary Josephine Agnes Elsie Trilby Louise Esmerelda Dickson Wright 1947- English celebrity chef. Trained as a lawyer, she became the youngest woman ever to be called to the Bar: *Mail on Sunday*, 24 September 2000

Girls bored me – they still do. I love Mickey Mouse more than any woman I've ever known.
Walt Disney 1901-66 American film producer, director, screenwriter, voice actor, animator, entrepreneur, entertainer and philanthropist

Man is tormented by no greater anxiety than to find someone quickly to whom he can hand over that great gift of freedom with which the ill-fated creature is born.
Fyodor Dostoevsky 1821-81 Russian novelist and essayist: *The Brothers Karamazov* (1880)

Would you *mind* if I flew the Atlantic?
Amelia Earhart 1898-1937 American aviatrix to her husband George Putnam; George P Putnam *Soaring Wings* (1939)

There is no expedient to which a man will not go to avoid the labour of thinking.
Thomas A Edison 1847-1931 American inventor, scientist and businessman

Every man who is not a monster, mathematician or a mad philosopher, is the slave of some woman or other.
George Eliot 1819-1880 English authoress: *Scenes of Clerical Life* (1857)

Misunderstood! It is a right fool's word. Is it so bad then to be misunderstood? Pythagoras was misunderstood, and Socrates, and Jesus, and Luther, and Copernicus, and Galileo, and Newton, and every pure and wise spirit that ever took flesh. To be great is to be misunderstood.
Essays (1841)

[Author's note: my uncle Henry is frequently misunderstood, but you wouldn't call him great. Stupid, possibly, but not great.]

There is always a certain meanness in the argument of conservatism, joined with a certain superiority in its fact.
The Conservative (1849)
Ralph Waldo Emerson 1803-82 American essayist, philosopher and poet

Many a man who falls in love with a dimple makes the mistake of marrying the whole girl.
Evan Esar 1899-1995 American humorist: *Esar's Comic Dictionary* (1943)

When a woman behaves like a man, why can't she behave like a *nice* man?
Dame Edith Evans 1888-1976 British actress

I've never struck a woman in my life, not even my own mother.

I was in love with a beautiful blonde once. She drove me to drink. 'Tis the one thing I'm indebted to her for.
Never Give a Sucker an Even Break (1941)

It reminds me of an aardvark's ass.
of Jeanette Macdonald's face

Women are like elephants to me: nice to look at, but I wouldn't want to own one.

I believe in clubs for women, but only if every other form of persuasion fails.
WC Fields 1880-1946 American comedian, actor, juggler and writer

Here's how men think. Sex, work – and those are reversible, depending on age – sex, work, food, sports and lastly, begrudgingly, relationships. And here's how women think. Relationships, relationships, relationships, work, sex, shopping, weight, food.
Carrie Fisher 1956- American actress, screenwriter and novelist: *Surrender the Pink* (1990)

The test of a first-rate intelligence is the ability to hold two opposed ideas in the mind at the same time, and still retain the ability to function.
F Scott Fitzgerald 1896-1940 American author

History is a voice forever sounding across the centuries the laws of right and wrong. Opinions alter, manners change, creeds rise and fall, but the moral law is written on the tablets of eternity.
James A Forude

Getting married for sex is like buying a 747 for the free peanuts.
Jeff Foxworthy 1958- American comedian and author

Emotion is a rotten base for politics.
Dick Francis 1920-2010 British horse racing crime writer and retired jockey

Perhaps the history of the errors of mankind, all things considered, is more valuable and interesting than that of their discoveries. Truth is uniform and narrow; it constantly exists, and does not seem to require so much an active energy, as a passive aptitude of the soul in order to encounter it. But error is endlessly diversified; it has no reality, but is the pure and simple creation of the mind that invents it. In this field the soul has room enough to expand herself, to display all her boundless faculties, and all her beautiful and interesting extravagancies and absurdities.
Benjamin Franklin 1706-1790 American author, printer, political theorist, politician, postmaster, scientist, musician, inventor, satirist, civic activist, statesman and diplomat: *Report to the King of France on Animal Magnetism* (1784)

The awe and dread with which the untutored savage contemplates his mother-in-law are amongst the most familiar facts of anthropology.
Sir James Frazer 1854-1941 Scottish classicist, anthropologist: *The Golden Bough* (1922)

Whatever they may be in public life, whatever their relations with men, in their relations with women, all men are rapists, and that's all they are. They rape us with their eyes, their laws, and their codes.

'I hate discussions of feminism that end up with who does the dishes,' she said. So do I. But at the end, there are always the damned dishes.
   The Women's Room (1977)
Marilyn French 1929- American writer

It is easier to live through someone else than to become complete yourself.

It is better for a woman to compete impersonally in society, as men do, than to compete for dominance in her own home with her husband, compete with her neighbours for empty status, and so smother her son that he cannot compete at all.
Betty Friedan 1921-2006 American writer, activist and feminist

A society that puts equality – in the sense of equality of outcome – ahead of freedom will end up with neither equality nor freedom.
Milton Friedman 1912-2006 American economist and statistician: *Free to Choose* (1980)

Male and female represent the two sides of the great radical dualism. But in fact they are perpetually passing into one another. Fluid hardens to solid, solid rushes to fluid. There is no wholly masculine man, no purely feminine woman.
Margaret Fuller 1810-50 American journalist, critic, and women's rights advocate: *Woman in the Nineteenth Century* (1845)

Under capitalism, man exploits man. Under communism, it's just the opposite.
John Kenneth Galbraith 1908-2006 Canadian-American economist

With reasonable men I will reason; with humane men I will plea; but to tyrants I will give no quarter, nor waste arguments where they will certainly be lost.
William Lloyd Garrison 1805-79 American anti-slavery campaigner

I'll not listen to reason... Reason always means what someone else has got to say.
Cranford (1853)

Your wife and I didn't hit it off the only time I ever saw her. I won't say she was silly, but I think one of us was silly, and it wasn't me.
Wives and Daughters (1866)
Elizabeth Gaskell 1810-65 British novelist

Man is the only animal whose desires increase as they are fed; the only animal that is never satisfied.
Henry George 1839-97 American writer, politician and political economist

Against criticism a man can neither protest nor defend himself; he must act in spite of it, and then it will gradually yield to him.

The phrases that men hear or repeat continually, end by becoming convictions and ossify the organs of intelligence.

The intelligent man finds almost everything ridiculous, the sensible man hardly anything.
Johann Wolfgang von Goethe 1749-1832 German writer, pictorial artist, biologist, theoretical physicist, and polymath

Commandment Number One of any truly civilised society is this: let people be different.
David Grayson 1870-1946 American journalist and author

So many new ideas are at first strange and horrible, though ultimately valuable, that a very heavy responsibility rests upon those who would prevent their dissemination.
JBS Haldane 1892-1964 British-born Indian geneticist and evolutionary biologist

It is not worth an intelligent man's time to be in the majority. By definition, there are already enough people to do that.
GH Hardy 1877-1947 English mathematician

Loving is misery for women always. I shall never forgive God for making me a woman and dearly am I beginning to pay for the honour of owning a pretty face.
Thomas Hardy 1840-1928 English novelist and poet: Bathsheba Everdene in *Far From the Madding Crowd* (1874)

Man is the only animal that laughs and weeps, for he is the only animal that is struck with the difference between what things are and what they ought to be.
William Hazlitt 1778-1830 English writer, essayist, critic and philosopher

A fair society is one in which some people fail – and they may fail in something other than precise, demographically representative proportions.
William A Henry III 1950-1994 American cultural critic and author: *In Defence of Elitism* (1994)

Humans live best when each has his place, when each knows where he belongs in the scheme of things. Destroy the place and destroy the person.
Frank Herbert 1920-1986 American science fiction author: *Dune* (1965)

By means of shrewd lies, unremittingly repeated, it is possible to make people believe that heaven is hell – and hell heaven. The greater the lie, the more readily it will be believed by the great masses.
Adolf Hitler 1889-1945 Austrian-born German politician, leader of the National Socialist Workers party: *Mein Kampf* (1925-6)

Man's mind, once stretched by a new idea, never regains its original dimensions.

When I think of talking, it is of course with a woman. For talking at its best being an inspiration, it wants a corresponding divine quality of receptiveness, and where will you find this but in a woman?
Oliver Wendell Holmes 1809-1894 American physician, professor, lecturer and author

The Blues ain't nothin' but a good woman on your mind.
Mississippi John Hurt 1893-1966 American country blues singer and guitarist

Single-mindedness is all very well in cows or baboons; in an animal claiming to belong to the same species as Shakespeare it is simply disgraceful.

At least two-thirds of our miseries spring from human stupidity, human malice and those great motivators and justifiers of malice and stupidity: idealism, dogmatism and proselytising zeal on behalf of religious or political ideas.

Most human beings have an almost infinite capacity for taking things for granted.
Aldous Huxley 1894-1963 English writer, humanist and pacifist

Any doctrine that will not bear investigation is not a fit tenant for the mind of an honest man.
Robert Ingersoll 1833-99 American Civil War veteran, political leader and orator during the Golden Age of Freethought

What courage can withstand the ever-enduring and all-besetting terrors of a woman's tongue?
  Rip Van Winkle (1819)

A woman's whole life is a history of the affections.
Washington Irving 1783-1859 American author, essayist, biographer and historian

Men and women. Women and men. It will never work.
Erica Jong 1942- American authoress and teacher

Jesus was a bachelor and never lived with a woman. Surely living with a woman is one of the most difficult things a man has to do, and he never did it.
James Joyce 1882-1941 Irish novelist and poet

Feminism: The Ugly Truth

Feminism: The Ugly Truth

I once complained to my father that I didn't seem to be able to do things the same way other people did. Dad's advice? 'Margo, don't be a sheep. People hate sheep. They eat sheep.'

The only thing worse than a man you can't control is a man you can.
Margo Kaufman American writer

When I was a kid I used to pray every night for a new bike. Then I realised that the Lord doesn't work that way, so I stole one and asked him to forgive me.
Peter Kay 1973- British comedian, comedy writer, producer, director and actor

Although the world is full of suffering, it is also full of the overcoming of it.
Helen Keller 1880-1968 American deaf blind author, political activist and lecturer

The ultimate measure of a man is not where he stands in moments of comfort and convenience, but where he stands at times of challenge and controversy.
Martin Luther King Jr 1929-1968 American clergyman and political activist: *Strength to Love* (1963)

Every woman knows all about everything.
Rudyard Kipling 1865-1936 English poet, short-story writer, and novelist: *The Eye of Allah* (1926)

Givers have to set limits because takers rarely do.
Irma Kurtz 1935- American-born British journalist and author

There's a great woman behind every idiot.
John Lennon 1940-1980 English musician and singer-songwriter

Why can't a woman be more like a man?
Men are so honest, so thoroughly square;
Eternally noble, historically fair.
Alan Jay Lerner 1918-86 American songwriter: 'A Hymn to Him' *My Fair Lady* (1956)

Somewhere on this globe, every ten seconds, there is a woman giving birth to a child. She must be found and stopped.
Sam Levenson 1911-1980 American humorist, writer, teacher, television host and journalist

Children need love and discipline. They need mothers and fathers. A welfare check is not a husband. The state is not a father.
Rush Limbaugh 1951- American radio host and conservative political commentator: *See, I Told You So* (1993)

New opinions are always suspected, and usually opposed, without any other reason but because they are not already common.
An Essay concerning Human Understanding (1690)

Earthly minds, like mud walls, resist the strongest batteries; and though, perhaps, sometimes the force of a clear argument may make some impression, yet they nevertheless stand firm, keep out the enemy, truth, that would captivate or disturb them.
John Locke 1632-1704 English philosopher

I define comfort as self-acceptance. When we finally learn that self-care begins and ends with ourselves, we no longer demand sustenance and happiness from others.
Jennifer Louden

Poor is the man whose pleasures depend on the permission of another.
Madonna 1958- American singer-songwriter, actress and entrepreneur

There is no greater importance in all the world like knowing you are right and that the wave of the world is wrong, yet the wave crashes upon you.
Norman Mailer 1923-2007 American novelist, journalist, essayist, poet, playwright, screenwriter and film director: *Armies Of The Night* (1968)

The human race progresses because and when the strongest human powers and the highest human faculties lead it . . . if all the ruling classes of today could be disposed of in a single massacre, and nobody left but those who at present call themselves the workers, these workers would be as helpless as a flock of shepherdless sheep.
William Hurrell Mallock 1849-1923 English author: *Aristocracy and Evolution* (1892)

I seek constantly to improve my manners and graces, for they are the sugar to which all are attracted.
Og Mandino 1923-1996 American author

The sign of an intelligent people is their ability to control emotions by the application of reason.
Marya Mannes 1904-90 American authoress and critic

There is one thing I would break up over, and that is if she caught me with another woman. I won't stand for that.
Steve Martin 1945- American actor, comedian, writer, playwright, producer, musician and composer

A woman can forgive a man for the harm he does her... but she can never forgive him for the sacrifices he makes on her account.
The Moon and Sixpence (1919)

One can be very much in love with a woman without wishing to spend the rest of one's life with her.
The Painted Veil (1925)
W Somerset Maugham 1874-1965 English playwright, novelist and short story writer

It is impossible to defeat an ignorant man in argument.
William G McAdoo 1863-1941 American lawyer and politician

I wanna be the leader
I wanna be the leader
Can I be the leader?
Can I? Can I?
Promise? Promise?
Yippee, I'm the leader
I'm the leader
OK, what shall we do now?
Roger McGough 1937- English poet: 'The Leader'

The human mind treats a new idea the same way the body treats a strange protein; it rejects it.
Peter Medawar 1915-1987 British biologist

The final test of truth is ridicule. Very few dogmas have ever faced it and survived.
Damn! A Book of Calumny (1918)

There is always a well-known solution to every human problem – neat, plausible, and wrong.
Prejudices: Second Series (1920)

An idealist is one who, on noticing that a rose smells better than a cabbage, concludes that it will also make better soup.
Chrestomathy (1949)

The worst government is often the most moral. One composed of cynics is often very tolerant and humane. But when fanatics are on top there is no limit to oppression.
Minority Report (1956)

One hears that the 'women of the United States' are up in arms about this or that; the plain fact is that eight fat women, meeting in a hotel parlor, have decided to kick up some dust.

Misogynist: A man who hates women as much as women hate one another.

Every decent man is ashamed of the government he lives under.

The most common of all follies is to believe passionately in the palpably not true. It is the chief occupation of mankind.
HL Mencken 1880-1956 American journalist, essayist, magazine editor, satirist, critic of American life and culture

I say 'girl' because I love to annoy people. I love the word 'girl'. 'Gal' is pretty great, too. I don't just want to be called a woman. It sounds like someone with a moustache.
Bette Midler 1945- American singer, actress and comedienne

The only way to be truly misogynistic is to be a woman.
Randy K Milholland webcomic author: *Something Positive*, 11 November 2004

Ask yourself if you are happy, and you cease to be so.
John Stuart Mill 1806-73 English philosopher and economist: *Autobiography* (1873)

Nobody can feel better than the man who is completely taken in. To be intelligent may be a boon, but to be completely trusting, gullible to the point of idiocy, to surrender without reservation, is one of the supreme joys of life.
Henry Miller 1891-1980 American novelist and painter: *Sexus (The Rosy Crucifixion)* (1949)

Give me the liberty to know, to utter, and to argue freely according to conscience, above all liberties.
Areopagitica (1644)

Where there is much desire to learn, there of necessity will be much arguing, much writing, many opinions; for opinions in good men is but knowledge in the making.
John Milton 1608-74 English poet

I don't mind living in a man's world as long as I can be a woman in it.
Marilyn Monroe 1926-1962 American actress, singer and model

A man who has never made a woman angry is a failure in life.
Christopher Morley 1890-1957 American journalist, novelist, essayist and poet

The cry of equality pulls everyone down.
Iris Murdoch 1919-99 Irish-born British authoress and philosopher

A certain amount of opposition is a great help to a man; it is what he wants and must have to be good for anything. Hardship and opposition are the native soil of manhood and self-reliance.
John Neal 1793-1876 American author and critic

Insanity in individuals is something rare – but in groups, parties, nations and epochs, it is the rule.

The irrationality of a thing is no argument against its existence, rather a condition of it.
Friedrich Nietzsche 1844 -1900 German philosopher and writer

To be conservative, then, is to prefer the familiar to the unknown, to prefer the tried to the untried, fact to mystery, the actual to the possible, the limited to the unbounded, the near to the distant, the sufficient to the superabundant, the convenient to the perfect, present laughter to utopian bliss.
Michael Oakeshott 1901-1990 English philosopher: 'On Being Conservative' (1956)

The vote, I think, means nothing to women. We should be armed.
Edna O'Brien 1932– Irish novelist and short story writer

If men were shouted down for being sexist when they used the word 'postman', then asking if there was any chance of a quick shag seemed like a bit of a non-starter.
John O'Farrell 1962- British author, broadcaster and comedy scriptwriter

Being politically correct means always having to say you're sorry.
Charles Osgood 1933- American radio and television commentator

We are slow to believe that which, if believed, would hurt our feelings.
Ovid 43BC - 17AD Roman poet

President Obama has been in office for over a year. I'd like to ask him, 'So, Mr President, how's the hopey, changey stuff been working out?'
Sarah Palin 1964- American Republican politician, speech February 2010

Oh, life is a glorious cycle of song,
A medley of extemporanea;
And love is a thing that can never go wrong –
And I am Marie of Romania
   Not So Deep as a Well (1937)

Woman lives but in her lord;
Count to ten, and man is bored.
With this the gist and sum of it,
What earthly good can come of it?
General Review of the Sex Situation (1937)

I hate women. They get on my nerves.
quoted in *Women's Wicked Wit* ed. Michelle Lovric (2000)
Dorothy Parker 1893 – 1967 American writer

Pain makes man think. Thought makes man wise. Wisdom makes life endurable.
John Patrick

Behind every successful man is a surprised woman.
Maryon Pearson 1901-89 wife of Lester Bowles Pearson, 14th Prime Minister of Canada

He who does not bellow the truth when he knows the truth makes himself the accomplice of liars and forgers.
Charles Péguy 1873–1914 French poet and essayist: *Basic Verities*

Grandmother's brain was dead, but her heart was still beating. It was the first time we ever had a Democrat in the family.

Women: you can't live with them, and you can't get them to dress up in a skimpy Nazi uniform and beat you with a warm squash.
Emo Philips 1956- American comedian

It's comforting to know you are out there working along the same lines as I am. It's discomforting to know David Cameron is indeed oblivious to what is happening. How can he hope to repair his broken society if he doesn't accept that it is radical feminists who first caused the break and continue to dismantle the future for our children?
communication with the author, 1 October 2011

To me a good family is the basis of democracy and is democratic to the core. That's why the feminists had to destroy it.
Erin Pizzey 1939- British family care activist and a best-selling novelist. She became internationally famous for having started one of the first Women's refuges in the modern world, Chiswick Women's Aid, in 1971. She has been the subject of death threats and boycotts because of her conclusions that most domestic violence is reciprocal, and that women are equally as capable of violence as men.

I have no faith in human perfectibility. I think that human exertion will have no appreciable effect upon humanity. Man is now only more active – not more happy – nor more wise, than he was 6,000 years ago.
Edgar Allan Poe 1809-1849 American author, poet, editor and literary critic

There are three roads to ruin: women, gambling and technicians. The most pleasant is with women, the quickest is with gambling, but the surest is with technicians.
Georges Pompidou 1911-74 French President

Human beings are perhaps never more frightening than when they are convinced beyond doubt that they are right.
Laurens Van der Post 1906-96 Afrikaner author, farmer, war hero, political adviser to British heads of government, close friend of Prince Charles, godfather of Prince William, educator, journalist, humanitarian, philosopher, explorer and conservationist: *The Lost World of the Kalahari* (1958)

Properly, we should read for power. Man reading should be man intensely alive. The book should be a ball of light in one's hand.
Ezra Pound 1885-1972 American poet and critic

But never fear, gentlemen; castration was really not the point of feminism, and we women are too busy eviscerating one another to take you on.
Anna Quindlen 1953- American authoress, journalist and opinion columnist

I hope that while so many people are out smelling the flowers, someone is taking the time to plant some.
Herbert Rappaport 1908-83 Austrian-Soviet screenwriter and film director

You cannot claim both full equality and special dispensation.
William Raspberry 1935- African-American Pulitzer Prize-winning columnist: *Washington Post* 20 September 1989

I didn't intend for this to take on a political tone. I'm here for the drugs.
on being asked a political question at a 'Just Say No' rally
Nancy Reagan 1921- widow of former United States President Ronald Reagan

It isn't so much that Liberals are ignorant. It's just that they know so much that isn't so.
televised speech, eve of the 1964 election

The nine most terrifying words in the English language are, 'I'm from the government and I'm here to help.'
Ronald Reagan 1911-89 Actor, American Democratic Party then Republican Party politician, 40th President of the United States 1981-89

There is not one female comic who was beautiful as a little girl.

A man can sleep around, no questions asked, but if a woman makes nineteen or twenty mistakes she's a tramp.
Joan Rivers 1935- American comedienne, television personality and actress

Feminism is a socialist, anti-family, political movement that encourages women to leave their husbands, kill their children, practice witchcraft, destroy capitalism and become lesbians.
Pat Robertson 1930- American media mogul, televangelist, ex-Baptist minister and businessman

Most of our so-called reasoning consists in finding arguments for going on believing as we already do.
James Harvey Robinson 1863-1936 American historian

You can't say that civilization don't advance, however, for in every war they kill you in a new way.
Will Rogers 1879-1935 American cowboy, comedian, humorist, social commentator, vaudeville performer and actor: *New York Times* 23 December 1929

Man is born free, but everywhere he is in chains.

To renounce liberty is to renounce being a man, to surrender the rights of humanity and even its duties. For he who renounces everything no indemnity is possible. Such a renunciation is incompatible with man's nature; to remove all liberty from his will is to remove all morality from his acts.

As soon as any man says of the affairs of the State, 'What does it matter to me?', the State may be given up for lost.
Jean Jacques Rousseau 1712-78 Genevan philosopher, plonker, and author of the book which, it has been argued, paved the way for the demonic philosophy of communism: *The Social Contract* (1762)

It takes a woman twenty years to make a man of her son, and another woman twenty minutes to make a fool of him.
Helen Rowland 1876-1950 American journalist and humorist

One of the things a writer is for is to say the unsayable, speak the unspeakable and ask difficult questions.
Salman Rushdie 1947– Indian-born British novelist: *Independent on Sunday* 10 September 1995

The greatest thing a human soul ever does in this world is to see something and tell what it saw in a plain way. Hundreds of people can talk for one who can think, but thousands can think for one who can see. To see clearly is poetry, prophecy and religion, all in one.
John Ruskin 1819-1900 English art critic, draughtsman, watercolourist, prominent social thinker and philanthropist

The opinions that are held with passion are always those for which no good ground exists; indeed the passion is the measure of the holder's lack of rational conviction.
Sceptical Essays (1928)

It is a waste of energy to be angry with a man who behaves badly, just as it is to be angry with a car that won't go.

All movements go too far.
Bertrand Russell 1872-1970 British philosopher, logician, mathematician, historian, free trade champion, pacifist and social critic

In science it often happens that scientists say, 'You know, that's a really good argument; my position is mistaken,' and then they would actually change their minds and you never hear that old view from them again. They really do it. It doesn't happen as often as it should, because scientists are human and change is sometimes painful. But it happens every day. I cannot recall the last time something like that happened in politics or religion.
Carl Sagan 1934 -96 American scientist and writer: 1987 CSICOP Keynote Address

Being defeated is often a temporary condition. Giving up is what makes it permanent.
Marilyn vos Savant 1946- American columnist, author, lecturer and playwright

Man is a clever animal who behaves like an imbecile.
Albert Schweitzer 1875-1965 Alsatian theologian, organist, philosopher, physician, and medical missionary

Finally, in conclusion, let me say just this.
Peter Sellers 1925-80 English comedian and actor

What does reason demand of a man? A very easy thing – to live in accord with his nature.
Seneca 5BC - 65AD Roman Stoic philosopher, statesman, dramatist and humorist

This royal throne of kings, this sceptered isle,
This earth of majesty, this seat of Mars,
This other Eden, demi-paradise,
This fortress built by Nature for herself
Against infection and the hand of war,
This happy breed of men, this little world,
This precious stone set in the silver sea,
Which serves it in the office of a wall
Or as a moat defensive to a house,
Against the envy of less happier lands,
This blessed plot, this earth, this realm, this England.
  King Richard II (1595)

What a piece of work is a man! how noble in reason! how infinite in
faculty! in form and moving how express and admirable! in action how
like an angel! in apprehension how like a god!
  Hamlet (1601)
William Shakespeare 1564-1616 English poet and playwright

The reasonable man adapts himself to the world; the unreasonable one
persists in trying to adapt the world to himself. Therefore all progress
depends on the unreasonable man.
  Man and Superman (1903), 'Maxims for Revolutionists'

Women upset everything. When you let them into your life, you find that
the woman is driving at one thing and you're driving at another.
  Pygmalion (1912)

Remember that you are a human being with a soul and the divine gift of
articulate speech: that your native language is the language of
Shakespeare and Milton and The Bible; and don't sit there crooning like
a bilious pigeon.
  Professor Higgins to Eliza Doolittle in *Pygmalion* (1912)

All great truths begin as blasphemies.
  Annajanska (1919)

The moment we want to believe something, we suddenly see all the
arguments for it, and become blind to the arguments against it.

If the lesser mind could measure the greater as a footrule can measure a
pyramid, there would be finality in universal suffrage. As it is, the political
problem remains unsolved.
George Bernard Shaw 1856-1950 Irish playwright

I like American women. They do things sexually that Russian girls never dream of doing – like showering.
Yakov Smirnoff 1951- Ukrainian-born American comedian, painter and teacher

When you think of the long and gloomy history of man, you will find more hideous crimes have been committed in the name of obedience than have ever been committed in the name of rebellion.
CP Snow 1905-80 English physicist and novelist

Remember that there is nothing stable in human affairs; therefore avoid undue elation in prosperity, or undue depression in adversity.
Sophocles 470 – 399BC Greek philosopher and tragedian

Nobody likes the man who brings bad news.

Numberless are the world's wonders, but none more wonderful than man.
Sophocles 496 - 406BC Greek tragedian: *Antigone* (442BC)

I am glad that I am not a man, for if I were I should have to marry a woman.
Madame de Stael 1766-1817 Swiss authoress

To be intelligent is to be open-minded, active, memoried, and persistently experimental.
Leopold Stein

To have respect for ourselves guides our morals; and to have a deference for others governs our manners.
Laurence Sterne (1713-1768) Anglo-Irish novelist and an Anglican clergyman

From the beginning of our history the country has been afflicted with compromise. It is by compromise that human rights have been abandoned. I insist that this shall cease. The country needs repose after all its trials; it deserves repose. And repose can only be found in everlasting principles.
Charles Sumner 1811-74 American statesman

I don't want to get to a position when we have women in senior roles because they're women, we want to have women because they are able and as well equipped as men and sometimes better.
Margaret Thatcher 1925- British Conservative politician, Leader of the Conservative Party 1975-90, Prime Minister of the United Kingdom 1979-90

I wouldn't recommend sex, drugs or insanity for everyone, but they've always worked for me.
Hunter S Thompson 1939-2005 American journalist and author

If a man does not keep pace with his companions, perhaps it is because he hears a different drummer. Let him step to the music which he hears, however measured or far away.
Conclusion (1854)

How many a man has dated a new era in his life from the reading of a book.
Henry Thoreau 1817-62 American author, poet, naturalist, tax resister, development critic, surveyor, historian, philosopher, and leading transcendentalist

A woman's place is in the wrong.
James Thurber 1894-1961 American author and cartoonist

America is great because she is good. If America ceases to be good, America will cease to be great.

Americans are so enamoured of equality that they would rather be equal in slavery than unequal in freedom.

On my arrival in the United States I was struck by the degree of ability among the governed and the lack of it among the governing.
Alexis de Tocqueville 1805-59 French political thinker and historian: *Democracy in America* (1835)

Men don't know women, or they would be harder to them.
Anthony Trollope 1815-82 English novelist: Lady Ongar in *The Claverings* (1867)

Noise proves nothing. Often a hen who has merely laid an egg cackles as if she had laid an asteroid.
Following the Equator (1897)

Humanity has unquestionably one really effective weapon – laughter. Power, money, persuasion, supplication, persecution – these can lift at a colossal humbug – push it a little – weaken it a little, century by century; but only laughter can blow it to rags and atoms at a blast. Against the assault of laughter nothing can stand.
The Mysterious Stranger (1910)
Mark Twain 1835-1910 American author and humorist

A successful man is one who makes more money than his wife can spend. A successful woman is one who can find such a man.
Lana Turner 1921-95 American actress

In fevered depravity the last Liberals ran riot through the 1970s gibbering: consciousness-raising! self-realization! group-therapy! sexuality! human rights! animal rights! water beds! wheat grass enemas! sanitary napkins shaped from genuine sea sponges! . . . This is light years removed from the New Deal.
R Emmett Tyrrell Jr 1943- American conservative magazine editor

I can understand companionship. I can understand bought sex in the afternoon. I cannot understand the love affair.

There is no human problem which could not be solved if people would simply do as I advise.
Gore Vidal 1925- American author, playwright, essayist, screenwriter and political activist

Like so many Americans, she was trying to construct a life that made sense from things she found in gift shops.
Slaughterhouse-Five (1969)

Thanks to TV and for the convenience of TV, you can only be one of two kinds of human beings, either a liberal or a conservative.
In These Times, 10 May 2004, 'Cold Turkey'
Kurt Vonnegut 1922-2007 American writer

Our cause is noble; it is the cause of mankind!
George Washington 1732-99 dominant military and political leader of the new United States of America from 1775 to 1799

A strong conviction that something must be done is the parent of many bad measures.
Daniel Webster 1782-1852 American politician

Human history becomes more and more a race between education and catastrophe.
HG Wells 1866 – 1946 English author: *Outline of History* (1920)

My dear boy, no woman is a genius. They are a decorative sex. They never have anything to say, but they say it charmingly. Women represent the triumph of matter over mind, just as men represent the triumph of mind over morals.
The Picture of Dorian Gray (1890)

A man can be happy with any woman as long as he does not love her.

One is tempted to define man as a rational animal who always loses his temper when he is called upon to act in accordance with the dictates of reason.
'The Critic as Artist' (1891)

Disobedience, in the eyes of anyone who has read history, is man's original virtue. It is through disobedience and rebellion that progress has been made.
'The Soul of Man Under Socialism' (1891)
Oscar Wilde 1854-1900 Irish writer, poet and playwright

Wherever you come near the human race there's layers and layers of nonsense.
Thornton Wilder 1897-1975 American playwright and novelist: *Our Town* (1938)

Americans are overreachers; overreaching is the most admirable of the many American excesses.
George F Will 1941- American newspaper columnist, journalist and author: *Statecraft as Soulcraft* (1983)

Belief is the death of intelligence.
Robert Anton Wilson 1932-2007 American author and polymath

No man can sit down and withhold his hands from the warfare against wrong and get peace from his acquiescence.
Woodrow Wilson 1856-1924 President of the United States (1913-21)

If you know somebody is going to be awfully annoyed by something you write, that's obviously very satisfying, and if they howl with rage or cry, that's honey.
AN Wilson 1950- British author and newspaper columnist

At the age of eleven or thereabouts women acquire a poise and an ability to handle difficult situations which a man, if he is lucky, manages to achieve somewhere in the later seventies.
Uneasy Money (1916)

I was in rare fettle and the heart had touched a new high. I don't know anything that braces one up like finding you haven't got to get married after all.
Jeeves in the Offing (1960)

Rose was the sweetest girl in a world where sweet girls are rather rare, but experience had taught him that, given the right conditions, she was capable of making her presence felt as perceptibly as one of those hurricanes which become so emotional on reaching Cape Hatteras.

Plum Pie (1966)

Sir Pelham Grenville ('PG') Wodehouse KBE 1881-1975 English writer whose body of work included novels, collections of short stories and musical theatre

Do you know what it means to come home at night to a woman who'll give you a little love, a little affection, a little tenderness? It means you're in the wrong house, that's what it means.

Henny Youngman 1906-98 British-born American comedian and violinist

APPENDIX 2| THE LETTER TO
THE RT HON THERESA MAY MP

The Rt Hon Theresa May MP
Home Secretary and Minister for Women and Equality
The House of Commons
London SW1A 0AA

1 February 2012

Dear Mrs May,

I hope this finds you well. This letter is an 'open letter' and is being displayed on my blog.[1] Copies are being sent to all 306 Conservative MPs, and it will appear in my forthcoming book *Feminism: The Ugly Truth.*

The coalition's continuing pursuit of the radical feminist agendas of the previous administration is baffling to many voters, particularly those – a substantial majority – who don't hold extreme left-wing views. Labour governments had no democratic mandate for those agendas over 1997-2010, and the coalition doesn't have one now. It may be that an exaggerated sensitivity over the 'women's vote' is driving the pursuit of feminist agendas, but it hardly needs pointing out that the estimable Margaret Thatcher was popular with female voters, despite never considering herself a feminist. Conservative voters in particular are deeply hostile to the continuing assaults on many things they hold dear.

Quite apart from the feminist-inspired gender-related employment provisions of the Equality Bill 2010 – 90% of which was enacted with unseemly haste after the last general election – there continues the initiative to force 'gender balance in the boardroom' on companies. Feminists continue to assert that discrimination by men against women (the 'glass ceiling')

---

[1] http://fightingfeminism.wordpress.com

prevents more women from reaching the boardroom. It's a discredited conspiracy theory and the 'solution' favoured by the coalition – to *force* companies to increase the proportion of women in the boardroom if they don't do so 'voluntarily' – will serve only to place in the boardroom women who wouldn't have reached it on the basis of merit, and to keep out men out who *would* have done so on the basis of merit. It's an assault on the independence of the business sector, the only wealth-creating sector.

I covered the issue of women reaching senior positions in my last book, *The Glass Ceiling Delusion*, and cover it again in *Feminism: The Ugly Truth*, due to be published shortly. The following is an extract from the latter book:

> Feminists continue to assert that discrimination against women accounts for women's low representation in some areas, although they only ever highlight lines of work which are highly paid and in pleasant and safe environments, never those which are poorly paid or in unpleasant and dangerous environments.
>
> There's a long-running feminist campaign to 'improve' the gender balance of corporate boardrooms, feminists repeatedly claiming that the historically low representation of women in boardrooms results from men's discrimination against women: the 'glass ceiling'.
>
> I contend that the 'glass ceiling' is a baseless conspiracy theory – as are other assertions about discrimination by men against women in the workplace – but what do women *themselves* think about discrimination on the grounds of gender? To answer this question we turn to the 2009-10 Citizenship Survey report 'Race, Religion and Equalities' produced by the Department for Communities and Local Government. Paragraph 5.57 of the 123 page report states:
>
>> Males and females were equally likely to cite gender as a reason for discrimination in relation to being refused a job (in both cases 1%), while female employees were slightly more likely than male employees to cite gender as a reason for discrimination regarding promotion (2% of females compared with 1% of males*).

How can these findings be squared with feminists' demands for special treatment for women in recruitment and promotion terms, which continue to drive government policies? They can't.

The government appears blissfully unaware, so far as I can tell, of the growing consciousness among voters about the harm inflicted on many areas of British life by man-hating radical feminists over many years. The following is but a small selection from the many websites and blogs of interest to people with an interest in gender politics, mostly critical of feminists' activities and manipulations:

http://brightonmanplan.wordpress.com
http://ncfm.org
http://opposingfeminism.ning.com
http://theantifeminist.com
http://therightsofman.typepad.co.uk
http://www.antifeministtech.info
http://www.avoiceformen.com
http://www.brainsexmatters.com
http://www.erinpizzey.com
http://www.fnf.org.uk
http://www.mankind.org.uk/
http://www.manwomanmyth.com
http://www.parity-uk.org

I look forward to learning the coalition's intentions with respect to the pursuit of radical feminist agendas, and I hope to hear from you before the end of February. I shall be happy to post your response (if any) on my blog. Thank you.

Yours sincerely,

Mike Buchanan

APPENDIX 3| IF THE BATTLE OF TRAFALGAR HAD BEEN FOUGHT IN A POLITICALLY CORRECT AGE...

The death of Nelson was felt in England as something more than a public calamity; men started at the intelligence, and turned pale, as if they had heard of the loss of a dear friend.
Richard Southey 1774 – 1843 *The Life of Nelson* (1813)

From Wikipedia:

> The Battle of Trafalgar (21 October 1805) was a sea battle fought between the British Royal Navy and the combined fleets of the French Navy and Spanish Navy, in the War of the Third Coalition . . . of the Napoleonic Wars (1803–1815). It was the most decisive British naval victory of the war. 27 British ships of the line led by Admiral Lord Nelson aboard HMS Victory defeated 33 French and Spanish ships of the line under French Admiral Pierre Villeneuve off the south-west coast of Spain, just west of Cape Trafalgar. The Franco-Spanish fleet lost 22 ships, no British vessels being lost.

On the *Mail Online* site on 29 April 2007, English author, broadcaster, journalist Richard Littlejohn (1954-) speculated on how Admiral Nelson might have fared at Trafalgar if he had been subject to modern health and safety regulations. The scene is set on the deck of the recently renamed British flagship, HMS Appeasement, shortly before the battle:

Order the signal, Hardy.

Aye, aye, Sir.

Hold on, that's not what I dictated to the signal officer. What's the meaning of this?

Sorry Sir?

England expects every person to do his or her duty, regardless of race, gender, sexual orientation, religious persuasion or disability.

What gobbledegook is this?

Admiralty policy, I'm afraid, Sir. We're an equal opportunities employer now. We had the devil's own job getting 'England' past the censors, lest it be considered racist.

Gadzooks, Hardy. Hand me my pipe and tobacco.

Sorry sir. All naval vessels have now been designated smoke-free working environments.

In that case, break open the rum ration. Let us splice the mainbrace to steel the men before battle.

The rum ration has been abolished, Admiral. It's part of the Government's policy on binge drinking.

Good heavens, Hardy. I suppose we'd better get on with it. Full speed ahead.

I think you'll find that there's a four knot speed limit in this stretch of water, Sir.

Damn it man! We are on the eve of the greatest sea battle in history. We must advance with all dispatch. Report from the crow's nest, please.

That won't be possible, sir.

What?

Health and Safety have closed the crow's nest, Sir. No harness. And they said that the rope ladders don't meet regulations. They won't let anyone up there until proper scaffolding can be erected.

Then get me the ship's carpenter without delay, Hardy.

He's busy knocking up a wheelchair access to the fo'c'sle, Admiral.

Wheelchair access? I've never heard anything so absurd.

Health and Safety again, sir. We have to provide a barrier-free environment for the differently abled.

Differently abled? I've only one arm and one eye and I refuse even to hear mention of the term. I didn't rise to the rank of

Admiral because of the disability card.

Actually, sir, you did. The Royal Navy is under-represented in the areas of visual impairment and limb deficiency.

Whatever next! Give me full sail. The salt spray beckons.

A couple of problems there too, sir. Health and Safety won't let the crew up the rigging without hard hats. And they don't want anyone breathing in too much salt – haven't you seen the latest adverts?

I've never heard such infamy. Break out the cannon and tell the men to stand by to engage the enemy.

The men are a bit worried about shooting at anyone, Admiral.

What? This is mutiny.

It's not that, sir. It's just that they're afraid of being charged with murder if they actually kill anyone. There's a couple of legal aid lawyers on board, watching everyone like hawks.

Then how are we to sink the Frenchies and the Spanish?

Actually, sir, we're not.

We're not?

No, sir. The French and the Spanish are our European partners now. According to the Common Fisheries Policy, we shouldn't even be in this stretch of water. We could get hit with a claim for compensation.

But you must hate a Frenchman as you hate the devil.

I wouldn't let the ship's diversity co-ordinator hear you saying that sir. You'll be up on a disciplinary.

You must consider every man an enemy who speaks ill of your King.

Not any more, sir. We must be inclusive in this multicultural age. Now put on your Kevlar vest; it's the rules.

Don't tell me – Health and Safety. Whatever happened to rum, sodomy and the lash?

As I explained, sir, rum is off the menu. And there's a ban on corporal punishment.

What about sodomy?

I believe it's to be encouraged, sir.

In that case . . . kiss me, Hardy.

Supplementary notes from Richard Littlejohn:

Shortly after I wrote this, the organisers of the official Trafalgar bicentenary celebrations decided that rather than reconstruct the battle in which the British fleet defeated a much larger Franco-Spanish fleet, they would simply stage a simulated confrontation between a Red Fleet and a Blue Fleet, so as not to upset the sensibilities of French and Spanish visitors.

In Devon, Totnes council announced that it was refusing to mark the anniversary of the battle in case it upset their twin town in Normandy, France.

If Nelson were alive today, he'd wonder why he ever bothered.

APPENDIX 4 | THE LETTER TO
THE RT HON DAVID MILIBAND MP

The Rt Hon David Miliband MP
Secretary of State
Department for Environment, Food and Rural Affairs
Nobel House
17 Smith Square
London SW1P 3JR

16 May 2007

Dear Secretary of State,

My friend, who is in farming at the moment, recently received a cheque for £3,000 from the Rural Payments Agency, for not rearing pigs. I would now like to join the 'not rearing pigs' business.

In your opinion, what is the best kind of farm not to rear pigs on, and which is the best breed of pig not to rear? I want to be sure I approach this endeavour in keeping with all government policies, as dictated by the EU under the Common Agricultural Policy.

I would prefer not to rear bacon pigs, but if this is not the type you want not rearing, I will just as gladly not rear porkers. Are there any advantages in not rearing rare breeds such as Saddlebacks or Gloucester Old Spots, or are there too many people already not rearing these?

As I see it, the hardest part of this programme will be keeping an accurate record of how many pigs I haven't reared. Are there any Government or Local Authority courses on this? My friend is very satisfied with this business. He had been rearing pigs for 40 years or so, and the best he ever made on them was £1,422, in 1968. That is, until this year, when he received a cheque for not rearing any. If I get £3,000 for not rearing 50 pigs, will I get £6,000 for not rearing 100?

I plan to operate on a small scale at first, holding myself down to about 4,000 pigs not raised, which will mean about £240,000 in the first year. As I become more expert in not rearing pigs, I plan to be more ambitious, perhaps increasing to, say, 40,000 pigs not reared in my second year, for which I should expect about £2.4 million from your department.

Incidentally, I wonder if I would be able to receive tradable carbon credits for all these pigs not producing harmful and polluting methane gases? Another point: these pigs that I plan not to rear will not eat 2,000 tonnes of cereals. I understand that you also pay farmers for not growing crops. Will I qualify for payments for not growing cereals to not feed the pigs I don't rear?

I am also considering the 'not milking cows' business, so please send any information you have on that too. Please could you also include the current DEFRA advice on set-aside fields? Can this be done on an e-commerce basis with virtual fields (of which I seem to have several thousand hectares)?

In view of the above, you will realise that I will be totally unemployed, and will therefore qualify for unemployment benefits. I shall of course be voting for your party at the next general election.

Yours faithfully,

Nigel Johnson-Hill

APPENDIX 5| INTRODUCTION TO THE J4MB GENERAL ELECTION MANIFESTO (2015)

(The 80-page-long manifesto is available online.[1])

The human rights of men and boys in the United Kingdom have been increasingly assaulted by the state's actions and inactions for over 30 years, as they have across much of the developed world. J4MB is the only political party in the English-speaking world campaigning for the human rights of men and boys, including the right of all children to enjoy good access to both parents following family breakdowns, and the restoration of fatherhood and strong families.

The British state has become ever more hostile towards men and boys, although it's largely funded by men, through income tax receipts. Of all the income tax collected by the state, men collectively pay 72%, women 28%.[2] In 2011/12 British men paid £68 billion more income tax than women, yet the state disadvantages men and boys in many areas, usually to advantage women and girls.

There are no areas in which the state disadvantages women and girls.

A state which is hostile towards half its citizens also affects women who are mothers of boys, or who are men's partners, relatives, colleagues, friends or acquaintances. In the case of abortion, foetal alcohol syndrome, and fatherlessness, girls (including those yet unborn) are also assaulted by the actions and inactions of the state. The result is both inevitable and

---

[1] http://tinyurl.com/j4mb2015manifesto
[2] http://tinyurl.com/j4mbincometax

predictable – an ever more dysfunctional society, with increasing alienation of the sexes.

In this manifesto we provide details of the state's disadvantaging of men and boys in 20 areas, and we make proposals in each of them. The areas are presented in a broadly chronological order:

1. Abortion
2. Foetal alcohol syndrome
3. Genital mutilation
4. Fatherlessness, restoring strong families
5. Education
6. Employment
7. Access to children after family breakdowns
8. Domestic violence
9. Sexual abuse
10. Healthcare provision
11. Armed Forces veterans' mental health issues
12. Homelessness
13. Suicide
14. Criminal justice system
15. Paternity fraud
16. Anonymity for suspected sexual offenders
17. Divorce settlements
18. Political representation
19. State interference in company director appointments
20. Expectation of retirement years

The social engineering programmes which seek equality of gender outcomes are having an increasingly damaging impact on British society, and the Conservative-led coalition is no less keen on driving those programmes than the preceding Labour administrations. We have a vision of Britain as a nation that doesn't disadvantage half its citizens. A society in which men and women are equals in opportunity but able to make their own choices in life, without state intervention to advantage one sex over the other.

It's said that under the 'first past the post' system, votes for parties other than the major parties are wasted, but voting is the only mechanism democracy affords citizens to seriously challenge politicians who embrace the all-pervading anti-male ideology which has dictated the state's policy directions for over 30 years.

The major parties are institutionally committed to advantaging women and girls at the expense of men and boys, regardless of the consequences, as we recognized after engaging in parliamentary inquiries which demonstrated that the government simply doesn't respond to rational arguments against anti-male policy directions. The only choice for citizens concerned about the state's assaults on the human rights of men and boys is to vote – and to vote for J4MB.

In the short to medium term, our challenge is to improve public understanding about the state's assaults on the human rights of men and boys. We do that in various ways, including the use of social media. Our television and radio appearances may be found on our YouTube channel.[1]

Our longer term strategy, however, is to develop our party to the point that we can field many candidates in general elections, in marginal constituencies, where the major parties are vulnerable. Politicians will then have no choice but to take heed of the voices we represent, engage with us, and seek to appease them by modifying their parties' policies, and their direction of travel.

At the 2015 general election we'll be fielding two candidates in adjacent constituencies near Nottingham where, in 2010, MPs were elected with very slim majorities:

- I'll be standing in Ashfield, where Gloria De Piero retained the seat for Labour with 192 more votes than a Liberal Democrat candidate. She's the Shadow Minister for Women & Equalities.

---

[1] http://tinyurl.com/j4mbyoutube

- Ray Barry, leader of the campaign group Real Fathers for Justice, will be standing against a Conservative, Anna Soubry, in Broxtowe.

I should like to take this opportunity to thank all the men and women who have supported J4MB since its launch in February 2013, including those who have contributed to this manifesto. We've gone to considerable lengths to ensure that all the information we present is factually correct. If you should find any mistakes, or you believe any of the content is misleading, please draw this to our attention.

If you wish to support J4MB in any way, please contact us. Wherever you live in the world, you can become a party member,[1] or make one-off donations,[2] which will support our work. Nobody associated with J4MB has ever drawn any personal income from donations, and we don't expect that to change in the foreseeable future, if ever.

Thank you for your support, and for seeking justice for men and boys (and the women who love them).

Mike Buchanan

Party Leader

Telephone:	07967 026163
Email:	info@j4mb.org.uk
Web:	http://j4mb.org.uk
YouTube:	http://tinyurl.com/j4mbyoutube
Facebook:	https://www.facebook.com/mike.buchanan.9066
Twitter:	@mikebuchanan11

---

[1] https://j4mb.wordpress.com/party-membership/
[2] http://j4mb.wordpress.com/donate

APPENDIX 6| J4MB - THE 2020 GENERAL ELECTION STRATEGY

(The following was published on the J4MB website shortly after the 2015 general election.)

Following a strategic review, we're changing our position on the political parties we challenge at general elections. Until now we've taken the position that we'll decide some time before general elections whether we'll target the marginal seats of the Conservatives or the Labour party. Our new strategy is to always challenge the party in power – i.e. the Conservatives until 7 May 2020 – or parties, if and when we again have a coalition government. At the 2020 general election we plan to field candidates in the 20 most marginal Conservative constituencies following the 2015 general election. We have income streams in place to fund all 20 candidates' £500 deposits.

The thinking behind our new strategy:

1. Only the party in government can change legislation and policies, to remove anti-male bias. Politicians have a long and ignominious track record of making commitments to men's rights groups when in opposition, only to renege on them once in office. In 2010 the Conservatives reneged on promises made to fathers' rights groups, and the commitment in the Coalition Agreement to re-introduce anonymity for people suspected of having committed sexual offences (until and unless committed of the crimes) was dropped. We will not be persuaded by what politicians say, but by what they do. An obvious early sign of goodwill towards men and boys would be to make MGM on religious or cultural grounds illegal.

2. There is little to separate the Conservatives and the Labour party with respect to their anti-male positions. Each party is

worse than the other in some areas. Freed from the shackles of the coalition with the Liberal Democrats, David Cameron promptly re-appointed Nicky Morgan as Minister for Women & Equalities, and handed a third of ministerial positions to women, although only one in five Conservative MPs are women. Female Conservative MPs are 62% more likely than male Conservative MPs to be given a ministerial position.

3. The state is the principal driver of anti-male disadvantaging, so we shouldn't be surprised at the reluctance of politicians to engage with those campaigning for an end to that disadvantaging. On the rare occasions politicians engage it's invariably a sham, as when House of Commons and House of Lords inquiries listened to Campaign for Merit in Business[1] – an associated organization – outlining the evidence of a causal link between increasing female representation on corporate boards and financial decline, then continued with the same policy direction. Under threats of legislated gender quotas, FTSE100 companies complied with the government's demand (The Davies Review, 2011) to increase the proportion of women on their boards from 12% to 25% by 2015. The government is now forcing FTSE350 companies to have women occupy a third of the positions on their boards by 2020.

4. By targeting Conservative marginal seats in 2020 we'll increase the possibility that the party won't be re-elected, and it will then have five years in opposition to reconsider its anti-male policy positions.

5. Over the coming five years we'll relentlessly challenge ministers and their officials, as well as other prominent figures, and issue press releases relating to those challenges. We anticipate more mainstream media attention, as well as more social media attention, which will bring more pressure to bear

---

[1] http://c4mb.wordpress.com

on ministers, and increase public awareness of the state's assaults on the human rights of men and boys.

6. Because we'll always be challenging the party in power, we'll build a lengthy public record of how ministers have failed to end anti-male legislation and policy directions. Challenges may be as detailed as the one we presented in September 2014 to Theresa May, Home Secretary, with respect to the Home Office's charade of a consultation exercise.[1] The link will also take you to the 154-page report we later sent to her concerning the anti-male bias of politicians and public bodies which leads to denial of support for male victims of domestic violence.

We've also reconsidered the number of candidates to field at the 2020 general election, and have decided on a target of 20. They'll stand in the seats won by the Conservatives in 2015 with the smallest majorities, those secured with between 27 and 1,925 votes. The seats include two in Wales and one in Scotland, that of David Mundell, the only remaining Conservative MP in Scotland. They include Bedford & Kempston, my home town, where I'll be standing. A list of the 20 seats in constituency order is here,[2] and in winning votes order here.[3]

We're looking for people – men and women – to stand as candidates at the 2020 election. If this appeals to you, please email me (mike@j4mb.org.uk) or call me (07967 026163). Depending on our financial situation in the months before that election – and if you're not in a position to finance your candidature – we may be able to help you.

We shall certainly be able to fund your £500 deposit – refunded if you secure at least 5% of the votes cast – and may be able to contribute towards the cost of your campaign

---

[1] http://tinyurl.com/j4mbhomeofficeconsultation
[2] http://tinyurl.com/j4mb2020constituencyorder
[3] http://tinyurl.com/j4mb2020votesorder

literature, including the cost (c. £2,000) of the literature which the Royal Mail will deliver at no charge to every household in your constituency. You don't need to live in a constituency to stand as a candidate there. You don't even need to be a British citizen, or live in the UK.

Thanks to party members, we have funding streams in place to pay for our 20 candidates' £500 deposits. We appeal to you to support our work, by becoming a party member yourself – details here.[1] Membership costs from as little as £5.00 monthly, about 16 pence per day. Lump sum donations to support our work can be made here.[2]

Thank you for your support.

---

[1] https://j4mb.wordpress.com/party-membership/
[2] https://j4mb.wordpress.com/donate/

APPENDIX 7 | MIKE BUCHANAN

(This section is drawn from the 2015 general election manifesto of the British political party Justice for Men & Boys – J4MB – which was published in December 2014.)

Mike Buchanan (1957-) is a men's human rights advocate, writer,[1] and publisher.[2]

After obtaining a Chemistry degree in 1979, Mike embarked upon a business career during which he worked for a number of blue chip organizations including SmithKline Beecham, Gillette, Exel Logistics and Revlon. He spent the final ten years of his 30-year-long career working as an independent business consultant, and over 2006-8 he worked for the Conservative party. Along with many other Conservative party members, he resigned his party membership in the autumn of 2009, when David Cameron announced his intention to introduce all-women shortlists for prospective parliamentary candidates.

Mike took early retirement in 2010 to concentrate on fighting the scourge of radical feminism, a female supremacy ideology driven by misandry (the hatred of men). He's written ten books, five of them particularly concerned with gender-related matters:

The Marriage Delusion: the fraud of the rings? (2009)
David and Goliatha: David Cameron – heir to Harman? (2010)
The Glass Ceiling Delusion – the _real_ reasons more women don't reach senior positions (2011)
Feminism – the ugly truth (2012)
J4MB general election manifesto (2015)

---

[1] http://www.amazon.co.uk/Mike-Buchanan/e/B001JCG3AY
[2] http://lpspublishing.co.uk/titles.html

Testimonials for *The Glass Ceiling Delusion* include the following:

Every doctoral study I have read about women in management in the past fifteen years proves that successful women have EXACTLY the same characteristics as successful men. I have always admired successful women as much as successful men and have had the privilege of working for and with many of them. So I hope Mike Buchanan's book will call a halt to all this ridiculous social engineering nonsense which, in the twenty first century, is fast developing into a gross insult to our female colleagues. **Malcolm McDonald** Emeritus Professor, Cranfield School of Management

Equality of opportunity is a fine thing but equality of outcome is another matter entirely. There is little doubt that men and women have, on average, different talents and interests that make gender quotas in the workplace unfair and impractical.

The Glass Ceiling Delusion is a welcome, well-argued addition to the debate about whether women should be pushed up the social ladder just because they are women, and thus at a presumed disadvantage. This is rather an insult to women and Margaret Thatcher, for one, would not have agreed.

Individuals should be treated as individuals, not as members of a particular race, class or gender. Whatever the historic injustices, this is the only way that social structures can evolve naturally. **Glenn Wilson** Visiting Professor of Psychology, Gresham College, London

The Glass Ceiling Delusion attacks head-on the militant feminist myth that men and women have the same interests and capabilities. Reviewing a wide range of evidence, Mike Buchanan shows that the under-representation of women in senior positions in business has nothing to do with discrimination and 'glass ceilings', and that attempts to impose quotas are therefore fundamentally flawed. A polemical book with an important message.

Peter Saunders Emeritus Professor of Sociology, Sussex University

At long last, someone has taken on the myth of discrimination against women who aspire to senior positions in business, including the boardrooms of major corporations.

The Glass Ceiling Delusion demythologizes each of thirty elements the author has identified of the now generally accepted claim that women are discriminated against in the world of white-collar work. Much has been accomplished recently in disclosing the half-truths about women and domestic violence, for example, but Buchanan illuminates an area that other critics of ideological feminism have not considered.

Buchanan's analysis is based partly on his experience of working as an executive for major British and American multinational corporations for over 30 years until 2010. His book should inspire research on settings of corporate power everywhere.

Always witty and sometimes even biting in style, Buchanan's text is grounded in important texts in psychobiology, sociology, history and politics. It is an impassioned yet not angry argument that deserves the careful attention of policy-makers and a general readership.

Professor Miles Groth Editor, *New Male Studies: An International Journal*

The Glass Ceiling Delusion is an important and brave
book, the best book on social economics and society
in general published for decades. It's irresistibly
compelling, cogently argued and superbly put
together. It should be in all school and college
libraries. It should be compulsory reading for social
science, economics and politics students. It should be
force-fed to male and female politicians. This is
definitely a five-star book.
Brilliant. Brilliant. Brilliant. Brilliant. Brilliant.
Dr Vernon Coleman bestselling English author

Mike launched the Anti-Feminism League with a blog,
'Fighting Feminism', in January 2012.[1] The first piece was
titled, 'Militant Feminism: an assault on women?'[2] The blog
hasn't been updated since April 2013, when Mike started to
post new pieces on his other blogs.

In May 2012 he launched Campaign for Merit in Business,[3] –
C4MB – then (as now) the only organization in the world
campaigning for an end to government interference in the
appointment of corporate directors through initiatives such as
gender quotas – or, as in the UK, the threat of them, which has
proven equally effective. C4MB campaigns for an end to
government interference in this area due to compelling
evidence (longitudinal studies) showing a causal link between
increasing female representation on boards, and corporate
financial decline.[4]

Proponents of 'more women on boards' regularly claim that
studies show that increasing female representation on boards
leads to financial performance improvement. They point to

[1] http://fightingfeminism.wordpress.com
[2] https://fightingfeminism.wordpress.com/2012/01/09/militant-feminism-an-assault-on-women/
[3] http://c4mb.wordpress.com
[4] https://c4mb.wordpress.com/improving-gender-diversity-on-boards-leads-to-a-decline-in-corporate-performance-the-evidence/

studies and reports which show a correlation, but all the studies of which C4MB is aware point out that correlation isn't evidence of causation, nor can it be taken to even *imply* causation. There are more credible reasons for the observed correlations than some mysterious 'female factor', for example that more profitable companies are in a better position to indulge in social engineering, and there is public relations value for some companies (e.g. major retailers) in appointing more women to their boards, when the customer base largely consists of women.

C4MB has challenged many prominent proponents of 'more women on boards' to provide evidence of a causal link with enhanced financial performance,[1] and none have ever done so. They include Professor Susan Vinnicombe of the Cranfield International Centre for Women Leaders, who admitted to a House of Lords inquiry that she knew of no such evidence.[2]

Mike presented the evidence for a causal link between increasing female representation on boards and financial performance declines to House of Lords and House of Commons inquiries. A video of him giving verbal testimony to the House of Commons inquiry is on the J4MB YouTube channel.[3] In January 2013 he appeared on the BBC television programme *Daily Politics*, challenging the government's initiative to drive up the proportion of women on corporate boards.[4]

The factual evidence Mike presented to the two government inquiries had no influence on the government's policy direction. Women have been appointed to FTSE100 boards in response to the government's demands for a minimum 25% female representation on those boards by 2015, and the threat

---

[1] https://c4mb.wordpress.com/our-public-challenges-of-high-profile-proponents-of-improved-gender-diversity-in-boardrooms/
[2] https://c4mb.wordpress.com/2012/07/20/a-remarkable-statement-by-a-leading-proponent-of-improved-gender-diversity-in-the-boardroom/
[3] https://www.youtube.com/watch?v=zwqTi6HN0pM
[4] https://www.youtube.com/watch?v=vcwfWEPg3t4

of legislated gender quotas if the companies fail to comply. It is known that the government's longer term target is gender parity on the boards of FTSE350 companies, which has led to C4MB calling on owners of FTSE350 shares to sell them.[1]

Mike concluded from his engagement with inquiries that governments will not alter policies advantaging women at the expense of men, even when faced with concrete evidence that the policies are damaging the interests of men, or having other negative consequences. The same problem is evident in the state's refusal to ensure fathers have reasonable access to their children following family breakdowns, the lack of support for male victims of domestic violence, and in many of the other areas explored in this manifesto.

Mike decided to launch a political party, Justice for Men & Boys (and the women who love them)[2] – J4MB – with the long-term objective of contesting enough of the marginal seats of major political parties, that they would have no choice but to engage with the party. It was registered with the Electoral Commission in February 2013.

In the short to medium term the challenge is to raise public awareness of the state's assaults on the human rights of men and boys, and the Conservative party under David Cameron's leadership is deeply anti-male. J4MB will contest two Conservative and Labour seats at the May 2015 general election. Mike will be standing in Ashfield, a historically safe Labour seat which Gloria De Piero, currently Shadow Minister for Women & Equalities, retained with only 192 votes in 2010. He has committed to work for the party, as leader or in another role, until at least the 2030 general election, when he'll be 72.

---

[1] http://www.avoiceformen.com/feminism/feminist-governance-feminism/do-you-own-any-ftse350-shares-if-so-sell-them-now/
[2] http://j4mb.org.uk

Mike's media appearances, along with those of Ray Barry, who'll also be standing as a candidate for J4MB at the 2015 general election, are on the J4MB YouTube channel.[1]

Mike is a firm supporter of an American website, A Voice for Men – AVfM.[2] It is, with good reason, the most-visited and most influential men's human rights advocacy website in the world, and publishes material relating to men's human rights around the world. By December 2014 the site had published over 50 of Mike's articles.[3]

AVfM is led by Paul Elam, a former mental health professional. He and his colleagues organized the first international conference on men's issues, held near Detroit in June 2014. The conference was judged a major success, and Mike Buchanan was among the speakers.

---

[1] http://tinyurl.com/j4mbyoutubechannel
[2] http://avoiceformen.com
[3] http://www.avoiceformen.com/author/mikebuchanan1957/

APPENDIX 8| THE MEN'S HUMAN RIGHTS MOVEMENT, A VOICE FOR MEN, FEMINISM, GYNOCENTRISM, MISANDRY, MORAL AGENCY, SEXISM, THE RED PILL...

(The material in this Appendix is drawn from the J4MB 2015 general election manifesto, pp.71-4.[1])

J4MB is currently the only political party in the English-speaking world campaigning for the human rights of men and boys on many fronts, but it is only one element in a burgeoning global men's human rights movement (MHRM). In our view, the most important website in the MHRM is an American website, A Voice for Men – AVfM.[2] The organization was launched in 2009 by Paul Elam, a former mental health practitioner, and he leads it to this day.

In five years AVfM has become the world's most-visited and most influential website advocating for the human rights of men and boys, and it's published over 50 of Mike Buchanan's articles.[3] Paul Elam and his colleagues organised the world's first international conference on men's issues, held near Detroit in June 2014. The conference was a huge success. Erin Pizzey,[4] Karen Straughan,[5] and Mike Buchanan[6] were among the

---

[1] http://tinyurl.com/j4mb2015manifesto

[2] http://avoiceformen.com

[3] http://www.avoiceformen.com/author/mikebuchanan1957/

[4] http://www.avoiceformen.com/a-voice-for-men/erin-pizzey-presentation-to-the-international-conference-on-mens-issues-2014/

[5] http://www.avoiceformen.com/a-voice-for-men/karen-straughan-presentation-to-the-international-conference-on-mens-issues-2014-womenagainstfeminism/

[6] http://tinyurl.com/j4mbicmi14detroit

speakers, and a keynote speaker was Anne Cools, a Canadian senator.[1]

There is an increasing number of female anti-feminists, some of whom are men's human rights advocates (MHRAs) – they are often referred to as 'Honey Badgers'[2] – and some are associated with AVfM in various capacities.[3] They include:

-   Erin Pizzey, the founder of the world's first refuge for battered women and their children, in Chiswick, London, in 1972. She was ousted by radical feminists who decided to copy the example of American radical feminists, and use refuges as sources of income. They do so to this day, across most of the developed world.[4]
-   Karen Straughan (Girl Writes What): a Canadian video maker.[5]
-   Alison Tieman (Typhon Blue): a Canadian video maker.[6]
-   Janet Bloomfield: a Canadian blogger.[7]

There are a number of terms in common usage in the MHRM which are not in common usage outside it, for a variety of reasons. To explain our analyses and political direction, we need to explain their meanings.

The first term is gynocentrism, an issue explored extensively by AVfM and other websites, and to which at least one website is devoted.[8] The website reveals that the term has been in use

---

[1] http://www.avoiceformen.com/a-voice-for-men/senator-anne-cools-presentation-to-the-international-conference-on-mens-issues-2014/
[2] https://j4mb.wordpress.com/2015/05/12/honey-badgers-the-video-3/
[3] http://honeybadgerbrigade.com/badgerfesto/
[4] http://erinpizzey.com
[5] http://youtube.com/user/girlwriteswhat
[6] http://www.avoiceformen.com/feminism/mens-rights-versus-feminism-explained-using-magnets/
[7] http://judgybitch.com
[8] http://gynocentrism.com/2013/08/16/gynocentrism-definitions-and-early-mentions/

since at least the 19th century. The Wikipedia entry on gynocentrism includes this:[1]

> Gynocentrism is the ideological practice, conscious or otherwise, of asserting the female point of view on a wide range of social issues. The perceptions, needs, and desires of women have primacy in this approach, where the female view is the point of departure or lens through which issues are addressed or analyzed. The antonymic perspective to gynocentrism is androcentrism, where the male view is the central reference point.
>
> Ideologically, gynocentrism prioritizes females hierarchically as the overriding focus, at the exclusion of all else; and as a result emulates or may be interpreted as misandry, the hatred and prejudice towards men. Katherine K Young and Paul Nathanson claim that gynocentrism is a worldview based on the implicit or explicit belief that the world revolves around women, and is a cultural theme so well entrenched that it has become 'de rigueur' behind the scenes in law courts and government bureaucracies, which has resulted in systemic discrimination against men.

The reader will surely recognize gynocentrism as the 'ideological practise, conscious or otherwise' upon which the disadvantaging of men and boys detailed in this manifesto is based. Alison Tieman produced a memorable video – 'Men's Rights versus Feminism explained using magnets' – on the cultural paradigm of men being seen as 'actors', and women as 'acted upon'.[2]

One invidious aspect of gynocentrism is that it infantilizes women, robbing them of moral agency, so that in many respects women are effectively considered not so much above the law, but not under its rule.[3] Gynocentrism explains in large part why, as William Collins demonstrated, if male criminals

---

[1] http://en.wikipedia.org/wiki/Gynocentrism
[2] http://www.avoiceformen.com/feminism/mens-rights-versus-feminism-explained-using-magnets/
[3] https://j4mb.wordpress.com/2015/12/13/why-are-women-above-the-law-3/

were treated as leniently as female criminals, five out of six men in British prisons wouldn't be there.[1] He also wrote a piece on the infamous Corston Report (2007) on the handling of female criminals by the justice system, 'The Corston Report: A Case Study in Gynocentrism'.[2]

The Wikipedia entry introduces us to another term not in common usage, though it deserves to be – misandry, 'the hatred and prejudice towards men'. Misandry is evident in how men and boys are treated in the UK today – and also, for that matter, the rest of the developed world, and an increasing part of the developing world. Gynocentrism and misandry combine when states disadvantage men and boys to advantage women and girls, regardless of the consequences.

Germaine Greer claimed in *The Female Eunuch* (1970) that men as a class are deeply misogynistic, that they hate women as a class. Nothing could be further from the truth. It's clear that feminists' belief that men are commonly misogynists is nothing less than a projection onto men of their own hatred of the opposite sex.

Feminism is popularly believed to be an ideology concerned with gender equality. As long ago as 1913 – 101 years ago – the Marxist philosopher Ernest Belfort Bax revealed in *The Fraud of Feminism* that 'modern feminism' was seeking the further extension of women's special privileges. The book is downloadable at no cost.[3]

In 1994 Christine Hoff Sommers, an American professor of philosophy and feminist, published *Who Stole Feminism? How Women Have Betrayed Women*. She distinguished between two classes of feminists:

---

[1] http://mra-uk.co.uk/?p=215
[2] http://mra-uk.co.uk/?p=226
[3] https://fightingfeminism.wordpress.com/the-fraud-of-feminism-book-1913/

- **Equity feminists:** women who believe in equality of
  opportunity for women. In the UK we might more
  usually employ the term 'feminist', or 'equality
  feminist'. Hoff Sommers self-identified as an equity
  feminist in 1994 – as she still does today, 20 years later.
- **Gender feminists:** women who believed in privileging
  of women on the ground of gender, regardless of the
  consequences. In the UK we'd more usually use the
  term 'radical' or militant' feminists, and we'll use the
  former term for the remainder of this section.

J4MB has never had an exchange with a feminist who wasn't
clearly in one camp or the other.

For over 30 years in the UK, the only feminists of significance
in politics, academia, the law, the mainstream media, and much
else, have been radical feminists. They have systematically and
ruthlessly exploited the gynocentric culture of the UK, and
their appetite for advantaging women and girls over men and
boys is insatiable. Radical feminists are in key positions in all
major political parties, the government, and public bodies,
from where many of the anti-male discriminations we have
seen in this document derive. They have long manipulated male
politicians into doing their bidding, raising the spectre of the
'women's vote' if politicians fail to advantage women over
men.

The Labour party, long dominated in its senior reaches by men,
introduced all-women shortlists for prospective parliamentary
candidates, while the current Conservative-led coalition – going
further than its Labour predecessors – continues to bully
FTSE100 companies into appointing more women to their
boards, despite Mike Buchanan (on behalf of Campaign for
Merit in Business) having presented to House of Commons
and House of Lords inquiries compelling evidence (from major
longitudinal studies) that one predictable consequence of

increasing female representation on boards is corporate financial decline.[1]

Anyone who harbours any doubts that feminism is a movement with the ultimate aim of female supremacy, and is driven by misandry, would do well to watch a video by the legendary British videomaker ManWomanMyth,[2] and read the output of a British blogger, Herbert Purdy.[3] In one particularly insightful piece, Purdy drew accurate parallels between feminists and Nazis.[4]

Feminism is built upon baseless conspiracy theories – such as patriarchy theory, the idea that men (as a class) oppress women (as a class) – as well as fantasies, lies, delusions and myths. For over 40 years feminists have lied relentlessly about issues such as rape and domestic violence, making women excessively fearful of men, and in consequence hateful towards men as a class. Radical feminists never retract their lies, even when challenged with evidence proving them to be liars, which illustrates the propaganda nature of what they say. This is reflected in the mainstream media which very rarely expose the lies of feminists, however outrageous the lies might be.

Because the media have manifestly failed to hold feminists to account for their lies, J4MB publicly challenges prominent feminists[5] – and their male collaborators, such as Mark Carney, governor of the Bank of England[6] – and presents 'Lying Feminist of the Month' awards.[7] None of this activity has ever led to a substantive response from those publicly exposed as liars.

---

[1] https://c4mb.wordpress.com/improving-gender-diversity-on-boards-leads-to-a-decline-in-corporate-performance-the-evidence/
[2] Sadly, ManWomanMyth took down his material from the internet in 2015.
[3] http://herbertpurdy.com
[4] http://herbertpurdy.com/?p=1148
[5] http://tinyurl.com/j4mbpublicchallenges
[6] http://tinyurl.com/j4mbmarkcarney
[7] https://j4mb.wordpress.com/lying-woman-of-the-month/

Laura Bates, the founder of the Everyday Sexism Project,[1] is a particularly active example of current radical feminism. J4MB has presented her with two 'Lying Feminist of the Month' awards, and three to another prominent feminist, Caroline Criado-Perez. Other winners of the award include Gloria De Piero MP, Kat Banyard, and Franki Hackett, a Woman's Aid spokeswoman. Details of why all the award winners won their awards are accessible through the final link on the last page.

Sexism causes far more harm to men and boys than to women and girls.[2] What are the state's anti-male policy directions outlined in this manifesto, if not sexist?

We end this section with the expression, 'taking the red pill'. Men and women who have the courage to see the world as it really is, and thereby accept that many assaults are inflicted on the human rights of men and boys, are said to have taken the red pill. The term is derived from a scene in the film *Matrix*.[3]

If you haven't already taken the red pill, are you prepared to do so now, for the sake of justice for men and boys, and the women who love them?

---

[1] http://everydaysexism.com
[2] http://thealternativesexismproject.wordpress.com
[3] https://www.youtube.com/watch?v=zE7PKRjrid4

APPENDIX 9 |
AMNESTY INTERNATIONAL REJECT OUR REQUEST FOR 2016 CONFERENCE FACILITIES

In late 2015 we were engaged in seeking a venue for the 2016 International Conference on Men's Issues, to be held in London. We were seeking a modestly priced venue with an auditorium to hold a maximum of 250 people, and a number of smaller rooms.

Then we alighted on what would have been a perfect venue, the Human Rights Action Centre,[1] operated by Amnesty International. To cut a long story short, Amnesty refused to even consider a booking application, claiming that J4MB conflicted with their 'ethos', and therefore – in line with their booking terms – they were unable to make facilities available to us.

In their first email, they wrote the following:

> Unfortunately, the Justice for Men and Boys' message seems incompatible with our very public campaigns specifically for women's human rights here.[2] As you will see from our terms and conditions, we are not able to accommodate any organisation that goes against AIUK's ethos.

We sent them a copy of our 2015 general election manifesto, and tried to make them see we weren't anti-women, but all to no avail. They weren't prepared to have a telephone discussion, or a meeting.

The full email exchange is on the J4MB website.[3] Amnesty's final email:

---

[1] http://tinyurl.com/jrjosoo
[2] https://www.amnesty.org.uk/issues/women-human-rights
[3] http://tinyurl.com/ailrejection

Apologies for the delay in getting back to you but I have been (and am still) working a conference and have limited access to my inbox. Unfortunately, we will not be able to accommodate your organisation within the Human Rights Action Centre.

I must clarify that this is not because you campaign for the rights of men but because your organisation is explicitly anti-feminist whereas Amnesty International UK is explicitly a pro-feminist organisation.

The building and all the work we do is paid for by our members and we have to be accountable to them. Our members would not approve of an anti-feminist organisation making use of our facilities for their own purposes.

We wish you all the best with your venue search and we consider this matter to be at an end.

Amnesty International could not have been clearer. The human rights of women and girls (as a class) are important, while the human rights of men and boys (as a class) are not, and they would not host a conference alerting more people to the matter.

We were contacted by many people to say they'd terminated their memberships of the organization.

BIBLIOGRAPHY AND
FURTHER READING
(updated)

Adams, Steven (2010), *Women First, Men Last* (Kindle).

Baron-Cohen, Simon (2003), *The Essential Difference* (London: Allen Lane).

Barrett, Louise, and Dunbar, Robin, and Lycett, John (2002), *Human Evolutionary Psychology* (Basingstoke and New York: Palgrave).

Baumeister, Roy (2010), *Is There Anything Good About Men? How Cultures Flourish by Exploiting Men* (Kindle).

Bax, Ernest Belfort (<u>1913</u>), *The Fraud of Feminism* – downloadable at no cost.[1]

Benatar, David (2012), *The Second Sexism: Discrimination Against Men and Boys* (John Wiley & Sons).

Brizendine, Louann (2007), *The Female Brain* (London: Bantam Press).

Brooks-Gordon, Belinda (2006), *The Price of Sex: Prostitution, Policy and Society* (Willan).

Browne, Anthony (2006), *The Retreat of Reason: Political Correctness and the Corruption of Public Debate in Modern Britain* (London: Civitas).

Buchanan, Mike (2009), *The Marriage Delusion: The Fraud of the Rings?* (London: LPS publishing).

Buchanan, Mike (2010), *The Joy of Self-Publishing* (London: LPS publishing).

Buchanan, Mike (2010), *David and Goliatha: David Cameron – heir to Harman?* (London: LPS publishing).

Buchanan, Mike (2011), *The Glass Ceiling Delusion: the <u>real</u> reasons more women don't reach senior positions* (London: LPS publishing).

Buchanan, Mike (2012), *Feminism: The Ugly Truth* (London: LPS publishing).

---

[1] http://j4mb.wordpress.com/2013/07/10/the-fraud-of-feminism-1913/

Buchanan, Mike (2015), *2015 General Election Manifesto* (London: LPS publishing).

Ceccherini-Nelli, Alfonso, and Priebe, Stefan (2010), 'Economic factors and suicide rates: associations over time in four countries', *Social Psychiatry and Psychiatric Epidemiology* (London: Springer-Verlag).

Cleary, Mary T (2015), *That Bitch: protect yourself against women with malicious intent* (Centre Publishing).

Cook, Philip W (2009), *Abused Men: The Hidden Side of Domestic Violence* (USA: Praeger).

Cook, Philip W, and Hodo, Tammy L (2013) *When Women Sexually Assault Men: The Hidden Side of Rape, Harassment, and Sexual Assault* (USA: Praeger).

Cooper, Joel (2007), *Cognitive Dissonance: Fifty Years of a Classic Theory* (London: Sage Publications).

Crawford, Edith (2006), *Truth and Prejudice: Men's Experiences of Domestic Violence* (AuthorHouse).

Creveld, Martin van (2013), *The Privileged Sex* (CreateSpace).

Cumming, Alan (2013), *May the Foreskin be With You: why circumcision makes no sense, and what you can do about it* (Magnus Books).

Davidson, Nicholas (1987), *The Failure of Feminism* (New York: Prometheus Books).

Dench, Geoff (1998), *Transforming Men: Changing Patterns of Dependency and Dominance in Gender Relations* (Transaction Publishers).

Elliott, Michele (1994), *Female Sexual Abuse of Children* (Guilford Press).

Farrell, Warren (1993), *The Myth of Male Power: Why Men Are The Disposable Sex* (Simon & Schuster).

Farrell, Warren (2005), *Why Men Earn More: The Startling Truth Behind The Pay Gap And What Women Can Do About It* (Amacom).

Freedman, Estelle (2013), *Redefining Rape: Sexual Violence in the Era of Suffrage and Segregation* (Harvard University Press).

Graglia, F Carolyn (1998), *Domestic Tranquility: A Brief Against Feminism* (Spence Publishing).

Hakim, Catherine (2000), *Lifestyle Choices in the 21st Century – Preference Theory* (Oxford: Oxford University Press).

Hakim, Catherine (2003), *Models of the Family in Modern Society* (Farnham: Ashgate Publishing).

Hakim, Catherine (2011), *Feminist Myths and Magic Medicine: The Flawed Thinking Behind Calls for Further Equality Legislation* (London: Centre for Policy Studies).

Hitchens, Peter (2009), *How British Politics Lost Its Way* (London, New York: Continuum Publishing).

Hitchens, Peter (2010), *The Cameron Delusion* (London, New York: Continuum Publishing).

(*The Cameron Delusion* is an updated edition of *The Broken Compass*).

James, Oliver (1998), *Britain on the Couch: why we are unhappier than we were in the 1950s – despite being richer. A treatment for the low-serotonin society* (London: Arrow).

Jones, January (2008), *Thou Shalt Not Whine: The Eleventh Commandment* (Beaufort Books).

Kelly, Irene (2015), *Sins of the Mother* (Pan).

Langford, Nick (2014), *An Exercise in Utter Futility: whatever happened to family justice?* (Nick Langford).

Lloyd, Peter (2014), *Stand by Your Manhood: A Game-changer for Modern Men* (London: Biteback Publishing).

Lyndon, Neil (1992), *No More Sex War: The Failures of Feminism* (Sinclair-Stevenson).

(We particularly recommend the following title by Neil Lyndon, which contains the original full and uncensored text of *No More Sex War.*)

Lyndon, Neil (2014), *Sexual Impolitics: Heresies on sex, gender and feminism* (Kindle).

Masterson, Dick (2008), *Men Are Better Than Women* (New York: Simon & Schuster)

McCain, Robert Stacy (2015), *Sex Trouble: Essays on Radical Feminism and the War Against Human Nature* (CreateSpace).

Moir, Anne, and Moir, Bill (1998), *Why Men Don't Iron: The Real Science of Gender Studies* (London: HarperCollins).

Moore, Charles (2013), *Margaret Thatcher: The Authorized Biography. Volume One – Not for Turning* (London: Allen Lane).

Moore, Charles (2015), *Margaret Thatcher: The Authorized Biography. Volume Two – Everything She Wants* (London: Allen Lane).

Moore, E.M. (2008), *A Call for InJustice: Domestic Violence Against Men* (AuthorHouse).

Moxon, Steve (2008), *The Woman Racket* (Exeter: Imprint Academic).

Nathanson, Paul, and Katherine K Young (2002), *Spreading Misandry: The Teaching of Contempt for Men in Popular Culture* (Montreal / Kingston: McGill-Queen's University Press).

Nathanson, Paul, and Katherine K Young (2006), *Legalizing Misandry: From Public Shame to Systemic Discrimination Against Men* (Montreal / Kingston: McGill-Queen's University Press).

Nathanson, Paul, and Katherine K Young (2009), *Sanctifying Misandry: Goddess Ideology and the Fall of Man* (Montreal / Kingston: McGill-Queen's University Press).

O'Beirne, Kate (2005), *Women Who Make The World Worse* (New York: Sentinel HC).

O'Pie, Swayne (2011), *Why Britain Hates Men: Exposing Feminism* (Bath: The Men's Press). The book is available in ebook editions, and outside the UK in a paperback edition, with the title *Exposing Feminism: The Thirty Years' War Against Men* (2012).

Ofshe, Richard, and Watters, Ethan (1995), *Making Monsters: False Memories, Psychotherapy and Sexual Hysteria* (Andre Deutsch).

Parker, Kathleen (2010), *Save the Males: Why Men Matter, Why Women Should Care* (Random House).

Patai, Daphne (1998), *Heterophobia: Sexual Harassment and the Future of Feminism* (Lanham: Rowman & Littlefield).

Patai, Daphne, and Koertge, Noretta (2003), *Professing Feminism* (Plymouth: Lexington Books).

Pinker, Steven (2003), *The Blank Slate: The Modern Denial of Human Nature* (London: Penguin).

Pinker, Susan (2008), *The Sexual Paradox: Men, Women, and the Real Gender Gap* (New York: Scribner).

Pizzey, Erin, and Shapiro, Jeff (1982), *Prone to Violence* (London: Hamlyn Publishers).

Pizzey, Erin (1983), *Scream Quietly or the Neighbours Will Hear* (London: Penguin).

Pizzey, Erin (2011), *This Way to the Revolution: A Memoir* (London: Peter Owen Publishers).

Purdy, Herbert (2016), *Their Angry Creed* (London: LPS publishing).

Saunders, Peter (2011), *The Rise of the Equalities Industry* (London: Civitas).

Sax, Leonard (2006), *Why Gender Matters: What Parents and Teachers Need To Know About The Emerging Science Of Sex Differences* (New York: Three Rivers Press).

Schlafly, Phyllis (2003), *Feminist Fantasies* (Spence Publishing).

Servadio, Anthony (2015), *How to Grow and Master Your Relationships: Thirteen Steps for Men* (Archway Publishing)

Smith, Helen (2013), *Men on Strike: Why Men are Boycotting Marriage, Fatherhood, and the American Dream, and Why it Matters* (USA: Encounter Books).

Snowdon, Christopher (2010), *The Spirit Level Delusion: Fact-checking the Left's new theory of everything* (London: Democracy Institute).

Sommers, Christina Hoff (1994), *Who Stole Feminism? How Women Have Betrayed Women* (New York: Simon & Schuster).

Sommers, Christina Hoff (2001), *The War Against Boys: How Misguided Feminism Is Harming Our Young Men* (New York: Simon & Schuster).

Stolba, Christine (2002), *Lying in a Room of One's Own: How Women's Studies Textbooks Miseducate Students* (Independent Women's Forum). Free to download.[1]

Strafford, John (2009), *Our Fight For Democracy: A History of Democracy in the United Kingdom* (London: J Strafford Holdings Ltd).

---

[1] http://tinyurl.com/j4mbstolbabook

Swaab, Dick (2014), *We Are Our Brains: From the Womb to Alzheimer's* (Allen Lane).

Tate, JP (2014), *Feminism **is** Sexism* (Kindle).

Venker, Suzanne, and Schlafly, Phyllis (2011), *The Flipside of Feminism – What Conservative Women Know, And Men Can't Say* (Washington: WND Books).

Venker, Suzanne (2013), *How to Choose a Husband: And Make Peace with Marriage* (Washington: WND Books)

Venker, Suzanne (2013), *The War on Men* (Kindle)

Vilar, Esther (2008), *The Manipulated Man* (Germany: C Bertelsman Verlag) – this is the third edition of a book first published in 1971.

Wadham, Lucy (2009), *The Secret Life of France* (London: Faber & Faber).

Watson, Lindsay R. (2014), *Unspeakable Mutilations: Circumcised Men Speak Out* (CreateSpace).

Weissman, Myrna, and Paykel, E.S. (1974), *Depressed Woman: Study of Social Relationships* (Chicago: University of Chicago Press).

Weldon, Fay (2006), *What Makes Women Happy* (London: HarperCollins).

Wright, Peter, and Elam, Paul (2014), *Go Your Own Way: Understanding MGTOW* (AVFM Press).

Zubaty, Rich (1994), *Surviving the Feminization of America: How to Keep Women From Ruining Your Life* (Zubaty Publishing).

Zubaty, Rich (2001), *What Men Know That Women Don't: How to Love Women Without Losing Your Soul* (virtualbookworm.com Publishing).

INDEX OF CITED PUBLICATIONS

INDEX

HOW TO ORDER BOOKS BY MIKE BUCHANAN AND OTHER AUTHORS PUBLISHED BY LPS PUBLISHING

These books are available from a number of sources:

1. Direct from the publisher, in which case the book(s) can be signed and dedicated, if you wish. On the publisher's website[1] payment may be made by PayPal or a credit / debit card. Alternatively send a sterling postal order or a cheque – a sterling cheque drawn on a British bank account, please – made out to 'Mike Buchanan', and mail it to:

   Mike Buchanan
   Justice for Men & Boys
   Kemp House
   152 City Road
   London EC1V 2NX

   Prices includes p&p to addresses in the United Kingdom, add an additional £2.50 p&p for delivery to addresses in Europe (exc. UK), or an additional £5.00 p&p for delivery to addresses outside Europe.

2. Amazon and other online book sellers.

3. Ebook editions may be read on e-readers including Amazon's Kindle devices. Amazon and most other e-reader retailers offer free-to-download software for reading ebooks on devices such as PCs and tablets.

---

[1] http://lpspublishing.co.uk/titles.html

REVIEWS OF A NUMBER OF MIKE BUCHANAN'S BOOKS

Two Men in a Car
(a businessman, a chauffeur, and their holidays in France)

A splendid romp. *Vive la France!*
Peter Mayle 1939- British author famous for his series of books detailing life in Provence, including the international bestseller *A Year in Provence* (1989)

Mike Buchanan is the best kind of opinionated, middle-aged, middle-class Englishman abroad: the funny kind.
Andrew Heslop 1966- Yorkshire-based businessman and author

If you have a sense of humour this book will put a big smile on your face. I laughed out loud many times. A refreshing absence of political correctness.
The lovely **Maureen Padley** 1968-

Reviews from buyers on Amazon.co.uk

5.0 stars out of 5
Seriously funny and fabulous France
7 May 2010
By Karon Grieve
This is definitely a holiday read of the first order. If you're stuck at home it will make you wish for sunshine and holidays, if you're reading it on holiday you won't get off your deck chair. Two men: different views, different outlooks, but together they create the funniest mix. This is a tour of the French countryside with a difference. It's real, it's funny, and so politically incorrect you won't stop laughing. Add to that lots of local colour and tempting details on food and wine, it will have you booking a flight or a ferry to *la belle France* right away.

5.0 stars out of 5
Brilliantly funny
23 Jan 2010
By Mrs. Rosemary Kind 'Kind of Rosie'
I read this book in 3 days – I couldn't put it down. It was just so funny. My husband kept wondering what I was laughing at as I read the book in bed, so I had to keep reading excerpts to him. It's a well written book,

interesting for those people who enjoy food & fine wines, and very amusing. Well worth buying.

5.0 stars out of 5
A gem of a book
25 June 2009
By Rosanne Lyden-Brown

Mike Buchanan's little gem of a book is a definite 'can't put it downer!' I read it during a recent spell of incarceration in hospital and it made me laugh my surgical socks off. An epicure and a man of discernment if ever there was one, Buchanan's tale of his holiday in France, accompanied by his driver and fellow traveller Paul (whose preferred fodder would appear to be steak and chips and a cup of strong English breakfast tea... in the absence of a good British corner caff cheese sandwich!) is a witty, amusing, and highly informative account of how two quite different people can, in their own quite different ways, enjoy *la belle France*. Those of us who love our Gallic neighbours and their splendid country (and even those who do not!) will find something in this book that will make them smile, laugh, and long to be back there again.

5.0 stars out of 5
Happy holiday reading
25 Aug 2009
By jan wright

The book is written with a sense of humour guaranteed to bring a smile to your face. The good rapport and the differences of character between Paul and Mike underlie the entertaining reading. Mike gives the reader a sense of the 'real' France as they tour the regions chosen for their holidays. There's a spin-off too, with a good deal of informative information on each of the areas visited. An honest account describing the many restaurants and good quality wines they tasted along the way. The book is a must for anyone who loves France and thinking of holidaying there. Certainly a book to be packed in the case.

5.0 stars out of 5
Two Men in a Car – Priceless!
10 Aug 2009
By Mr H 'ribble valley rover' (Lancashire)

Thanks Mr Buchanan! A cracking read. What could be better than lying back in a sunlounger by the pool, in the beautiful Dordogne valley, and having fellow holidaymakers look at you with puzzlement every two minutes or so because you are laughing out loud? They were so jealous! That is what *Two Men in a Car* does to you. But beware – alongside the quirky stories and lovely descriptions of the *belles* of France (of whom

there are many) Mike Buchanan gives an insight into the history of the
fabulous country and takes you to places off the beaten track as well as
the more 'touristy' bits. My wife and I particularly liked 'The French
Helpfulness Index' to which we referred many times during our own
Tour de France this summer – very witty but true. It was so refreshing to
be part of a boys' road trip across a wonderful country. Bryson-esque!

5.0 stars out of 5
Two Men in a Car (and bar)
26 Mar 2009
By Mr Christopher David 'Celticman' (Wales)
A great read especially, but not exclusively, for those of you who like to
travel in France. It's confirmation that I haven't joined the realms of the
politically correct as I find the anecdotes are marvellously honest and
funny. Like the author, I am now in my third age (yes, that's the one
after you've been sensible for years, and are now reverting back to the
first age of your life) and could identify with the romps of our two men.
It's educational as well. Thoroughly recommended.

5.0 stars out of 5
Two Men in a Car... it's a Classic... or should that be a Vintage!!!
12 May 2009
By Leo – the Black Labrador's lead holder! 'Alan' (Lancaster)
What a joy to read, especially given that I can say... we were there, and
have pointed out to everyone who has visited in the last week that our
dog is the unwitting star of the book (for us, at least) – Leo, the Black
Labrador, it may only be on one page, but that's good enough for us!
Beyond that, what an easy read... full of fun, and I can imagine Mike
and Paul sat by the pool recalling their many adventures, it's just like they
were here... but without the guitars. Thanks Mike for adding a further
reminder to a memorable holiday, I can't wait for the next instalment.

5.0 stars out of 5
A cracking read
21 April 2009
By G.R. Morris 'Molepole' (Kent)
A wonderful meander through the backwaters of France. Two more
unlikely companions you couldn't imagine. One a Francophile
connoisseur of food and wine who likes to indulge in both, the other an
egg, chips, and cup of tea man! The only thing they seem to have in
common is being politically incorrect (and thank god or whatever deity
you are into for that!) A very amusing book, enough to make me want to
get *Guitar Gods in Beds*. Hope there will be some more travelogues from

Mr Buchanan soon. What about Italy? Plenty of good food & wine there and probably some very attractive *senoritas* as well!

Review from a lady buyer on Amazon.com

5.0 stars out of 5

A pleasant holiday for the reader

January 25, 2010

By Laurie A. Helgoe

Mike Buchanan's road memoir allowed me a chance to get away and explore France without the packing and expense. Traveling with Buchanan and his friend/chauffeur Paul Carrington made my trip especially entertaining. The author describes himself as 'highly unfit and averse to physical effort' and as a lover of food, wine and France; Carrington enjoys a variety of sports but is indifferent to food and wine. They do have in common their single status and accumulation of ex-wives – five between the two. The author cleverly uses charts to contrast the attributes of the two travelers and their packing lists, and includes a French Helpfulness Index. Buchanan's penchant for detail helps bring the reader along, not just through the beautiful landscapes but also into the frustrating, funny, and interesting situations that make up travel. If you need to get away and have a laugh, buy *Two Men in a Car*.

The Marriage Delusion: The Fraud of the Rings?

A highly original and stimulating critique of the modern marriage crisis, supported by important yet sometimes uncomfortable truths.
Oliver James, clinical psychologist, broadcaster, author of *Affluenza*, *Britain on the Couch*, *They F*** You Up, How Not to F*** Them Up*

Mike Buchanan's analysis of marriage in western industrialised society is courageous and thoughtful. His perspectives on the challenges associated with marriage, and solutions to them, draw on important scientific evidence and arguments from some of our leading psychologists and wisest philosophers. This is a 'must-read' for all concerned with modern marriage.
Alan Carr, Professor of Clinical Psychology, University College, Dublin, author of *The Handbook of Adult Clinical Psychology*, *Family Therapy* and *Positive Psychology*

Reviews from buyers on Amazon.com

5.0 stars out of 5
An honest assessment of modern marriage – at last!!!!
January 10, 2010
By Mary B 'Book Chaser' (North Carolina)
This is a brilliant and honest look at the realities of modern marriage. Mr Buchanan bravely exposes the painful truths of why marriage isn't working for most of us. He paints with very broad strokes to depict the sometimes subtle inconsistencies between our assumptions about marriage and the realities. For example, why some unhappily married people continue to extol the virtues of marriage. Particularly relevant for me was the description of introversion versus extroversion and the impact the different personality traits can have on marriage. As a happily divorced introvert, I feel vindicated. I now accept and appreciate that my singleness is a valid lifestyle choice for me as an introvert, and that my yen for solitude doesn't make me a bad person. The book is filled with excellent excerpts from other writers that corroborate Mr Buchanan's observations. The writing defies political correctness, and it is well balanced. Buchanan's candor is delightfully naughty. This is truly the most uniquely written book I've read in years.

5.0 stars out of 5

A Brilliant Exploration and Realistic Assessment of Marriage

October 30, 2009

By dancing bees – See all my reviews

As one who has made almost a vocation of studying marriage and reading books on every aspect of it, I found Mr. Buchanan's book to be a welcome breath of fresh air on a subject that is too often occluded by starry-eyed optimism and unrealistic expectations. Herein the reader will find a bracingly honest discussion of the principal factors that can undermine a given individual's chances of creating a rewarding marriage, including the inherent personality characteristic of introversion. This is a topic that has been neglected in the current climate of happy talk which leads us all to believe that, given enough work, almost any marriage can become fulfilling. In view of all the negative fallout resulting from an incomplete understanding of how personality impacts on marriage, the author has made a significant contribution to future human happiness by emphasizing this underrated aspect of what can contribute to – or detract from – what most people consider their most important relationship.

This important book includes an overview of facets that are seldom sufficiently touched upon in the many superficial works on marriage. One of these is the different natures of men and women. I found this chapter especially relevant and fascinating due to the unique slant the author has taken. The chapter covering the role of political correctness in the present day and its disastrous effects on male/female interactions is in itself a courageous *tour de force*. The conclusion, dealing with the future of marriage, outlines practical and intelligent suggestions for overhauling this nearly anachronistic institution. Interestingly, the author quotes Bertrand Russell's views on marriage at some length in this chapter. It's striking how compelling and pertinent his observations still are today, even nearly 80 years after he penned them!

While the subject matter is sobering, the author's elegant writing style and sometimes laugh-out-loud witticisms make for a read that is both edifying and enjoyable. My hope is that this book will soon find its way onto bookshelves everywhere in the U.S. because marriage, if it is to survive much longer, is in dire need of a reality check. Mr. Buchanan's book is an outstanding first step in that direction.

5.0 stars out of 5

A Challenging 'Must Read'

October 4, 2009

By Brandi Love (NC USA)

I found this book to be intense and thought-provoking. Mr Buchanan brings to light many of the issues that lead to failed marriages, in a bold and sometimes unexpected manner. It's always effective (perhaps not liked) to be honest and to communicate about all topics. So many couples go into marriage with a desired 'concept', this book is an awesome read to ensure ones understanding of what marriage IS and / or CAN be. Agree with the author's philosophies or not, you can count on many meaningful and potentially life changing conversations between you and your mate. Discussions that most likely will lead to a deeper love, understanding and appreciation for one another. It's about time someone wrote a book with Mr. Buchanan's sharp, sometimes cutting facts. Open his book, open your mind and change the relationships in your life for the better. I definitely recommend.

Reviews from buyers on Amazon.co.uk

4.0 stars out of 5
The Marriage Delusion
30 Jun 2010
By Snowboot Girl
I would seriously recommend readers of both genders to read this book. Firstly it is always interesting reading about relationships from a man's point of view, because as the author rightly points out, there is little out there by men that give an honest account. Mr Buchanan has clearly spent a great deal of time reading up on his subject and the book contains extracts from other books / newspaper articles / studies. As my husband reluctantly discusses anything to do with relationships, particularly ours, it's encouraging that there are plenty of men who are interested in the subject. Many of the book's contributors are men.

I chose this book, interested by the fact that it was about marriage and didn't have the title, 'Why men… and women don't…'! Also because it was challenging the fact that marriage should exist at all in the modern world. [Author's note: the last sentence is incorrect. I simply assert that most people in the developed world in the modern era are unsuited to the institution of marriage.]

Having finished the book today I am left with the feeling that the author chose his extracts largely to support his theory about the reasons marriage is increasingly failing and divorce rates increasing. Many of the reasons are valid but I am not left feeling entirely convinced. For example he talks about marriages that fail and those that succeed and the reasons for both often being compared. However he doesn't really touch on the fact that within many marriages there are good times and bad times.

Marriages are either set for failure or not seems to be the general consensus. Divorce rates have been rising since the 60s yes, but that's a comparatively short time in the history of marriage. Personally I feel that in the short time divorce has become easier we haven't yet seen the effects of / or much research into people who have divorced only to regret it later. He also does not touch very much on children and how many people's lives are made worse by divorce because of the effect it has on them.

This book was written because the author wanted to explore why his own two marriages failed and why divorce is increasing. His argument that introverted men are unhappier in marriage is interesting and yet he claims that extraverted people are more likely to be adulterous – surely a situation that increases (or results from) unhappiness in a marriage?

The book is sceptical (obviously from the title) about lifetime marriage commitment. I'm divorced and have remarried with children from both marriages (statistically I'm therefore more likely than first time marrieds to divorce again). This book has made me really appreciate what my husband and I do have rather than highlight what we don't have and I feel rather sad that so many people lose physical passion and are not able to maintain willpower to save their marriages. Selfishness – something that is not really mentioned in the book but seems to come through from between the pages – is one reason I personally would suggest.

On a massive positive – a very thought-provoking book which I could not put down and has really helped me understand how men including my husband think and feel. He deserves more slack from me, more freedom and more gratitude. I have put loads of pencil marks in the margin so I can pick it up any time I want to look at those issues that are particularly relevant to us.

4.0 stars out of 5
The case for a long and happy 'relationship'
27 Oct 2009
By 'Single Man'

A couple of days before a dinner during which I was planning to propose to my girlfriend, I was in Waterstone's in Piccadilly, looking in the 'self help' section for books about relationships and marriage. In the middle of a multitude of books in the *Ten Sure Steps To An Awesome Marriage* genre was this book. The cover intrigued me and I was soon flicking through the book. I sat down with it and an hour passed by in a flash, before one of the sales assistants started looking askance at me, so I bought it.

After I read it I realised that I (in common with most people contemplating marriage in the modern era) was suffering from 'the marriage delusion' - the expectation that we would enjoy a long and happy marriage. I came to understand why (like most people) I'm unsuited to the institution of marriage, and why the prospects of long-term happiness with my partner were poor. My girlfriend spotted the book in my bookshelf after I'd read it, then asked if she could read it herself.

A week later – having read the book herself – she brought round a bottle of chilled champagne, and said, 'Can I make a proposal, darling?' I gulped and before I could reply, she continued, 'Can I propose that we never get married?' We both laughed, I accepted her proposal, and we've never been happier. Mr Buchanan, thank you for saving me from a lot of unhappiness, and probably financial ruin too!

5.0 stars out of 5
The Marriage Delusion
27 Oct 2009
By 'Mr. M'
I've been reading this book with interest. It deals with many aspects of relationships and the institution of marriage. The book has been well researched and has many quotes and extracts from other relevant authors on the subject. It challenges many conformist and social historic approaches to the subject and contrasts the differences between male and female views and outlooks. As I am in a happy second-time relationship it is possible to be more understanding and use one's own experience and be philosophical in looking at these issues. It seems the author highlights the difference between reality and expectation as causing a great number of problems for both individuals and consequently couples. A book to stir up opinions and discussion on what's sometimes a thorny area full of so-called experts. A very valuable read and helpful background to getting married and co-habiting.

5.0 stars out of 5
The Marriage Delusion
15 Oct 2009
Mr R Corfe
The Marriage Delusion by Mike Buchanan is a brilliantly written book and a 'no-put-down-read' with quotations and longer passages on every aspect of marriage and personal relationships between the sexes. He's not only put his own mind to the problems of marriage, but in the cause of objectivity has engaged in extensive research. This is a must read for anyone who is already married or who contemplates marriage in the near future.

5.0 stars out of 5
Thought provoking
27 Sep 2009
By A. Heslop

The title of this book should provide an indication of the writer's perspective, but overall this is a challenging and interesting review of a difficult subject. Mike Buchanan has clearly completed a deep review of literature on the subject, from academic tomes to 'how to improve your marriage' books from the 'self help' section of bookstores. His approach is not to offer recipes to improve a marriage or even focus on the morality of whether marriage is a good thing ethically speaking – he simply asserts that most marriages are unhappy, about half fail completely, and he goes on to explore why this situation occurs. His perspective on understanding the problem focuses on personality types, gender-related factors and religious beliefs. Oh, and he rants quite a bit about the Rt. Hon. Harriet Harman MP.

I didn't expect to identify with the book's key themes as I've been happily married for 20 years and my parents have been for 50 years, but many of my contemporaries have been divorced, and the subject is worthy of consideration by everyone, happily married or otherwise. Overall the book is well written, interesting, thought provoking and at times amusing. Depending on your perspective, it may help you better understand why you've been unhappy in your own marriage, or send you into apoplexy. You will probably find his final recommendations either extremely sensible or totally outrageous: views will be polarised.

5.0 stars out of 5
1 Oct 2009
By Mr H 'ribble valley rover' (Lancashire)

I have to agree with all the comments made by A. Heslop; I too am happily married and I thoroughly enjoyed the way the author challenged my views and perception of marriage. Through extensive research (and obviously years of experience) Mr Buchanan gives an interesting thesis on the institution of marriage which created many lively discussions between my wife and I. At times I had to agree with the author, however, I often found myself 'hoping' to disagree with his argument!

Reading *The Marriage Delusion* is a thought-provoking and often enlightening experience. Mr Buchanan's wit gives the book a light touch besides the more serious topics discussed. I would recommend this book to anybody thinking of getting married, is happily (or not so happily) married, and to anybody who likes to challenge institutionalism in today's society. A great read.

5.0 stars out of 5
At last – some realism about marriage
1 Oct 2009
By Mr Gary P Lewis

Mike Buchanan pulls no punches in this book. His central assertion – that most people are unsuited to marriage – at first seems astonishing, even if the high divorce rate across the developed world suggests he might be on to something important. The book goes a long way to explaining the misery of married couples I've known (a number of whom have divorced). I learnt a lot about marriage in this book. It had – to take just one example – never occurred to me that marriage originated in an era when people couldn't expect to live many years after their offspring were independent. And yet today people are told it's natural to have a rewarding (and even sexually exciting) relationship for 30-40 years after the kids have left home. It's about as natural as flying.

I was particularly interested in the lengthy exploration of introversion and extraversion. It seems obvious that these personality types will impact on marital happiness, but I'd never come across the point before. The book explains how both personality types can be a problem in marriage.

The book contains some welcome humour to balance the serious messages. This includes a lengthy appendix of quotations about Love, Sex and Marriage. My personal favourite, from Shelley Winters: 'In Hollywood, all the marriages are happy. It's trying to live together afterwards that causes all the problems.'

5.0 stars of 5
A fresh view on an old institution
24 September 2009
By D Lomax

Mike Buchanan's take on married life is undoubtedly coloured by his two divorces (so far), so he certainly speaks from experience, but by combining his own views with existing material and interviews with other interested parties, he has put together a fascinating insight into why he feels a large number of modern marriages are destined for failure.

Maybe failure is the wrong word because Mr Buchanan attempts to show us that actually we shouldn't expect so much from the institution of marriage in the first place, while exploding a number of myths along the way. The book is well researched and it is sprinkled liberally with quotes and references to other works.

This would be great subject matter for a book club as the issues raised almost demand to be discussed further and every page has the ability to divide opinion. Mr Buchanan stokes all kinds of fires within the reader – religious, political, idealist – then stands back and lets the sparks fly.

Depending on your status – male, female, married, single or divorced – this book will either have you nodding and smiling in agreement, or tearing the pages out, but you won't put it down.

The Marriage Delusion is unashamedly written from a male perspective which is surprising as blokes aren't good at buying, much less reading books on relationships, but maybe that's part of the problem Mr Buchanan is trying to explore, and if you have an interest in how men and women ever manage to get along, you should certainly buy this to provide a bit of balance to your bookshelf.

It's not for men only though. The style of the book is more akin to a technical thesis, and anyone studying relationships would be well advised to get hold of a copy. This book should also be compulsory reading for any couple contemplating that all too short walk down the aisle, although you'll wonder why church aisles don't have an escape lane after reading this. I can also recommend it as a great resource for a best man's speech, particularly if you don't like the bride.

The Marriage Delusion lacks the laugh-out-loud humour of some of Mr Buchanan's other books, but that's because he approaches this complex subject with detail and accuracy, making it easy to connect with his way of thinking, even if it is not in line with your own. It's not without humour though and I couldn't help noticing that Mr Buchanan seems to have an unhealthy fascination with Harriet Harman MP, delivering a number of very funny jibes and comments that pull Harman's speeches and policy apart. (She was given the right to reply, but never bothered.) A picture comes to mind of Buchanan as a schoolboy, teasing Harman in the playground because secretly he quite likes her. Hang on, that's the answer – Mike should ask Ms Harman to be the next Mrs Buchanan. Now there's a book...

5.0 stars of 5
Compulsory reading
19 Sept 2009
By G. Williams

Informative, amusing, and invaluable. This book offers great insight into the long-term pitfalls of an age-old tradition that so many people seem to naively drift into. Its objectivity provides a real wake-up call for those struggling with an unhappy relationship and a warning to those who've not yet taken their vows. This should be a compulsory read for anyone considering marriage – it could save you thousands in divorce lawyers' fees!

The Joy of Self-Publishing

I've been publishing my own books for over 20 years, after having been published by more than a dozen of London's leading publishers including Pan, Penguin, Corgi, Arrow etc. I've had books on both the *Bookseller* and *Sunday Times* bestseller lists. During the last two decades I've self-published scores of books and sold millions of copies around the world. I wish I'd had Mike Buchanan's book *The Joy of Self-Publishing* when I started. It's the best damned book on publishing in existence. It's brilliant. I'm learning stuff from it every time I open it. Writers who try self-publishing without reading it first – and without keeping it on their desks as they go on – are giving themselves an extra handicap. And in the business of self-publishing we all start with enough handicaps.
Dr Vernon Coleman bestselling English author

Reviews from buyers on Amazon.co.uk

5.0 out of 5 stars
Helpful, easy to understand, and amusing
5 Aug 2011
By Richard W Hardwick
As a published writer setting myself up as a self-publishing writer I've bought at least eight books on self-publishing and book design. And now I've designed my book I'm finding this one is the one I'm turning to more than any other. I didn't even plan to buy it. Mike answered a question of mine in a Yahoo group on self-publishing and then he gave me his phone number so I could go over some issues in more detail. I only bought his book because I felt I ought to. But here's why it worked so well. It really is the easiest one to understand. And self-publishing (if you're new to it) is so complicated you wonder why you ever decided to bother half the time. It made me smile a number of times too, and I'm pretty miserable so that's no mean feat. If you're new to self-publishing buy this book and then scout around the rest of them and buy one more too, one that's specifically designed for what you want. You'll get there (I almost am) and a book like this will help you.

5.0 out of 5 stars
Great reading for all budding writers
9 Sep 2010
By A Heslop
Technology has opened up a whole new world for writers and self-publishers – until I read this book I didn't realise by just how much. So, if there's a book in you – write it. Begin to write it now, whilst the creative urge is flowing. But before you get too far, read Mike

Buchanan's book *The Joy of Self-Publishing*. You'll learn more about writing and publishing by investing just a few hours, than you normally would in ten years of self-discovery: Buchanan has been there, done it, and learnt how to make it work. This book provides inspiration (should you need it) but above all is commercial and honest about successful book publishing – it will both motivate you and help you avoid costly and annoying mistakes. And I've been there. I wrote a book that was published by a mainstream publishing house. They did a good job and the book sold okay, but their overheads were so high that by the time I received my royalties I'd worked for less than the minimum wage. Mainstream publishing makes no sense when the tools exist to do it profitably yourself – and I sense that Buchanan gets as much pleasure from the publishing process as he does from writing. My next book will be self published and the process set out in *The Joy of Self-Publishing* is exactly how I'll do it.

5.0 out of 5 stars
At long last, a comprehensive and practical guide to self-publishing
19 Feb 2011
By KateS
Unlike other books I've bought on the subject of self-publishing, this book provides practical solutions to all the problems self-publishers face, and is right up-to-date on the options available. Its coverage of Print-on-Demand ('POD') is authoritative and its comparison of the economics of different book specification options (e.g. paperbacks, hardbacks, plate sections) is very helpful. The writer delivers his knowledge of the subject with a good deal of humour and I laughed out loud on a number of occasions. The appendix of quotations on publishing, book writing etc. could be a boon for self-publishers: many are funny, many insightful.

4.0 out of 5 stars
A must read for a wannabee author
31 Mar 2011
By Mrs H Owens
I received Mike Buchanan's book *The Joy of Self-Publishing* a couple of months ago and such a valuable pack of information shouldn't be wasted on the shelf! I've been considering writing a book of my own for many months, but with the vast information available didn't know where or how to start. I especially wanted a guide to tell me about specific resources but with the internet searches I got all lost and confused and came to the edge of giving up before even starting. *The Joy of Self-Publishing* reached me just in time and I can't recommend it more highly to anyone who is wondering where to start. It's obvious that Mike has worked hard to give practical advice and detailed information on

process, formatting, other resources including even the costs! Like everything in life, writing and publishing a book requires effort but with the aid of Mike Buchanan's book it seems not just possible but achievable. The invaluable resource *The Joy of Self-Publishing* gave me the hope that I (and anyone) can now make a book visible and available to book buyers around the world at minimal cost. *The Joy of Self-Publishing* takes you through the options and explain their relative advantages and disadvantages realistically. This book also provides guidance on selecting book topics with strong sales potential; writing distinctively as well as writing content-rich non-fiction. It even offers help choosing between hardback and paperback and other formats. With the aid of *The Joy of Self-Publishing* I am hoping to say, it's all much easier than it sounds! Thank you, Mike Buchanan.

Review from a lady buyer on Amazon.com

5.0 out of 5 stars
Fabulous, encouraging, and hysterical (yes – this book is helpful AND very funny)
February 27, 2011
By Kelly McCarthy Barner (Shrewsbury, MA United States)
I read Mike Buchanan's first book *Profitable Buying Strategies* about a year ago, and when I was thinking of writing my own book on procurement I found he'd written another book that would help me out. I received my copy of this book not quite a week ago and I've already finished it. More than once I actually laughed out loud while reading it, which caused my husband to think I was hiding another book inside this one's cover, which I wasn't. Really.

If you're even considering writing a book of your own, I can't recommend this one more highly. Mike's practical advice and detailed information on process, formatting, other resources, and costs make the effort required to get a book into print sound just challenging enough to risk trying. The book is made available using the same POD process he outlines in the book so you're holding the last piece of encouragement you need right in your hands.

I've now proofed my review (because who would take me seriously as a potential writer if I made obvious mistakes in a simple review?) and plan to go right back to Mike's book – next to which is the pile of notes I will turn into a book of my own thanks to Mike's help.